GEORGES VANIER:
SOLDIER

GEORGES VANIER: SOLDIER

THE WARTIME LETTERS AND DIARIES 1915–1919

EDITED BY
DEBORAH COWLEY

DUNDURN PRESS
TORONTO · OXFORD

Copyright © Deborah Cowley, 2000

All rights reserved. No part of this publication may be reproduced, stored in a retrieval system, or transmitted in any form or by any means, electronic, mechanical, photocopying, recording, or otherwise (except for brief passages for purposes of review) without the prior permission of Dundurn Press. Permission to photocopy should be requested from the Canadian Copyright Licensing Agency.

Design: Jennifer Scott
Printer: Transcontinental

Canadian Cataloguing in Publication Data

Vanier, Georges P. (Georges Philias), 1888-1967
  Georges Vanier, soldier: the wartime letters and diaries, 1915-1919

ISBN 1-55002-343-8

1. Vanier, Georges P. (Georges Philias), 1888-1967 — Correspondence. 2. Vanier, Georges P. (Georges Philias), 1888-1967 — Diaries. 3. World war, 1914–1918 — Personal narratives, Canadian. 4. Soldiers — Canada — Correspondence. 5. Soldiers — Canada — Diaries. I. Cowley, Deborah. II. Title.

D640.V35 2000   940.4'8171   C00-931844-5

1   2   3   4   5   04   03   02   01   00

ONTARIO ARTS COUNCIL
CONSEIL DES ARTS DE L'ONTARIO

We acknowledge the support of the *Canada Council for the Arts* and the *Ontario Arts Council* for our publishing program. We also acknowledge the financial support of the *Government of Canada* through the *Book Publishing Industry Development Program, The Association for the Export of Canadian Books*, and the *Government of Ontario* through the *Ontario Book Publishers Tax Credit* program.

Care has been taken to trace the ownership of copyright material used in this book. The author and the publisher welcome any information enabling them to rectify any references or credit in subsequent editions.
                              J. Kirk Howard, President

Printed and bound in Canada.
Printed on recycled paper. ❀

www.dundurn.com

Dundurn Press	Dundurn Press	Dundurn Press
8 Market Street	73 Lime Walk	2250 Military Road
Suite 200	Headington, Oxford,	Tonawanda NY
Toronto, Ontario, Canada	England	U.S.A. 14150
M5E 1M6	OX3 7AD	

"It is a privilege to be of this age when, instead of mediocre colourless lives, we can forget the dollars and the soil and think of principles and the stars. We have been looking at the ground so long that we have forgotten that the stars still shine."
                      Georges Vanier to his mother,
                      20 May 1915

This drawing of Georges Vanier by the Belgian artist Alfred Bastien is one of many drawings and paintings Bastien made in July/August 1918 while he was attached as a war artist to the 22nd Battalion. On the front, he has written a dedication to Vanier: "A Major G. Vanier, Souvenir de mon joyeux séjour en France, Alfred Bastien." (In memory of my happy stay in France, Alfred Bastien.) On the outside border, he has added: "Ce dessin a été fait d'après nature — en face des boches à Monchy-le-Preux — près d'Arras, dans la tranchée de 1 ère ligne." (This drawing was made from life — facing the Boches at Monchy-le-Preux — near Arras, in one of the front line trenches.)

CONTENTS

Editor's Notes ... 10
Prologue — The Call of War ... 13
The War So Far ... 31

1. The Van Doos Sail for Europe — May 1915 ... 33

2. "To Be at Last in France" — September 1915 ... 59

3. "Oh, the Mud of Flanders" — October 1915 ... 79

4. A "Special Task" — January 1916 ... 99

5. The Big Push — February 1916 ... 121

6. Trench Warfare Intensifies — April 1916 ... 129

7. Convalescence in Britain — June 1916 ... 147

8. Return to the Battlefield — October 1916 ... 171

9. The Campaign Heats Up — Spring 1917 ... 181

10. "Such Frightful Carnage" — March 1918 ... 219

11. Casualty of War — August 1918 ... 241

12. Continued Convalescence, and Armistice —
     November 1918 ... 269

Epilogue ... 295
Chronology ... 305
Endnotes ... 309
Acknowledgements ... 321
Suggested Reading ... 322
Index ... 325

EDITOR'S NOTES

It was almost two years ago that Thérèse Vanier, the only daughter and eldest of Georges Vanier's five children, asked me to look at some of her father's wartime letters. He had written regularly to his family from the trenches during World War I and kept a diary for most of that period. It was Thérèse's feeling that this material might reveal a side of her father that few people knew.

My first hesitation was that I am neither a historian nor a military expert. Nonetheless, I quickly sought out those who were versed in both disciplines to help steer me through the minutiae of military lore. My second concern was that, at first glance, many of Vanier's letters did not appear to reveal much of what the writer really felt. They seemed to mask the day-to-day realities of war and often sounded too up-beat to be true. But the more I sifted through the voluminous material — there were over three hundred letters as well as meticulously detailed diary notes — the more I realized that they did in fact offer insights into the man. They also, of course, represented important records of a period. So for almost two years, I immersed myself in the First World War and followed the daily wartime exploits of Georges Vanier, the soldier.

The letters and diaries I have selected appear almost exactly as they do in the originals. I have taken a few small liberties, correcting occasional spelling mistakes or dates or place names. I have also removed repetitious material (indicated by square brackets and dots) to help move the story along. Where necessary, I have added brief comments (shown in italics within square brackets). When I felt more complete explanations were called for, I have provided endnotes.

The letters Vanier wrote to his mother were all written in English, and those to his father in French. Where the original letter was written in French, I have shown the opening salutation in French but continued with an English translation. Most of his diaries were written in French so these appear in translation.

I have chosen to spell Georges Vanier's first name in the French way, with an "s". He generally signed his wartime letters without an "s" but for the latter part of his life, he tended to use the French version. A reporter once asked him which spelling he preferred. "I have no preference," he replied. "I like to leave a certain latitude."

One small note: throughout the war, Vanier, like most of his fellow soldiers, made frequent use of the words "Hun" and "Boche" when referring to the Germans. This was a slang usage, that was freely used in wartime.

Finally, if any errors have crept into the text, I offer my apologies and take full responsibility.

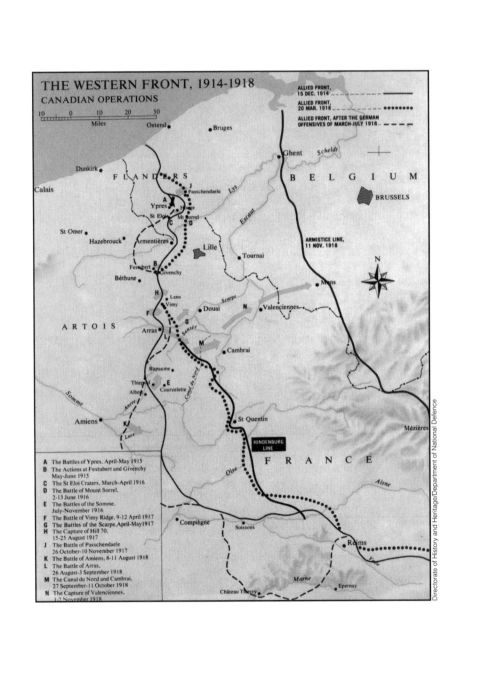

PROLOGUE
THE CALL OF WAR

Georges Vanier was a military man to the depths of his soul. He was intensely proud of his regiment, the Royal 22nd, and he often described the four years he spent on the battlefields of Europe as the most rewarding of his life. He was fighting for a cause — the defence of his beloved France — and even as the war dragged on into its fourth year, he never appeared to doubt the legitimacy of his mission. He was a loyal and dedicated soldier.

Vanier's strong allegiance to his regiment and to the military continued long past the silencing of the guns in November 1918. In fact, it remained with him throughout his life. It is not surprising, therefore, that at his investiture as governor-general on September 15, 1959 — and at most other ceremonial occasions — he chose to wear full military uniform, sword slung at his side and a row of medals strung proudly across his chest. At his state funeral in March 1967, he was mourned in true military style: a simple walnut coffin draped with the Canadian flag, his military cap and sword placed on top, travelled on a gun carriage through the snow-bound streets of Ottawa escorted by over two thousand members of the armed forces. As they slowly marched to the beat of muffled drums, air force jets flew by overhead and a booming seventy-eight-gun salute — one for each year of Georges Vanier's life — crackled through the frosty air. It was a fitting tribute to a great soldier.

But for most people, Georges Vanier will long be remembered as Canada's most respected and deeply loved governor-general. He held office for more than seven years — from 1959 to 1967 — and during that time he travelled constantly across Canada, visiting the most remote communities despite being well into his seventies and hampered by an artificial leg. Everywhere he went, this tall, white-haired, grandfatherly figure sparked the imagination of those he met. In town halls and auditoriums, schools and factories, he gave stirring speeches about service and duty, about human rights and the family, and, above all, about the need for unity between the country's two language groups. *Maclean's* magazine described him as "Canada's moral compass."

But what of the less well-known Vanier, the young man who passed up a promising career in law to become a soldier, who spent four and a half years on the battlefields watching many of his best comrades die; the man who was himself wounded twice but still managed to comfort those around him? What of the man who chose not to return home to Canada because he felt it was his duty to rejoin his battalion, and who wrote to his mother in May 1919 that "I am happy ... that God gave me the strength of body and of mind to do my duty under fire"? Indeed, what of Georges Vanier, the soldier?

Rumblings of War

It is now more than thirty years since Georges Vanier's death and nearly ninety since the first rumblings of impending war in Europe reached Canada. When World War I finally broke out in August 1914, Vanier was a fledgling Montreal lawyer of 26. Neither he, nor anyone else, could have envisaged that it would take four long years — a staggering 1,559 days of slogging through the battlefields of Ypres and Passchendaele, of Vimy and the Somme — to resolve a conflict that was to cost the lives of at least ten million young men, including sixty thousand Canadians.

Many realized that Europe in the spring of 1914 was on the brink of disaster. The Great Powers had ranged themselves in two opposing camps: Germany, Austria/Hungary and Italy formed the Triple

Alliance while France, Russia and Great Britain were to become known as the Triple Entente. The two sides had been smouldering for years when a single event ignited a flame: the assassination of Austrian Archduke Franz Ferdinand, heir to the Austro-Hungarian throne.

That single gunshot — on June 28, 1914 in the Serbian city of Sarajevo — triggered a conflict that was to touch every continent. A month later, Austria declared war on Serbia. Germany followed by declaring war on Russia and, on August 1, upon France. As the German army moved towards France, first invading Belgium, a country whose neutrality had been guaranteed by the Great Powers, Britain joined the fray. Outraged at the violation of Belgian neutrality, the British Government issued an ultimatum to Germany demanding the withdrawal of German troops. This demand was ignored and at 11 p.m. on August 4, 1914, Britain too was at war.

It did not take long for what became known as the Great War to take on global proportions. Japan joined France, Russia and Great Britain in 1914, and was followed by Italy in 1915. In November 1915, the Triple Entente declared war on Turkey, which was already aligned with Germany and Austria. On April 6, 1917, the United States entered the war as an "Associated Power." By then, it had truly become a World War.

Britain began mobilizing troops in early August of 1914 while pundits predicted that the war would be short and the boys would be home by Christmas. They were not to know that what lay ahead was a war that would become four long years of death and destruction or that it would be characterized by high-explosive shells, rapid-fire machine guns, and a new and most lethal weapon, poison gas. Nor were they to know that it would destroy almost a whole generation of young men.

CANADIANS RALLY TO THE CALL

As news of Britain's entry into the war reached Canada, Prime Minister Sir Robert Borden called on Canadians, as members of the British Empire, to support Britain and France. Within two months, more than 32,000 men, two-thirds of them recent British-born immigrants, stepped forward and formed the Canadian Expeditionary

Force. By early October they were boarding the first troop ships bound for England. There they were to undergo rigorous training before heading to the front where they served as part of the British Expeditionary Force.

Not all segments of the Canadian population rushed to join Bordeu's call to arms: French-speaking Quebecers were only scantily represented among those first volunteers. Most French-Canadians had little enthusiasm for this distant war. They saw it as a British war and did not feel connected to Britain or the British Empire as did those from English Canada. Nor did they feel welcome among the ranks: English was the only language of instruction at the Valcartier training camp in Quebec and senior French-Canadian officers were generally given meaningless administrative positions with little prospect of advancement.

Alongside that was a bitter controversy raging over Ruling 17, which forbade the use of French in the schools of Ontario. Here was another reason to ignore the call to arms.

It took an open letter to Prime Minister Borden from Colonel Arthur Mignault in the Montreal newspaper, *La Presse*, to galvanize the French-speaking population. In it, Colonel Mignault, a medical officer with the 65th Carabiniers Mont-Royal, sought authorization from the Prime Minister to mount a battalion composed exclusively of French-Canadians. Sir Wilfrid Laurier, the popular Leader of the Opposition, publicly endorsed the idea and Borden agreed.

Recruitment for the new battalion began at once. On October 15, just as the first Canadian soldiers were reaching Europe, twenty thousand people gathered in Montreal's Parc Sohmer to applaud a rousing speech by Laurier and to hear Arthur Mignault share his dream. By evening's end they had formed a contingent calling itself the 22nd (French-Canadian) Battalion. It quickly became known by its more popular name, the "Van Doos" ("vingt-deux" or "twenty-two") and by its insignia — a crown mounted on a beaver with the motto, *"Je Me Souviens"* below.

The men who responded to the call were all French-Canadian and most were Roman Catholic civilians who, like Vanier, had little or no military experience. The officers, with an average age of 27, came largely from Montreal and Quebec City and included civil servants and students, engineers, lawyers, doctors and bank clerks.

The men were mostly labourers and farmers, aged 24 on average, drawn from across the province of Quebec. What united that small group was a strong determination to come to the aid of France, the land of their forefathers, rather than to support the British Empire.

Twenty-six-year old Georges Vanier was completing his second year in the Montreal law firm of Dessaules and Garneau at the time of the Montreal meeting on October 15 and he was among the first to join the new battalion. Years later, in a speech honouring the fiftieth anniversary of what became, in 1921, the Royal 22nd Regiment, he was to recall that historic gathering. "We were a group representing the descendants of the French language in a war where the life of France was threatened.... We believed that the best way of showing one's love for one's motherland was to go to her defence even at the risk of one's life."

An Unlikely Volunteer

While Georges Vanier was an enthusiastic volunteer, he seemed an unlikely candidate for a military career. He had been a serious student at the Jesuit-run Loyola College, a private English secondary school in Montreal where he not only excelled in mathematics and philosophy but also showed a strong literary bent. He enjoyed music and the theatre, wrote poetry and plays, and delighted in combing through second-hand bookshops in search of his favourite authors, especially the nineteenth century satirical British novelist William Makepeace Thackeray.[1] He was also a true romantic. He loved the poetry of Shelley and Keats and was known to carry a small red leather-bound copy of Shelley's poems in his breast pocket throughout the war.

Young Vanier was soon to add to his love of the English classics a keen interest in French culture and literature. This evolved partly through his close friendship with Father Pierre Gaume,[2] a warm-hearted French-born Jesuit who taught at Loyola and shared his love of Shakespeare and the English Victorian novelists with his precocious student. Even more influential was Camille Martin, a retired professor from Paris who coached the young Georges during his school years. This tall, commanding tutor was passionate about his native France and the two spent many long hours reading French authors and discussing French philosophers. Camille Martin, more than anyone, instilled in Georges a lifelong love of French history and literature and helped him begin to identify — ever so proudly — with his French ancestors.

In 1906, Vanier graduated from Loyola with a flourish, and delivered the valedictory address for his graduating class. Like many young men at Catholic schools, he considered a religious vocation but chose instead to study law on the Montreal campus of the French-speaking Laval University. Here he continued to cultivate his interest in French culture and delivered a speech on the role of the French-Canadian student in Canada. "It seems to me that our mission here is clear," he told his fellow students. "We must spread the spirit of the Latin countries, we must develop the Latin civilization, and the culture of our forbears, by the mediation and the use of the most beautiful language which has ever existed for the translation of human thought...." Vanier left Laval in 1910 to join the law firm of Dessaules and Garneau and was admitted to the bar in February 1912. He was still working at Dessaules and Garneau in 1914 when he decided to enlist.

Father Pierre Gaume, a French-born Jesuit who taught at Loyola, shared his love of Shakespeare and the English Victorian novelists with his precocious student.

Georges Vanier graduated from Loyola College in 1906 and was valedictorian for his class.

Family Influence

Vanier's cultural and bilingual background stemmed also from his family. His mother, Margaret ("Maggie") Maloney[3] was a sensitive and kindly woman, an anglophone from Cork, Ireland. His French-Canadian father Philias[4] was a great-grandson of Guillaume Vanier, who had embarked from the Normandy port of Honfleur at the end of the seventeenth century to sail for Quebec. Guillaume's great-grandson Philias settled in Montreal where he became a shrewd and successful real estate agent. He was a gentle man with a beguiling sense of humour that was passed on to his son, Georges. The family spoke English at home and Georges perfected his French at university. He and his siblings all grew up speaking both languages effortlessly.

Georges was the eldest of the five (one child died in infancy). They were a happy, close-knit family growing up in a large house, now demolished, at 861 Dorchester Street West in Montreal and spending memorable summers together either at Cacouna, on the south bank of the St. Lawrence River, or at "Pineleigh," the family farm on Lake Memphramagog in Quebec's Eastern Townships. There Philias Vanier delighted cottagers by arriving in one of the region's first Buick cars.

So what prompted this young man of 26, versed in the humanities and launched on a promising career in law, to join up to fight in this distant war?

Unlike many of the early volunteers, Georges Vanier was not looking for a life of adventure or seeking an escape from the futility of unemployment. He had other reasons to enlist. There is no doubt that he was angered by the German invasion of Belgium and the consequent suffering of innocent people. He was certainly aware that this could be the first step towards an attack on his beloved France. As he confessed much later in a letter to his sister, Frances: "During the last months of 1914, I could not read the accounts of Belgian sufferings without a deep compassion and an active desire to right, as far as it was in my power, the heinous wrong done."

It is also clear that Vanier saw wartime service as a duty. On August 16, 1915 he wrote to his mother: "I feel it is my duty to see this sacred war through and with God's help, I shall." His sense of duty extended even further. On September 17, 1915, only days after stepping from the ship onto the soil of France, he wrote, again to his

Vanier's mother, Margaret Maloney, signed her photo "To my dear boy. Mother." Throughout the war, Georges kept the photo in a small leather case beside one of his sister Frances.
Courtesy: Mlle. Marcelle Trudeau

Georges' French-Canadian father, Philias Vanier, was a descendant of Guillaume Vanier, who sailed for Quebec from the Normandy port of Honfleur in the seventeenth century.
Courtesy: Thérèse Vanier

mother: "Never in my wildest flights of imagination could I have foretold that one day I would march through the country I love so much in order to fight in its defence. Perhaps I should not say in <u>its</u> defence because it is really in defence of human rights, not of French rights only."

Another factor prompted Georges Vanier to volunteer. He cared deeply about humanity, about the people who would become the unfortunate victims of war — the housewives who had lost family members in the cross-fire, the shopkeepers whose shops or homes had been destroyed. As the war dragged on, he expressed deep concern for the women — "In this war, a woman's lot is the most terrible," he told his mother in a letter dated September 20, 1916.

"She has neither the excitement nor the glory but only the awful suspense." And he saluted the peasants. "The more I see of the peasant class...." he wrote on January 14, 1918, "the greater is my admiration for the French nation."

Training Begins

There was, therefore, no question in Vanier's mind that he should join the military and contribute his share. He never doubted that his place was on the battlefield, so when the call came for volunteers to join the newly formed 22nd Regiment, he was an early and enthusiastic recruit. Vanier was commissioned as lieutenant on October 27, 1914 and was sent to the battalion's base in St. Jean, Quebec for a rigorous four-month training period. The Van Doos consisted of four companies of eight platoons with thirty-six officers and 1,093 non-commissioned officers and men. Vanier started out in "D" Company under Major Arthur-Edouard Dubuc, a former civil engineer. The commanding officer of the battalion was Colonel Frédéric Gaudet, a short, stocky man with a bristling moustache who had previously served in the Royal Canadian Artillery.

The first part of the training period ended in mid-December. On December 17, the battalion was inspected by the Governor-General of Canada, the Duke of Connaught[5] and, three months later, on March 2, 1915, they boarded a train for Amherst, Nova Scotia.

Amherst gave the Van Doos a heroes' welcome. "French Canadians Carry Amherst by Bloodless Storm," read a banner headline in the *Amherst Daily Mirror* after thousands crowded the railway station to greet the young soldiers. The officers lived in various hotels while the men were billeted in the shops of The Canada Car and Foundry Company. The new visitors quickly became popular fixtures on the local scene. "The officers are all gentlemen, tried and true," noted the paper. "Descendants of the first settlers in Canada, these French-Canadian officers bear names of the old French seigneuralty, and carry confirmed pride in their names as well as themselves."

They stayed in Amherst for a further two months of training, which involved such rigours as twenty-mile marches. By mid-May

GEORGES VANIER: SOLDIER

The Van Doos in training at St. Jean, Quebec in January 1915. Vanier has marked himself with an "x" and noted on the photo: "After a 10 mile march, lunch outside — temperature 0 degrees."

Colonel Frédéric Gaudet was the first commanding officer of the battalion.

The 22nd Battalion assembles at the station at St. Jean, Quebec, before to their departure for Amherst.

Prologue

On March 2, 1915, the 22nd Battalion boarded a train for Amherst, Nova Scotia.

The officers of the 22nd Battalion in Amherst, Nova Scotia. Georges Vanier is in the back row, third from the left.

The Van Doos' training in Amherst, Nova Scotia, included twenty-mile marches.

1915, the battalion was ready to leave for Europe. The night before their departure, Colonel Gaudet gave a large military ball for three hundred guests. The next morning, on May 20, 1915, the unit travelled by train to Halifax and prepared to board the *R.M.T. Saxonia*, bound for England.

FAITHFUL CORRESPONDENT

Georges Vanier was to spend the next four years overseas — almost 1,500 days. Whether on the front line facing a barrage of gunfire or recuperating from shellshock in a field hospital, he remained a faithful correspondent. There were periods when he kept a detailed diary in several slim rain-soaked pocket notebooks in which he jotted down the day's events — usually in French — on both sides of flimsy paper and in tiny spidery writing. These were written at considerable risk since private diaries were generally frowned upon by army regulations for fear of falling into enemy hands. Presumably he shipped them home at regular intervals with willing travellers.

He also wrote letter —, reams of them. He wrote frequently to his brothers Anthony and John and his sister Eva. His second sister

Prologue

Eva, George's elder sister, married Joseph Trudeau on January 17, 1916 while her brother was at the front.

Frances, the youngest in the family, was George's favourite sibling. He carried this photo, signed "To George with love Goo," throughout the war.

Frances, the youngest in the family and some fifteen years younger than George, was his favourite sibling. Georges sent her long rambling tomes, often using a special code ("Me a prised on did'n't yite.... Terribits well" was one message written on a postcard), and addressed her with such nicknames as "smink" or "goo" or "snookyookums." He wrote frequently to his father in Montreal, always in French. And throughout the four long years he wrote to his mother almost daily — except for occasional periods of unexplained silence. These long newsy letters were written in English in a broad, sloping script, frequently on pages torn from a lined exercise book. Happily for us, his mother saved them all.

Each letter begins "My dearest Mater ... " and closes with "very devotedly your son, Georges." He was meticulous about acknowledging the almost daily arrival of letters and cablegrams (none of which have survived), postcards and parcels from home — maple syrup was the most popular gift, closely followed by all-wool socks. In his letters to his mother, he never fails to send greetings to his father, whom he refers to as "The Governor," to his sisters and brothers whom he calls "all the dear children" and to "dear Sophie," the devoted family maid. He often enclosed an assortment of souvenirs — maps and menus, invitations and train tickets, paper currency and even his tiny Bank of Montreal bank book — asking that they be carefully

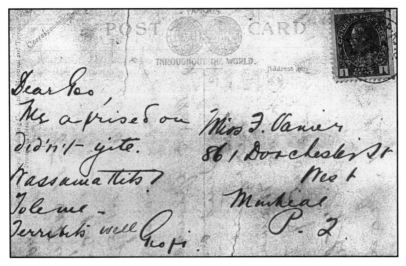

Georges often used a special code in his letters and cards to his sister, Frances.

pasted in his "war album" and kept for his return.

More often than not, Vanier wrote under the most awkward of circumstances. Some were letters he scribbled in pencil by the light of a solitary candle in some dreary billet. Others were written in pitch darkness, or by the spasmodic light of shell explosions. He wrote from the trenches on freezing nights, with water up to his knees or bent double in his mud-filled dugout frequently with enemy aircraft droning overhead.

He describes the deaths and serious injuries of close comrades and fellow soldiers. When his friend Captain Beaubien was killed on June 6, 1916, Georges noted in his diary: "Another of my old friends has gone.... I loved him very much and his death has struck me very hard." He also speaks of his own narrow escapes. On June 9, 1916, he notes that "a shell exploded a few feet away, deafening and shaking me and knocking me out completely. If the earth hadn't been so soft, I would have been killed." A month before, on May 17, 1916, he told his mother: "I have never done 50 yards in quicker time, the end being a dive onto the trench mat and a painful wait for the hellish explosion." Though he faced more than his share of danger, he carried throughout the war a firm conviction that he was being protected from above: "Providence — thanks to the prayers of all the dear ones at home — has protected me in a special manner...."

Casualty of War

If the prayers from home helped to keep him alive, his good luck nevertheless ran out less than three months before the Armistice of November 1918. On August 26, Vanier was leading the battalion in the capture of the French village of Chérisy when he was hit by a German machine-gun bullet in the shoulder and one arm. As he was being helped onto a stretcher, a bomb exploded, killing the stretcher-bearer and practically severing Vanier's right leg. It was to be amputated later at a field hospital. Vanier nevertheless continued to write home regularly, determined to reassure his family that he was well and in good spirits.

His letters were obviously intended to appease both his family and the censors (a requirement designed to ensure that sensitive military information was not passed on). Vanier must have experienced hours of fatigue and seemingly endless days of monotony and boredom. He must have suffered intense heartache when death became an almost daily reality, with close friends and comrades being killed before his eyes. Throughout it all, he appeared incredibly stoic. "God how the nights are long," scribbled in his diary on September 9, 1918, was one of his few expressions of discomfort after the amputation of his leg. Earlier, he wrote to Frances when he returned to the battlefield in October 1916 following the horrendous losses among his regiment during the Battle of the Somme: "The battalion is very much changed since I left. Most of the officers and men have either been killed or wounded. It is hard to be merry under these circumstances but it is <u>necessary</u> not to be downhearted, so we try to think of the present and of the living and not of the past and the dead."

Georges Vanier once told his old friend and former teacher, Father Gaume, that "intimate feelings — joys, sorrows, aspirations — are not things to write about. They can be spoken, and even so they are better understood by gestures, looks and the tone of voice." This, as well as the fact that censors were hovering over his shoulder (several of his envelopes had been re-sealed with a strip of bold black letters reading "OPENED BY CENSOR"), helps explain the fact that many of his letters and his reactions to events appear guarded. Nonetheless, he still manages to convey some of the excitement and exhilaration of war, as well as the tragedy and inhumanity. Fortunately for us, he was a skilled wordsmith. Barely a month after his first foray into the trenches, he was sitting under a starry sky observing a new moon and savouring the momentary silence — with the enemy poised less than half a mile away. That night, October 18, 1915, he confided in his diary: "If it were not so tragic and horrible, it would be beautiful."

It is a testimony to Vanier's strength — both physical and emotional — that his dedication to his regiment and to his beloved France never flagged, as the long and bloody war dragged on. He even declined the chance to accept an "honourable repatriation" home after his wounding in 1916 — one that would not reflect adversely on his performance — during the summer of 1916 when he was in England recuperating from shellshock. "I appreciate very much what my friends in Canada have done for me," he wrote to his mother. "But somehow, I can't go back. I must be at the front so long as I am fit. I should be unhappy anywhere else." He never regretted that decision. In May 1919, while still convalescing in England after the loss of his leg, he mused: "I am happy at the thought that I had the courage to return to my boys in 1916 and that God gave me the strength of body and of mind to do my duty under fire. It is a tremendous consolation that will comfort me until my dying day."

THE WAR SO FAR....
AUGUST 1914 — MAY 1915

The Van Doos had spent almost seven months in rigorous training, first in St. Jean, Quebec, and then in Amherst, Nova Scotia, when they gathered in Halifax on May 20, 1915 ready to leave for England. During this period, there was fighting on a number of main fronts, mostly in Europe.

The first five months of the war saw most of the expectations of the main warring powers — Germany, France and Russia — completely shattered. On the Eastern front, Allied hopes were dashed when the Germans under Paul von Hindenburg defeated the Russian army at Tannenberg on August 30, 1914. Serbia and Montenegro fell by the end of the year and the Allies' ambitious Gallipoli campaign the next year turned into a costly failure.

On the Western front, where most of the Canadian troops were engaged, Germany's movements were dictated by the "Schlieffen Plan," named after its architect, Field Marshall Alfred von Schlieffen, a one-time German Chief of Staff. The object of the plan was to strike quickly against France, through Belgium, destroy her armies, then turn their energies against the Russians on the eastern flank. The plan almost succeeded. German troops crossed into Belgium on August 4, 1914 and, early in September, advanced across that country into France but were held dangerously close to Paris at the First Battle of the Marne.

There followed the so-called "race to the sea" in which each side sought to outflank the northern flank of the other. By mid-October, the Belgian army under Belgian King Albert held only the western corner of the country in Flanders, north of Ypres. In the first Battle of Ypres and at great loss to both sides, the British Expeditionary Force (BEF) successfully prevented the Germans from reaching the French Channel ports.

By year's end, the long front had stabilized into lines of trenches running from the Belgian coast to the Swiss frontier.

The second Battle of Ypres, in April 1915, was another German attempt to reach the Channel ports. When the first Canadian troops joined the British and French forces, they managed together to hold the Salient around Ypres against a strong German assault. It was here, on April 22, that the Germans sought to break the stalemate by introducing a vicious new weapon, poison gas.

After the Battle of the Marne and both battles of Ypres (a third followed in October/November 1917), there was still no sign of a breakthrough. Instead, the two sides became firmly deadlocked along a six-hundred-kilometre front of impregnable trenches separated only by a narrow stretch of "No Man's Land." This stalemate would continue and the battle lines changed little over the next three years.

1

THE VAN DOOS SAIL FOR EUROPE
MAY 1915

> *"It was a touching and inspiring scene, this gathering of Canadian officers from every part of the Dominion and belonging to every walk in life, united in the mother country and proclaiming the solidarity of the English peoples."*
> Georges Vanier to his mother,
> 5 August, 1915

*I*t was May 20, 1915, and the 22nd (French-Canadian) Battalion — the "Van Doos" — was preparing to leave Canada for the battlefields of Europe. They had just completed a four months' training program in Amherst, Nova Scotia, and were excited at the prospects of their impending departure. Within hours, they would embark on their hazardous journey across the Atlantic, a course where the threat of submarine attack was very real. Only two weeks before, on May 7, the British passenger liner, the *Lusitania*, had been sunk by a German submarine off the coast of Ireland, claiming over one thousand lives.

For the moment, the troops were caught up in the ebullient send-off given them by the citizens of Amherst. As the battalion paraded along a route lined by the 6th Mounted Rifles, the Amherst Military Band struck up with "It's a Long Way to Tipperary" and "Soldiers of the King" while the whole town shouted and cheered.

"It was a very emotional departure," Georges Vanier noted in his diary that morning. "The streets are lined with people carrying flags, and the houses are covered with flags and bunting. If outward demonstration means anything, Amherst was sorry to lose us and that I think is the best compliment that could be paid us."

They boarded two trains for Halifax and arrived there the same afternoon. Here too the reception was euphoric with thousands of Halifax citizens swarming to the port, waving flags and cheering the soldiers as they boarded the troopship R.M.T. *Saxonia*. Later that night, Vanier was to describe the scene to his mother:

At Halifax, our train shunted right onto the wharf where the Saxonia was waiting for us, with the 25th Battalion (from Nova Scotia) already on board. We filed off the trains and onto the Saxonia, the gangway was removed and we steamed away. No disorder, no noise on the part of the men, discipline perfect.

Before the vessel was under way, Major-General Rutherford

On May 20, 1915, the Van Doos boarded the troopship *R.M.T. Saxonia*. Vanier called their departure "the most 'alive' moment of our existence so far."

gave three cheers for the King, then for the 22nd and 25th Battalions and the crowd responded with vim. The sight was impressive as we drew away to the sounds of "O Canada" played by our band. Then a quiet descended as we left the wharf, the people silently waving flags, handkerchiefs and hats. It was the most "alive" moment of our existence so far.

It is a privilege (Lloyd George[1] said so first) to be of this age, when instead of mediocre, colourless lives we can forget the dollars and the soil, and think of principles and the stars. We have been looking at the ground so long that we have forgotten that the stars still shine.

Diary entry: 22 May. On board troopship, R.M.T. Saxonia.

This morning we passed an iceberg, twelve miles to port. It looked like a gigantic snowbank through the field glasses. I played shuffleboard and quoits a great part of the day and I have never felt so well before on board a ship. Weather clear and cold, with not too much motion in the sea.

Diary entry: Sunday, 23 May

This morning we heard Mass on deck. All the men were gathered together on the forecastle. It was wonderful to hear Mass in the open air, with the sky and the clouds and the sea as sole witnesses. The most impressive moment was when the priest raised his hands to the sky preparatory to giving us his blessing just before the last gospel.

Diary entry: Empire Day, 24 May

Another day of delightful weather. Tonight the moon is shining in a perfect heaven and we sit on the upper deck idling the time away and thinking of our friends in Canada. We will be in the danger zone in a few days and the possibility of being torpedoed is far from

Mass on board the *R.M.T. Saxonia*. Vanier noted in his diary that "it was wonderful to hear Mass in the open air, with the sky and the clouds and the sea as sole witnesses."

remote. Probably our course will have been thoroughly scouted by destroyers and cruisers that will act as escort. So far, of course, we moved ahead without any protection whatsoever.

Information received today leads us to believe that Italy may enter the war on side of the Allies. Marconigram says the Italians and Austrians are fighting already. Such conflict may obviate the necessity for any formal declaration of war by the principal powers.

Diary entry: 25 May

War has been declared between Italy and Germany. This is unquestionably the greatest event since the 4th of August. Germany's doom is sealed. The past has shown that one nation cannot fight the whole of Europe. The humiliation of Germany is inevitable. No treaty with her will be of any value unless she is stripped of her power: she has not respected her signature in the past and she will not do so in the future unless she is too weak to make dishonesty profitable.

Diary entry: 26 May

Today I was one of the officers on the guard whose duty it is to maintain order on board. No incident of import except that about 10:30 p.m., we sighted to starboard a vessel which had the lines of a battle cruiser. Ships that we have met have signalled to us but we have given no sign of life, our orders being not to give away our identity or our position.

Diary entry: 27 May

Weather a little rougher today: I have no feeling of seasickness however. The Saxonia is a wonderfully steady boat and I would advise any of my friends to cross on her, especially those who fear seasickness.

Three or four of us got together and bought what is known as the "low field" in pool. Twenty numbers are auctioned off — in this case from 310 to 330 — which represent the miles the vessel will run from 12 o'clock noon to 12 noon.

We are getting into the danger zone: tonight most of us will sleep with our clothes on and our life belts at our side. All the portholes are darkened: unfortunately there is a magnificent moon shining and we must be plainly visible for a radius of many miles.

Diary entry: 28 May

The "low field" won: our run was 300 miles flat.

All our life-boats are swung out ready for use: personally I consider a life-boat as being practically useless until it is actually in the water. The ship's officers say it is very much better in case of accident to put on one's life belt and to jump from the deck when the ship is about to go down, without paying any attention to the boats.

2:30 p.m. We have just sighted a destroyer on our port side coming towards us at great speed. It turned out to be the British destroyer Lawford and she is the first war vessel we have seen since we left Canada. The Captain says she is a modern destroyer (class

1913) with three four inch caliber guns and a possible speed of 29 knots (35 miles). Everyone on board was delighted and we cheered like children. Before the arrival of the Lawford, we had no escort or protection of any kind. She is now following a parallel course to ours on our port side. Should a submarine attack us now we would see some actual fighting. Another destroyer has joined us and we are now proceeding with a destroyer on either side. The night is a clear moonlit one and we move along silently with our sentries watching.

The destroyers carry no lights. Silhouetted against the sky they look like gigantic greyhounds, with their noses pushed into the sea.

12 p.m. At midnight, we are about 80 miles from Plymouth and we can see the lights of Lizard Point.

Diary entry: 29 May

6 a.m. At dawn we steamed into Devonport, the naval base for the town of Plymouth.

I climbed up onto the bridge at 7 a.m. The landscape is beautiful, with fields of brilliant green. Here and there are rows of small houses, all identical, with tile roofs. Went ashore at 4:30 where we boarded the train. Travelled across the counties of Devon, Dorset, Wiltshire, Hampshire, Surrey and Kent to reach Shorncliffe. The countryside is smiling: the neatly trimmed hedges bordering properties are well cared for.

Diary entry: Sunday, 30 May. East Sandling camp, near Shorncliffe.

Arrived at East Sandling camp at 7 a.m. after a march of four miles (from the siding where we detrained). The location of the camp is ideal: high, dry ground, varied countryside. We are housed in small waterproof huts — excellent lodgings..

7:30 a.m. Observation point above our camp.

This morning, we left our camp and made for the highest point we could see — about one mile from camp. We crossed fields of lush green where hundreds of sheep were grazing. From the height a delightful panorama unrolls to the right and below us to the left is our camp. Folkestone and the English Channel are just four miles away on the sea.... The countryside is a warm, restful green, such as is seen nowhere in Canada. I saw a naval cruiser and a dozen anti-torpedo boats exercising in Folkestone Bay.

Mass in the room of Captain Doyon[2] [*the army chaplain*].

Diary entry: 31 May

Our regular life begins today. The men are settled in. We sleep in portable cots, a little hard but one gets used to it. East Sandling camp lies in one of the most beautiful parts of Kent. We are just 80 miles from the front.

Diary entry: 1 June

Captain Boyer and I are leaving for London to buy a motorcar for the regiment. We will be staying at the Savoy.

Diary entry: 2 June

Visit to Major Hamilton Gault, D.S.O.[3] at No. 17 Park Lane where he is recuperating. He has several wounds, among others a very serious one to his left arm. He doubts that he will be able to return to the front. He tells us that the Canadians have won an enviable reputation for courage and personal initiative.... That evening, we saw The Man Who Stayed at Home at the Royalty Theatre, a play about spies, with some very subtle intrigue.

Diary entry: 3 June. Still in London.

Today is the King's [*King George V*] birthday. This morning I visited the office of the Canadian Red Cross where I met Miss Fleet, the sister of Robbie Fleet, and Lady Drummond[4] who had just lost her son. Lady D. is marvellous and hides her grief and her sadness under a stoic exterior which masks her deep suffering. She is working hard for the Red Cross trying to forget....

Savoy Hotel, London
3 June, 1915

My dearest Mater,
As you know already from the cablegram asking for two hundred dollars, I have come up to London with Captain Boyer. The object of our stay here is to purchase a motor car for the regiment.... I cabled for the money because there were a number of things which I needed such as a portable bath, a periscope (really a hyposcope), a water bottle and a hundred and one other things. Besides I have been thinking seriously of purchasing a motorcycle which would be a very useful to me in many ways, firstly as a means of locomotion and secondly in order that I might learn the mechanism and running of it. You know great use is being made of them at the front and the knowledge obtained might be of incalculable value.

I have thought it unwise to deprive myself of anything that might be an aid to me in France: it would be misplaced economy. Hence the call for money.

[...] We have very comfortable quarters at East Sandling camp, near Folkestone, the well-known watering place. We are all living in waterproof huts in one of the most beautiful spots in the south of England, in sight of the English Channel (four miles away) and only thirty-five miles [*actually closer to seventy*] from the battle front.

You know of course that the night before last, there was a Zeppelin raid in London: very few knew anything about it. The Germans dropped some incendiary bombs but did very little damage, murdering a few women and children. There were a number of fires at the same time and I am inclined to believe that some of the fires were set not by the bombs but by Germans resident in London. [*Not factually correct but probably reflects atmosphere of widespread public suspicion.*] I think you will read of other raids in London during the month of June. No question of the front for a couple of months: in any case, I shall make it a point to keep you in touch with my movements.

At East Sandling camp, the Van Doos joined three other battalions: the 24th from Montreal, the 25th from Nova Scotia and the 26th from New Brunswick. These four battalions formed the 5th Infantry Brigade under the command of Brigadier-General David Watson,[5] former publisher of the Quebec City Chronicle *whose battalion had distinguished itself at Ypres. The 5th Brigade would be part of the 2nd Canadian Division. Their commanding officer was Major-General Sir Richard Turner,[6] a slight, bespectacled man who had been a Quebec City merchant before becoming a popular hero in Canada, having won the Victoria Cross in South Africa.*

The brigade's training was rigorous: a ten-mile march every morning, often under scorching sun and through choking dust, and platoon exercises, such as musketry, gymnastics, and bayonet and machine-gun skills in the afternoon. Vanier was chosen to follow a course in map-reading.

Diary entry: Sunday, 6 June

Mass in the open air on our parade ground (an Anglican touch). Standing on the parade ground, more than a thousand voices sang the Magnificat[7] — very moving. One amusing detail: at the end of the Mass, we sang "Nous vous invoquons tous" to the tune of "God Save the King" and the officers of the 24th Battalion thought we were singing "God Save the King" in French and, in their turn, played and sung the National Anthem at the end of their own service.

Diary entry: 10 June

Visit in the driving rain to Caesar's Camp [*probably a Roman camp*] with Captain Weekes and the members of the [*map-reading*] class. The fortifications that we found date from Caesar's time. Close to the camp, there is an airfield with a "garage" where pilots on their way to France can receive their orders.

Diary entry: 16 June

Last night, I went by bicycle to Westenhanger [*a village four miles from Folkestone*] to follow a course on the stars given by Captain Weekes which will complete his course on military mapping. Returned by bicycle at midnight. The rules for night marches — use them to study the stars and for periods of contemplation.

East Sandling camp
17 June, 1915

My dearest Mater,
This is an acknowledgement of a number of letters I have received lately and which I should have answered before, but the work here is so long that after parades we are very tired, and sometimes we forget to send news home.

I was very much surprised and very sorry to hear of Judge Beaudin's death. Extraordinary that he should have died of apoplexy when he was anything but full blooded....

Everything has been going splendidly, health excellent, progress satisfactory in matters military.

Tomorrow I intend to send you a cablegram which you will have received long before this letter. I repeat here the good wishes which I offered you on the occasion of your birthday. I trust that you may have very many happy returns of the day.

East Sandling camp,
22 June, 1915

My dearest Mother,
I have not bought a motor cycle yet but if I do I will bear in mind what you say about Anthony [*Vanier's youngest brother*]. Still, motor cycles are very useful at the front and I might obtain permission to bring it to France, in which case, Anthony would have to wait. Besides, it is not sure that I will purchase one — our hours are very long and I have very little time for play.

The Van Doos Sail for Europe — May 1915

This week we are at the Hythe [*target*] ranges: you have often heard of them. We rise at 4:30 a.m. and shoot until 1 p.m. when another battalion takes our place.... When I compare our lot with that of the Princess Pat's [*Princess Patricia's Canadian Light Infantry*] at Salisbury, I consider that we are wonderfully fortunate. Our mode of living here is perfect from a hygenic viewpoint — the open-air, exercise of every description and delightful surroundings.

My writing is a bit uncertain because I am writing in bed (9 p.m. — reveille tomorrow at 4:30 a.m.)

Diary entry: 24 June. Feast of St. John the Baptist.

Beginning of a course in machine-gunnery at the Napier Barracks in Shorncliffe under the direction of Captain Johnstone, wounded in the battle of the Marne.

In the evening, a St. Jean-Baptiste dinner at the mess.... French Canadian songs, French enthusiasm, speeches. For some of us, this might be the last St. Jean-Baptiste dinner.

On the way from East Sandling to London
25 June, 1915

My dearest Mater,
I am writing this on the train, which explains the erratic writing. I told you in a letter sent a few days ago that I was going to take a course in machine guns. Since yesterday morning I have been quartered at Napier Barracks (headquarters of the 30th Infantry Battalion) at Shorncliffe camp, and I will probably be there for two weeks. When one leaves East Sandling camp to take a course elsewhere he is attached for discipline to the regiment occupying the barracks where he lives. As it is always difficult to obtain leave from one's own Commanding Officer because of various duties, I decided to take advantage of my stay at Napier to go to London for a change of air.

Our daily grind continues. However, as long as the machine gun course lasts I shall have very much better hours. First lecture 9:15 a.m. — last lecture over at 4:15 p.m. I need not tell you how important a part machine guns are playing in the present war. Before the war such a battalion as ours had two machine guns: now we are attempting to send a battalion to the front equipped with sixteen — one per platoon. Judiciously handled, these guns can do the work of 30 men.

Evidently the imperial authorities have decided to give us a thorough training before allowing us to go to the front. Officers are taking courses continually — bayonet, fighting, map-reading, machine gun handling, musketry etc. I almost forgot to mention our St. Jean-Baptiste dinner last night. Colonel Landry, our Brigadier, was present as were a number of French-Canadian guests. We had a jolly time, sang old French-Canadian songs and turned East Sandling camp into a suburb of Quebec. It did us all good. And we were very jolly. As our Brigadier [*Brigadier-General David Watson*] happily put it, while some in Canada mourned, we were jovial because to be so is the right of all those going into combat.

Casernes Napier, Shorncliffe,
le 1 juillet 1915

Bien cher papa,
[...] The length of our period of training in England is still uncertain and probably depends on the losses of the 1st Division who are in France. The McGill company (Capt. Barclay, Capt. McDougall and my other friends) should be heading for the front shortly as reinforcements for the "Princess Pat's." I am told that Talbot Papineau[8] [*a Montreal lawyer and passionate pan-Canadian nationalist who enlisted with the Princess Pat's*] continues to make promises: he has been in all sorts of predicaments and has managed to come through unscathed. He is now Captain and will perhaps be Major before long.

Diary entry: 1 July

I fired my automatic Colt revolver for the first time. It works magnificently.

Diary entry: 2 July

I bought a half interest in a motorcycle which belongs to Lieutenant Buchanan of the 24th Battalion. I rode it for the first time this evening and it went very well. Tomorrow, I will probably go to Canterbury.

Diary entry: 5 July

Swam in the sea in Hythe, the first time in several years. Intense heat. Frigid water.

East Sandling camp,
10 July, 1915.

My dearest Mother,
I have received your very interesting letters dated June 19th and June 22nd. You ask me in the former if I receive my letters regularly. Of course: the postal service is perhaps the best organized service in the Army. I am told that one's mail is delivered in <u>the front line</u> trenches, being brought up at night under cover of darkness.

Of course, you will hear all sorts of rumours — that we have left for the front before we do, that the regiment has been wiped out and a lot of similar rot. The less attention you give to wild reports and newspaper talk the nearer you will be to the truth.

I think we will not leave for the front before the end of August. The intention evidently is to give the 2nd Division a very thorough training. We are anxious to get over, and when the time comes to leave, we will be so fed up with training that we will shout with joy.

Glad to hear you have left for Magog [*Lake Memphramagog, in Quebec's Eastern Townships, where the Vaniers spent their summers*]. But even in Magog I doubt if the weather can be any finer than the weather we have been having here. Only on one or two days have we suffered from the heat: the evenings are very cool and the beaches are only three or four miles away. Today is positively cold:

every night we sleep with one blanket at least and sometimes we throw our great-coat over that.

I am delighted to hear that Frances has been so successful at the convent and that she has run away with three firsts and two seconds. Congratulate her. Don't worry about Anthony: he will come through when he gets started.

Diary entry: 17 July

Reveille at 5 a.m. Depart for inspection grounds at 7 a.m. Inspection of the entire division at 10:30 a.m. by the Canadian Prime Minister, Sir Robert Borden[9] and his Minister of War, the Rt. Honorable Sam Hughes.[10] Before the inspection came a torrential rain, followed by brilliant sun.

East Sandling camp
25 July, 1915

My dearest Mater,
[...] Lately we have been bivouacking out at night: except when it rains, one sleeps very well under the stars. We expect to be inspected this week or next by the King and by Lord Kitchener.[11] Our training has become more arduous than it ever was before, outpost work at night, attacks at dawn, very long and hard marches etc. In spite of this work, I think I am still putting on flesh.

There has been nothing to mar our pleasant mode of life at East Sandling. We have a very good mess, cheerful and hygienic quarters and usually delightful weather. I have seen a number of chaps from the front who tell me that the life there is less strenuous than the one we are leading and that one gets used to conditions very quickly.

I was glad to hear that you had at last discovered a satisfactory chauffeur; however chauffeurs change their attitude so quickly that by the time you receive this you may no longer look upon the one you have as a paragon. They have a way of suddenly exploding and going up into thin air!

East Sandling camp
29 July, 1915

My dearest Mater,
We have been doing so much night-marching, outpost work, etc. that I have begun to lose track of the days and dates. Tuesday morning, we left for a long march on which I acted as officer in command (C.O.) of the left flank guard. At night we slept in bivouac: next morning we returned to camp and had a couple of hours' sleep: in the afternoon we practiced trench warfare and at night until midnight — attacks on enemy trenches. I have just got up from a well earned rest (11 a.m.) We are leaving in two hours on another march and we bivouac again tonight.

    There is no news of our departure yet but as I wish to inform you of any move of that kind and as the censor might not let through a direct message, I shall make use of the following code: "How is Arthur?" means leaving for France. "Expect you shortly" means leaving for the Dardanelles.[12] The cablegram may be signed by someone else but pay no attention to the signature and say nothing to anyone about the message for two or three days after its receipt. There has been some vague talk concerning our being sent to the Dardanelles. Personally I place no credence in the stories.

East Sandling camp on Tolsford Hill
5 August, 1915

My dearest Mater,
Yesterday we were reviewed by the Rt. Hon. Mr. Bonar Law[13] and by the Hon. Sam Hughes in the pouring rain. The Division looked even better than it did for the inspection by Sir Robert Borden.

    It was a repetition of the impressive ceremony of a few weeks ago: at the foot of Summerhouse Hill, the 2nd Canadian contingent was lined up, approximately 40,000 strong. We marched past in columns of platoons (any of your military friends will tell you what this formation is) and as each platoon commander saluted and gave the command "Eyes Right," Mr. Law removed his black bowler, had his head drenched and probably his back also, as the water was trickling down our spines. The men swung along splendidly: instead of dampening their ardour, the storm seemed to rouse them. The air was less oppressive after the first downpour.

Of course you know yesterday was the anniversary of the declaration of war by England and the review, consequently, had a very particular significance. To complete the day, Mr. Bonar Law spoke to us in the evening at the drill hall in Folkestone. His speech was retrospective and prospective: a synopsis of what England had done and what she was likely to do. He spoke with deep conviction. He is a quiet unassuming speaker, with little gesture and no theatrical tricks. He speaks in a conversational tone (very pleasant timbre) and unless you listen intently (specially at the back of the hall), you miss snatches here and there. He has a delightful sense of humour, a remarkable command of idiomatic English and a supple turn of mind. I felt as if I could have listened to him for three or four hours without tiring. He told us that he wished he were at liberty to tell us how many troops England had raised and equipped during the last year and that if the figures were known they would delight us and surprise our enemies.

The meeting was for officers only. It was a touching and inspiring scene, this gathering of Canadian officers from every part of the Dominion and belonging to every walk in life, united in the mother country and proclaiming the solidarity of the English peoples.

Everyone is quite confident of ultimate victory: there is only one end, the complete humiliation of Germany. It makes no difference whether it takes one year or ten years. Even should Germany succeed in completely dominating France and Russia, which is ridiculous, the war would only be beginning as far as England is concerned. This is the sentiment found in the speeches of Asquith,[14] Law, Lloyd George and Balfour.[15]

I receive "Le Temps" [*a daily paper from Paris*] regularly and there again the foremost thinkers of France make it quite clear that peace is impossible until Germany accepts unqualified defeat. There are no half measures for France this time: she is determined to destroy German autocracy or to go down irredeemably. The sword of Damocles has been hanging above the French head too long already. The only way France can obtain honourable security is by eradicating the Hun menace.

Hotel Cecil,
Strand, London W.C.
8 August, 1915

My dearest Mater,
I am spending the weekend in London.... During the last week I have been detached from my regular work to take a course in bomb-throwing. The work is very interesting. All the officers and most of the men are obliged to take instruction in it. At the front there are officers who carry bombs instead of revolvers. They are very simple to make and are very deadly. Shaving soap tins, and in fact any handy receptacle are used in the manufacture of these grenades.

The summer is getting well on, without any intimation of our departure so I imagine we will not suffer from the heat in the trenches but rather from the cold — which suits me very much better.

Diary entry: Sunday, 8 August

Mass at the Farm Street Church [*in London*]. In the afternoon, visited the poor quarters of London.
    7:15 p.m. Left for East Sandling.

East Sandling camp
10 August, 1915

My dearest Mater,
Last night I witnessed a marvellous sight, nothing less than a fight between a Zeppelin and the English gunners at Dover and in the Channel. It was just my luck (I should say "our luck" because the battalion was doing night work) to be in just the right position to get a splendid view of the fight. We left camp at 10 p.m. and marched to a point N.E. of our camp. Whilst preparing to make an attack on a defensive position of which a reconnaissance had been made by day, I saw the searchlights at Dover and along the coast playing on the skies. After five minutes of searching they found the Zeppelin they were looking for and kept it covered with their lights. A moment later (the

Zeppelin was flying very low) shells began to burst around it. The coast guns and the English men of war in the Channel were firing on the Zeppelin. I could follow the train of the shells from the ground to the Zeppelin and then see them bursting apparently very near the craft. After a number of shells had been fired, the Zeppelin suddenly appeared to dip: it was impossible to say whether it was struck or whether the aeronaut, seeing that the Zeppelin was discovered and that it would have a short life, decided to rise to a safe height. In any case it disappeared and the searchlights were unable to locate it again. All this we saw quite plainly at a distance of eight or nine miles. The Zeppelin stood out quite distinctly against the starry sky. This is the first glimpse we have had of actual warfare and although we were in no danger, it gave us a thrill.

11 August 1915

This morning's paper (I am enclosing a clipping from London's Daily Mirror) gives us the information that one of the Zeppelins was so badly crippled that it fell and was towed into Ostend where the Allied aeroplanes had a "go" at it and destroyed it.

Diary entry: 21 August

Drove to Hendon with Majors Tremblay,[16] Dubuc and Captain Boyer. All four of us went up in an aeroplane for the first time. Weather fine with a strong wind. The sensation of flying was very agreeable with its lightness and detachment from things material. The plane leaves the ground without the slightest jerk. The take-off is the most impressive moment: it is taking flight towards the unknown. Our bodies seem to leave us and become part of our souls. I didn't feel the least bit nervous; you go up up and you feel completely satisfied. The whole nervous system relaxes amazingly. It's like being in a rocking-chair, as you ascend, coast along, and come down again, without any shock or fear. It's like a beautiful and strange dream.

The Van Doos Sail for Europe — May 1915

Royal Automobile Club
Pall Mall, London S.W.
27 August, 1915

My dearest Mater,
[...] Last Friday night (Aug. 20th), Major Dubuc and myself obtained a six days' leave and became travelling companions. We came to London and went to the Savoy Hotel where we remained until Sunday morning. Sunday we left for Brighton Beach, one of the most important watering places in England. Brighton is 50 miles due south of London: wonderful train service, the fast train making the trip in one hour flat.

In peace time, many thousands of people go to Brighton for the baths and the sand (as a matter of fact the worst feature about Brighton is the shore which is covered with small pebbles and rocks that hurt the feet when you walk barefooted). In wartime however there are fewer people: economy has become the watchword in England and as a consequence certain branches of industry and of commerce are suffering badly.

We put up at the Metropole at Brighton. We lounged about the place, we lay on the seashore and we had very good sea baths. (Oh how the Governor would enjoy them! I remember how he always felt at Cacouna.)

I forgot to mention that Saturday afternoon we went out to Hendon and flew in an aeroplane. You know how anxious I have always been to go up. It had been one of the dreams of my life to take an aerial trip.... The most surprising thing about flying is that it hardly affects you at all in the way in which you might expect it to: you do not feel in the least nervous. In fact it keys one up: the people below you appear to be flies or babies according to the height at which you are. There is no nervous tension, you observe everything that goes on below and altogether the experience is most pleasant.

The one disagreeable feature is the terrific whirr of the powerful motor behind you. The sound almost deafens. Of course there is a tremendous wind blowing all the time and you imagine that your nose is turning white or red according to the temperatures.

We returned to London from Brighton Tuesday afternoon: since then I have been going to the theatre at night and shopping in the day-time. I cabled for money: I don't wish you to think that I am very extravagant in London because I am not. However the articles of kit that I have bought are rather expensive and as I wish to have as complete a kit as possible and the best goods I didn't hesitate to cable for money. To show you that I am not buying <u>inexpensive</u> effects I went to Burberry's today and purchased a very heavy raincoat with detachable fleece lining. The officers at the front recommend it very highly: it costs six pounds six shillings. You can see how a few purchases of this kind will make a hole in a subaltern's pay.

I think we shall be going in a few weeks — two or three. I hear however that we shall probably continue our training in France and not go into the firing line at once.

Give my affectionate regards to all — specially to the Governor to whom I will write in a day or so.

P.S. I am now staying at the Royal Automobile Club, Pall Mall: the members have graciously admitted all officers of the Imperial Army to the privileges of the club.

We have a gymnasium, Turkish baths, a large swimming tank and other conveniences: besides there is a homelike atmosphere about the Club that I like very much.

Diary entry: 2 September

Inspection of the 2nd Canadian Division by His Majesty the King. The King was accompanied by Lord Kitchener and by Major-General Turner, Commandant of the Division. The King appeared radiant, buoyant and confident. He told us that the inspection had been very successful, and that the men had marched well. As usual for inspections, it rained, but in all, it was a moving spectacle, the most beautiful day of my military life.

East Sandling camp,
4 September, 1915

My dearest Mater,

The Van Doos Sail for Europe — May 1915

[...] Yesterday I received two pairs of boots from Dangerfield — and very delighted I was to get them. I don't think I ever explained why I cabled for shoes to Montreal. This is why: I imagined in the first place that I could get a shoemaker in England who would make me a comfortable pair of boots after studying my foot. I went to a highly recommended man, gave my measure and he made me two different pairs of boots, one after the other, and was unable to give me satisfaction. I have worn Dangerfield's boots almost continuously since I purchased them: they have given me solid comfort. Dangerfield seems to have given me support exactly where it was needed.

I was sorry to hear of Father Fox's[17] [*one of Vanier's teachers at Loyola*] death: he was a saintly man and is certainly reaping the great reward he worked so hard for. I have seldom met such a self-sacrificing man as he: he wore himself down doing his own and specially other people's work. He was the sort of man who never could call his time his own, because if anyone wanted anything done he was good natured enough to volunteer himself, even if his comfort suffered. He was a man in several hundred thousand.

A death which surprised me very much and one of which you have probably not heard is that of Mayor Douglas[18] of Amherst. In my letters from Amherst I must have mentioned how he received us publicly and in his home. He was most kind to us all, and when on the boat, I wrote him a long letter which pleased him very much. He replied, expressing his thanks, and at this moment his unanswered letter lies before me. He was very sad when he said goodbye to us at Halifax (he accompanied us from Amherst with the federal member Mr. Rhodes[19]) and we little thought that long before we saw the trenches he would be gone. He died of pneumonia.

Thursday I was appointed machine gun officer of the 22nd in place of the incumbent officer for whom another berth was found. Of course I lose my platoon and I leave "D" Company. The new responsibility is greater and so is the interest. Each battalion will have sixteen machine guns, we are told, and this should afford splendid protection to the infantry.

I think we will leave for France in two weeks and that we will get another month's training over there before going into the firing line. As a matter of fact there is no need for more men in the first line trenches on the western front: things are very quiet there at present.

Of course if there were a German drive, supports and reserves would have to be brought up. I doubt very much if the Germans will ever break through in the west. To attempt such a thing would mean appalling losses.

About myself there is little to say, except that I am in radiant health and that I am very happy to be where I am.

P.S. Poor Judge Gervais[20] had been ill for such a long time that I was not surprised to hear of his death: an exceptional man with a very broad and receptive mind. A loss to French Canada.

Diary entry: Sunday, 5 September

Rode on horseback to Sandgate.... This morning at 11 a.m., Mass at which His Eminence Cardinal Bourne [*Roman Catholic Archbishop of Westminster*] presided. The Cardinal gave a lively sermon, speaking in both English and French (with a very good accent). After Mass, His Eminence gave us his benediction, then the troops gave three "hurrahs" for the Cardinal. It was a very moving sight for a Catholic soldier.

East Sandling camp
6 September 1915

My dearest Mater,
I received today your letter from Lake Memphramagog. You must have had a very lively weekend with fourteen in the house: I wish I had been there with all of you.

My appointment to the machine gun section has given me a bit more work: things are shaping very well and I expect to be "au fait" very shortly.

There are all sorts of rumours in connection with our departure. I think we shall leave next week (between the 13th and 20th). The training has been a little less violent recently, as we have been attending to the equipment of the men and for that matter of ourselves. I have bought about everything I shall require at the front and perhaps a great deal more that is quite unnecessary.

I have received very interesting letters from Mr. and Mrs. Marson [*family friends*] who have taken the trouble to send me clippings and newspapers. I gather from their letters that the Montreal newspapers, having little news to publish, spend their time frightening the people with stories of German attacks, enemy aeroplanes and such rot. Fortunately you pay no attention to these absurd stories.

P.S. I hope the long letter I wrote you dealing with Dangerfield's boots, Father Fox's death etc. did not go down on the "Hesperian."[21] Will you let me know please?

East Sandling camp,
12 September, 1915

My dearest Mater,
We leave for the front tomorrow afternoon — this is definite and of course by this time you will have received my cablegram informing you of the news.

There is nothing of special interest to relate — except of course the great event for which we have been waiting for so long.

The first section of the battalion left East Sandling camp by train for Southampton on September 13. The whole machine-gun section, which Lieutenant Vanier supervised as machine-gun officer, was on board — twenty-four privates, two sergeants, a corporal, a batman, and six drivers. Their equipment consisted of four guns, four limbered wagons and thirteen horses, twelve for draught and one for riding.

At Southampton, they prepared to board the ship Invention. *It had previously been used for trading with India but during the past year it was pressed into service to transport troops and munitions to France.*

Diary entry: 13 September

We are leaving for France in two hours. First to go are the cars, the transport, the munitions, the machine-guns. Tomorrow or the day after tomorrow, the rest of the battalion leaves. All the men are thrilled.... We spent the night on the wharf.... Our sleep was a little disturbed by the continuous arrival of trains. In spite of all the worries, a restful night.

Southampton Wharf
14 September 1915

My dearest Mater,
[...] The journey from East Sandling to Southampton was very enjoyable with the men naturally in the best of humour. We reached Southampton at midnight and detrained our transport in one hour without incident. I slept on the wharf and very well indeed with a horse blanket as mattress. Even at the Savoy with their three foot mattresses I have seldom had such a refreshing sleep. I shall begin to get very fat, I am afraid, with this outdoor life.

At the time of writing (11 a.m.), all our baggage is aboard the

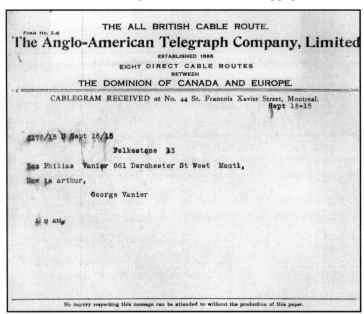

transport and we are ready to leave. Midnight, I think, will see us in France.

The departure from camp was very impressive and cheering. We got a rousing send-off from our brothers-in-arms. At every railway station where we stopped the people gave us a parting cheer.

The long training we have undergone should begin to bear fruit. If it does not it won't be the fault of the men, who are very keen for action.

The next morning, Vanier sent his mother a cable reading: "How is Arthur?" They were leaving for France.

2

"TO BE AT LAST IN FRANCE"
SEPTEMBER 1915

> "Never in my wildest flights of imagination could I have foretold that one day, I would march through the country I love so much in order to fight in its defence."
> Georges Vanier to his mother,
> 17 September, 1915

> "What France has gone through in this war no one will ever know; what her women have suffered without a murmur can never be adequately told...."
> Georges Vanier to his mother,
> 30 September, 1915

The Van Doos arrived in France in September 1915, a low point in the fortunes of the Anglo-French Entente. That summer had brought dismal news for the Allies from other fronts. An amphibious attack had stalled at Gallipoli on the northern side of the Dardanelles, the narrow strait that separates European Turkey from Asia. The campaign failed disastrously in the attempt to gain control of those straits and to capture the strategically important Turkish capital, Constantinople.

The picture was equally gloomy in the east along the front between the Central Powers and Russia. On May 2, German Chief of Staff General Erich von Falkenhayn ordered an attack at Gorlice, blowing apart the Russian front. His intention was to destroy the Russian army, then concentrate his full resources on the Western front. The attack nearly succeeded. Although Russia lost three-quarters of a million men and vast stretches of territory, there was no decisive victory. Despite near defeat, Russia was still in the war.

Meanwhile in France, preparations were underway for an Anglo-French offensive at Loos, a battle that would start on September 25 — once again, with disappointing results for the Allies.

The Van Doos crossed the English Channel on September 14. One section arrived in Boulogne the next morning and Vanier's contingent disembarked at Le Havre. It was a moving moment for the French-Canadian soldiers and one which Sir Maxwell Aitken[1] (later Lord Beaverbrook) described when he was acting as official "Canadian Eyewitness" at the front in the early years of the war.

> There is no parallel in history that matches the picture of the descendants of the men who founded Port Royal and Quebec under Champlain in the 17th century, returning after three hundred years of absence and a hundred and fifty years under a different flag, to fight once more for the soil whence their ancestors sprang.

Georges Vanier also wrote about the battalion's arrival in France in his diary the next day, September 16.

At night as we travelled across in the direction of the French countryside ... an indelible impression of this trip remains with me. To be at last in France and to fight for that beloved country is an inspiration!

Years later, when Vanier addressed the fiftieth anniversary of the Van Doos in 1964, he quoted one of his fellow officers, Major Maurice Dubrulé, who spoke about that moving day when the regiment first set foot in France:

"To Be at Last in France" — September 1915

Each one of us felt moved to tread for the first time on the soil of France which our ancestors had left to found New France. The curiosity of the Boulonnais was very lively. These brave cousins from France wondered who were these British soldiers who spoke French. Our men didn't hesitate to inform them. The news spread like wildfire in Boulogne and the crowds soon grew. Boulonnais and French Canadian soldiers felt immediately linked in friendship. Suddenly the orders of Colonel Gaudet rang out. We presented arms to a French flag which flapped from the mast of a ship. It was a salute from French Canada to the whole of France. Afterwards, a loud stentorian voice rose like a prayer from the ranks of the 22nd, with "O Canadiens rallions-nous."[2] The whole regiment, as if electrified, replied in unison with the refrain:

> Et près du vieux drapeau,
> Symbol d'espérance....

And with tears flowing, the proud evocation:

> Jadis, la France sur nos bords
> Jeta sa semence immortelle.

The regiment then marched through the streets of the town to the tune of "O Carillon" while the enthusiastic spectators lined the streets giving our soldiers an ecstatic ovation.

Diary entry: 15 September

Our section of troops landed at 8:30 a.m.... We walked through Le Havre as far as the Quai Maritime where we would be leaving for, where? Some say Rouen, or Abbéville. When we left Le Havre, the people shouted "good bye, good luck, safe return." They were all surprised to see that we spoke French and that we came from Canada!

The officers were very comfortably settled in a second class carriage while the men, on the other hand, were very uncomfortable in the baggage car (36 to 40 per car), with no seats and no lights.... However, they did not complain. On the contrary, they left the station at Le Havre singing "La Marseillaise" and "O Canada".... The women along the route were enthusiastic, cheering us up and encouraging us. At one small station, I bought a French newspaper from a woman who said with delight: "Ah Monsieur, we are happy to deal with a Frenchman en khaki." [*The French soldiers wore blue uniforms.*] The woman had tears in her eyes as she spoke....

They joined the rest of the battalion at the small station at Pont de Briques and continued by train to the town of St. Omer, twenty-five kilometres from Boulogne. At St. Omer, they linked up with their military transport — horses, mules and cars. Major Dubuc led this first contingent and Vanier, his machine-gun officer, rode on horseback. The bulk of the battalion marched the nine miles further to Wallon-Cappel just west of Hazebrouck in French Flanders where they spent the night.

It was at this point that Canada's 2nd Division, which included the Van Doos, joined the 1st Division to become the Canadian Army Corps. The newly formed Corps was headed by Lieutenant-General Sir Edwin Alderson,[3] *a fifty-five-year-old veteran who had commanded Canadians during the South African war. They made their headquarters in Bailleul, a small town southwest of Ypres, and took over a section of the front between Ploegsteert Wood (called "Plug Street" by the soldiers) and St. Eloi.*

Diary entry: 15 September. Wallon Cappel.

At Wallon Cappel, all the officers were installed at the Mairie where they slept on the hard floor with their mackintosh as a mattress. To sleep by 2 a.m. after looking after some food as well as the men's sleeping quarters. The region where we are staying was Flemish before the Napoleonic war and many of the people still speak Flemish.

"To Be at Last in France" — September 1915

Diary entry: 16 September

Last night, I went to bed at 9 p.m. and, with a few interruptions, slept very soundly all night. It was the first real sleep in three days and I was very tired. The French soldiers who keep watch (they are obviously not trained soldiers) are lively, intelligent, formidable opponents.

Diary entry: 17 September

Breakfast in a farm two steps away from the Mairie. The woman who served us has lived in this same spot since her childhood and refused to leave during the German advance last October. At this time, the Boche have been held back as far as Hazebrouck, four kilometres from here. Last night, we heard artillery shots very clearly to the north east. We are 16 1/2 miles [*twenty-five kilometres*] from the front.

    1:30 p.m. Departure from Wallon Cappel. We marched via Chemin Cinq Rues, Hazebrouck, Borre, Pradelles to our billets at Rouge-Croix where we spent the night.

Somewhere in France
17 September, 1915

My dearest Mater,
I presume you have received both cablegrams which I sent you. Consequently you will not be surprised to receive a letter from "somewhere in France." Without mishap the crossing from England to France was made and now we are quite near to the front — near enough to see the flare of the bombs and shells exploding near hostile aircraft and near enough to hear the roar of the artillery at night. I am billeted in a farm house with a few other officers and my men are in a neighbouring barn.

    I have never been so well in my life; the food is excellent. There are farmers quite near to the front who can supply you with delicious eggs, butter, coffee, milk, in fact any nutritious food. They say no one is ever so well fed as at the front, and I am beginning to think that what appeared absurd is quite true.

Since I have been appointed machine gun officer I have got into the very good habit of riding on an average of ten miles each day and the exercise (much less violent of course) agrees with me. I wish you to know particularly that I have not suffered in the least in reaching the point where I am: I mean by that, that I have not felt the slightest fatigue and the reason is quite simple: unmounted officers carry all their kit on their backs on the marches: mounted officers carry their effects in saddle bags slung across the horse. We carry on us our revolver, ammunition, a haversack and a water bottle — the horse carries the rest, even the raincoat.

The farmers of the district in which we are are very cordial and obliging — in a special manner perhaps because we speak the same tongue. Our reception throughout France has been splendid: the people hardly understand how we happen to speak French and wear khaki. Very many of the French inhabitants were ignorant of our political existence as a race apart in Canada. I think we have opened their eyes and their hearts.

I have lived some very thrilling moments in the last few days. All our training and hard work and drudgery were worth going through for the wonderful experiences that will mark our lives in such an indelible manner. Never in my wildest flights of imagination could I have foretold that one day I would march through the country I love so much in order to fight in its defence. Perhaps I should not say in its defence because it is really in defence of human rights, not of French rights solely.

The war has been lasting now so long that the organization is well nigh perfect. Every need is provided for and we are leading a very full and splendid life.

Regards to all at home, specially to the Governor. Don't forget Sophie who could say a little prayer for an extra dose of courage for the 22nd.

On September 19, the battalion left for Scherpenberg, 3 1/2 miles from the front. The next day, seven platoons, including Vanier's, made their first foray into the trenches near the town of Vierstraat in Flanders (Belgium).

The First World War was in fact a war of the trenches and for

"To Be at Last in France" — September 1915

most of the war, armies in Western Europe were locked in a series of trench systems that twisted and looped for several hundred miles from the North Sea to the border of Switzerland. A narrow strip of "No Man's Land" — varying from a few dozen yards to a mile wide — separated the two front lines and was threaded with masses of protective barbed wire.

A trench was usually about eight feet deep and four or five feet wide. There were parapets of sandbags packed to the front and rear where a flight of dirt stairs led down to a row of dugouts that were used for officers' quarters. Communication trenches ran at right angles to the front line and served to bring up supplies such as food and ammunition, and to bring back the dead and wounded. It was into this strange labyrinthine world that Vanier and his battalion plunged.

Diary entry: 20 September

Our first night in the trenches passed without incident. As the machine-gun officer of the 1st Kings Own Yorkshire Light Infantry was also on duty, I was allowed to sleep in for a few hours. Today I visited all the machine-gun posts. The secret of security in the trenches is to never show your head above the parapet. The bullets are harmless in a deep and straight trench. Your chief concern of life underground is to always stoop down. To forget this could be fatal. The Boche snipers train their machine guns on every inch of the parapet so lo and behold the unfortunate ones who show themselves.

Vanier's first impressions of life in the trenches were written, in French, to his father:

Flandres
le 18 [*probably* 20] septembre 1915

Bien cher papa,
I have just spent my first day in the front line of the trenches just 150 yards from the Boche. You very quickly get used to the bullets whistling past above your heads and the explosion of shells which

miss their target most of the time and to all the other diabolic machines used by the Germans.

At night the effect is ethereal — fireworks illuminating the German lines, the shells exploding in a burst of light which is fantastic and picturesque, the men singing and working and happy to be where they are — all this is deeply impressive. The game is well worth the candle: the intense reality of the life we are leading gives one a human outlook never to be lost. Don't imagine that the first sensations are unpleasant; they are not. A little astonishment and surprise at first, after which one is almost indifferent. (I say "almost" because there is still a little respect for these weapons of destruction.) You see, one gets so quickly accustomed to the most abnormal sort of life.

The life we are living in the trenches is exceptionally healthy. Our sector is very clean. We have all the provisions we need and of good quality too — a comfortable bed, relative security. What more could you ask?

Excuse this short note written in haste. I know that you will be happy to have my first impressions from the firing line and that you would be anxious to know the state of my soul and my morale under fire. Do not worry. I have never felt so strong.

In the trenches,
Flanders.
23 September, 1915

My dearest Mater,
I have been in the trenches four days and I am beginning to get used to the queer life. I received your letter dated August 30th at 1 o'clock last night as I was cleaning out one of my machine guns in an emplacement. First I had better answer your questions. I received both sums cabled to me and I should have acknowledged them before — mea culpa — many thanks. I received Dangerfield's boots and they were exactly what I wanted....

Now I shall recount briefly our mode of existence here. We are six days in the trenches and six days out in billets. During the six days in we seldom sleep at night: the Boche trenches are only 75 to 200 yards distant and of course relaxed vigilance might be a very serious thing, might end in a disaster of some kind.

The trenches (at least the sector we are in) are relatively safe and if a chap keeps his head well down he is not likely to be hit. This applies of course to rifle and machine gun fire: shell fire is harder to avoid and whether you are hit or not is largely a matter of chance.

This morning I witnessed a most striking scene: some time before dawn artillery duels were opened all around us and the sky was red with the thousand flashes from the cannon. Slowly dawn crept up, the flashes became more intermittent and less distinct and the morning broke on a plain zigzagged by trenches of all kinds. It is the sort of sunrise one does not forget.... I would not exchange the marvellous experiences I have gone through for five years of life.

Just at present we are marking time and watching one another like field mice. We nibble at one another occasionally, as General Joffre[4] [*French Commander-in-Chief*] would say. So far the weather has been very favourable and the trenches have been very dry, but as soon as the wet weather sets in we shall probably be ankle-deep in mud. Really it is very good sport.

Diary entry: 23 September

After a restful night, I left with Major Tremblay to reconnoitre the subsidiary lines of defence in our sector which stretch from a spot on the Vierstratt-Wytschaete road, 3/4 of a mile south east of Vierstraat to the Petit Bois which is occupied by the Germans. In case of an attack, the supplementary lines of defence are very strong, especially in the Bois Rossignol which is a little outside of our sector.

5:30 p.m. I saw my first Taube [*a type of German plane*]. It was flying very high. One of our planes chased it but without success. The Taube was much faster than our plane. The night was noisy with loud cannon firing. Fairy-like illuminations all along the front.

Diary entry: 29 September

The changeover of the machine-gun section with the 26th Battalion was scheduled for 8 p.m. When all the arrangements were made, I stayed in the trenches until 2:30 a.m. then left for camp at Scherpenberg, arriving exhausted at 6 a.m. Along the road, my machine-gunners were walking under such heavy loads of equipment, they kept collapsing with fatigue. It was only after many long stops that I was able to reach the camp with them. Arrived at 6 a.m. I threw myself down on the floorboards of the hut and slept soundly all night. <u>Sleep.</u>

A division usually had only four of its twelve battalions in the trenches at one time. Once relieved, almost always at night, troops filed their weary way back through a maze of communications trenches. There they formed up and marched to their billets which could be a battered farmhouse, a prefabricated hut, even a rain-soaked tent. Often there was no choice but to sleep in the fields under the stars.

About 3 1/2 miles from the front [*at Scherpenberg*]
30 September, 1915

My dearest Mater,
Tuesday night we came out of the trenches after a stay of ten days. I can admit that it was a relief to be able to raise one's head as high as one wanted to and to stretch the body, to walk, to run and to ride. One is necessarily cramped up in the trenches: the horizon is restricted to your dugout and to the top of the parapet with an occasional glance at the German lines through a loop-hole or through a periscope.

Since leaving the trenches I have taken as much exercise as possible. Today for instance I left camp at 10 a.m. and returned at 7 p.m. The country about is very beautiful and picturesque. There are all sorts of interesting spots, small chapels, windmills etc.

I forgot to mention that after a stay in the trenches we are brought out sufficiently far back to be freed of the worry caused by bullets, small shells and other little annoyances but we are still within range of the heavy artillery.

It is most striking at night to observe the battlefront: a continuous line of flares, of torpedoes, of artillery bursts indicates the mobile frontier which we hope to push onward shortly when the

"To Be at Last in France" — September 1915

French have continued their advance. The French are splendid, their dash and determination is wonderful and I feel like saluting every man and woman I meet from the most gallant and boldest nation in the world.

It is hard to believe that there are people in Canada who dare criticise the French: if we had more like them in Canada we would be another, a better race. What France has gone through in this war no one will ever know; what her women have suffered without murmur can never be adequately told. The French will start the offensive movement and we will follow it up. After twelve months of hardship and of privation, the old time dash of the most gallant of nations will carry us through — and we are <u>going</u> through.

Long walks, often while carrying heavy equipment, were part of a soldier's day.

Diary entry: 1 October

Our installation continues. We are living in Scherpenberg, some of us in huts, the others under tents. Six officers share our hut — Major Dubuc, Captains Plante [*Lucien*] and Beaubien, Lieutenants Dubrulé, de Martigny and me. We are 3 1/2 miles from the front.

At night, there is the sound of cannon-fire, fireworks, flashes of artillery.... Though we are outside the danger zone ... we are in the range of the heavy artillery but the Boche have not discovered our position and we rest in peace.

This afternoon, I rode on horseback to Westoutre [*Westouter, in Flemish*] to take a hot bath in a wash-tub fitted out in a large shed.

Diary entry: 2 October

This morning, I received orders to return to the trenches in the afternoon with the machine-gun section. Left Scherpenberg at 2:30 p.m. Close to Sandbag Villa [*an old house turned into Regimental Headquarters*], the Germans launched heavy shells which exploded 500 yards from where we were. In the communications trench, I met two stretcher-bearers who were carrying one of our men on their shoulders. It was Tremblay of no. 13 platoon. He had been killed while repairing the support trench. It was a "reversed bullet" [*a dum-dum?*] which killed him. Les Cochons! [*the swine*]

Two days later, on October 4, Vanier went out on his first patrol, near the village of Kemmel. He described his experiences in his diary:

Today I tried out the machine guns which worked wonderfully. The Germans are very active: there is light bombing in the countryside by their artillery. Tonight I must go out on patrol near the lines of defence. This will be a new and dangerous experience but useful for training purposes.

Out in front of the trenches from 9 till 11 p.m. As we were coming back one of our sentries fired on us at short range and Sergeant Rajotte [?] very nearly was killed. It could have been a fatal mistake. Beyond the parapet you have to drag yourself along on your stomach, your face in the mud. Bullets whistle past and cross by overhead. You are under incessant fire. Actually the danger is not as great as you might think. In creeping along you are pretty sure to avoid the fire of machine-guns and artillery. The German rifles are pointed at the top of our parapet and the bullets pass three or four feet above our heads. The only immediate danger is from stray bullets, and from the bombs and hand grenades that the Boche throw between the lines, precisely to catch the patrols. The sensation of being underneath this sort of fire — bullets, machine-guns, etc. — is exciting; it seizes your imagination, your nerves remain very firm, and you keep your head.

Diary entry: Tuesday, 5 October

Situation generally quiet. At 3:30 p.m., two Zeppelins passed over our lines at one hour's interval. Heavy shelling on the Kemmel Road.

Diary Entry: 6 October

We have our meals at the most extraordinary times — it's the reverse of our old system. We rise at 11 a.m. and have breakfast. We have lunch at 4 p.m. and at 11 p.m., we have dinner which is our best meal. We have it this late to keep ourselves awake and to help pass the long hours of the night. It's a jolly meal. The five members of the mess — Major Dubuc, Captains Plante and Beaubien, Lieutenant de Martigny and myself — get along splendidly, and during the meal we are very open and there is much ribaldry. This is what makes life in the trenches bearable.

    3:30 p.m. I have just learned that Major Roy [A.V. Roy, *Commander of Company "B"*] was killed while picking up a German grenade that landed close to him without exploding. The minute he picked it up, the grenade exploded and killed him. This was a very brave man who has left us. At the front, he was a fine example of devotion and courage. It is the first loss among the officers and it has been particularly painful for us.

Le 6 octobre 1915

Bien cher papa,
I have the sad duty of informing you that we have lost an officer of the 22nd today. It is our first loss among the officers and a painful

one for his comrades. Major Roy was killed this afternoon by a German grenade which fell a few feet in front of him. It did not go off at once and without thinking about it, the officer bent down to pick it up. The moment his hand touched it, it exploded, inflicting the most terrible wounds.

Our losses, up to now, however, have been minimal. Our sector of the front has been quite peaceful. Since the newspapers will nonetheless print all sorts of false and disquieting news, I thought it wise to reassure you to the contrary. First of all, we were not part of the Allied attack recently at Loos[5] and in any event we would not have been chosen to participate until we have learnt the fundamentals of trench warfare. At the moment, the Germans opposite us are doing the same work as we: making the trenches deeper and safer. In spite of the proximity of our work to the front lines, we are in relatively little danger. Losses will become serious only when our troops are asked to advance and attack. Thus you must not worry: if a soldier is killed or wounded, it will be either a case of bad luck or a result of lack of caution.

On a personal note, my spirit is at peace, my health is excellent, sleep comes easily and is very restorative.

A toute la famille mes amitiés. A vous et à Maman toute mon affection.

Diary Entry: 8 October

At 4 p.m. I received orders to leave the trenches as soon as the machine-gunners have been relieved by the 26th Battalion. By 5:30 p.m., the Boche had discovered what was going on and with heavy artillery pounded, among others, the trenches occupied by the 25th Battalion. Some thirty men were swallowed up by the bombardment but the actual losses are not yet known. For several minutes there was a series of explosions that shook the ground. The shock was frightening. The bombardment exploded several of our landmines and one explosion left a crater 150' by 30'. Our own artillery responded in kind. One unfortunate detail was that a flurry of English 4.5" Howitzer shells landed among our lines. Miraculously, only one exploded. It was equally miraculous that no one was wounded.

At 6:30 p.m., I reported to Colonel Gaudet who sent me back to the trenches with my section. After the explosions and bombings, we fear a possible attack and the Colonel wants the machine-gun section to be doubled.

10 p.m. On duty again, after an arduous journey slogging through the mud in the maze of dark trenches. Every minute, you slide into another hole of water.

Diary Entry: 9 October

We left the trenches at noon and returned to the camp at Scherpenberg. <u>Rest.</u>

Diary Entry: Sunday, 10 October

Mass at the parish church in Locre [*"Loker" in Flemish, a village near Bailleul*], 1 1/2 kilometres from Scherpenberg. The sermon given by l'Abbé Doyon was animated and very listenable. It had a sobering effect on the men who realized the serious work they have to accomplish. In the afternoon, General Turner, head of our division, came to congratulate us on our conduct in the trenches during the events of 8 October. Major Roy has been recommended for the Victoria Cross for his act of bravery....

In the trenches
Flanders
Undated. Probably early October 1915

My dearest Mater,
I received this morning your card dated 15th September from Hampton Beach and your letter from home dated 20th September.
I am delighted to hear that Anthony likes St. Mary's College better as he continues. Let him stick to it but do not allow him to leave off his French lessons at Miss Martin's.

There is nothing too startling to record. The Boche are very inoffensive in our sector and they (the authorities) will probably keep us here for some time yet until we become really seasoned troops. Our men are taking to the work very well indeed and the morale of the whole battalion is splendid.

We are getting a taste of cold weather, but so long as the atmosphere remains relatively dry we shan't complain: what is hard is being up to one's knees in mud and dirt. After six days in the trenches they take us out and we get a wonderful bath which lasts almost an hour. Each man receives clean underclothing and after six days rest is ready for the trenches once again.

I received a letter from Mr. Marson at the same time as yours and he gave me news of the Court House. He says the law offices are not nearly so prosperous as they used to be. It will be hard to eke out even a petty existence when I return to Montreal — eh what? as Frances would say.

This letter is written very much in haste on my knees which accounts for the strange penmanship.

Diary Entry: 11 October

The morning bath with my section at Westoutre [*Westouter in Flemish*]. The hygiene among the English troops is excellent, thanks perhaps to this regular bath. We sit for half an hour in the hot water. Each man then receives clean underwear and socks.

Flanders
13 October, 1915

My dearest Mater,
I have received your letters dated Sept. 26th and Sept. 28th from Montreal. It is splendid to get news so regularly from home. If you send me socks, and I should be very glad to receive some, please send very thick ones, <u>all wool</u>, and as much as possible, seamless. Socks are the soldier's greatest need in the trenches (perhaps I should say together with boots.)

I have been out of the trenches four days now and am going

back the day after tomorrow. Some battalions have four days in and four out, others two in and two out. I prefer our method because one has time to settle down in rest camp.

I have had no hardship so far: the weather has been favourable. It is perhaps better not to boast as the worst months I am told in Flanders are November, December and January.

I mess with the officers of "D" Company. We have had a mess basket sent from London. This basket is wonderfully complete in plates, cutlery and utensils of all kinds. It is very portable in size and in weight: great boon!

Diary Entry: Wednesday, 13 October

5:30 a.m. Woke early to meet with several of my section at the Church in Locre. Confession and Communion.

Our battalion is still being held in reserve at Scherpenberg. This afternoon, there was intense bombing of the German lines by our artillery. We could watch the effects of our shelling from the slopes du Mont Aigu (near Scherpenberg) where we had a superb view of the front occupied by our 5th Brigade. It was a moving and imposing spectacle. You can hear the explosions, and see the smoke which is white or black or sometimes green. The front is marked by a long trail of powder. There is an autumn sun on the green and restful countryside. How picturesque! The Boche have replied by a bombardment that caused many losses among the 26th and 24th regiments.

Diary entry: 14 October

At 3 p.m., I received orders to return to the trenches with my section.... I took over command at 7 p.m. We have learned that the losses among the 26th have been heavy. The machine-gun officer of the 26th has been wounded in the hip.

Diary entry: 15 October

The 22nd Battalion is in the trenches by 7 p.m. I am not displeased. Our "Mess" is very jolly and makes the slightly monotonous life in the trenches almost agreeable.

Diary entry: 17 October

Excursion over the parapet of "C" Company with Brosseau under cover of the early morning mist. We went a distance of 400 yards where we saw several German corpses in an advanced state of decay lying close to a hole two feet deep. They had evidently been trying to dig a trench when the machine-gun surprised them. They must have been lying in the open for several months. I took a few buttons and a Missal from one of the bodies and we will bury them in the mist tomorrow.

Dans les Flandres
le 18 octobre 1915

Bien chere papa,
[...] Our life underground continues without too many tragic incidents. Our losses are light, the sector where we are is very quiet. The daily bombardments that we receive are not too aggravating. Our artillery is definitely superior to the Boche artillery.

We continue a routine of six days in the trenches and six days of rest at a camp four miles from the firing line. We have not yet taken part in an attack but the men are very anxious to jump over the parapet and push back the enemy. I do not think that the order to advance will come before we have received more complete training.

Father Gaume regularly sends me his genial and patriotic letters which remind me of the good times we spent together in Paris [*when he visited with his father in 1912*].

The news of the French victory in Champagne[6] has bolstered the troops: we are expecting other attacks and a definitive victory.

The question of the Balkans is a little complicated and unfortunate but cannot influence the final result. We will surely win.

Diary entry: 18 October

The weather continues to be fine and tonight there is a new moon. It is difficult to believe that while we are sitting in the trenches under the stars the Boche are barely yards away. At certain times, there is complete silence, not a single rifle shot much less a fussilade for several minutes.

If it was not so tragic and horrible, it would be beautiful.

3

"OH, THE MUD OF FLANDERS"
OCTOBER 1915

"A heavy rain continues to fall. The water rises, the tide of mud appears to flood us completely. I return to my dugout and find five inches of water and all my personal effects — sox, books, etc. — floating around.... Mud, mud and more mud."
     Georges Vanier in his diary,
     10 November, 1915

"I have attended midnight Masses when the singing was better, when the lighting was more brilliant, when the crowd was gayer and the clothes brighter. But never have I attended a more stirring or a more impressive Mass than last night's."
     Georges Vanier to his mother,
     Christmas Day, 1915

Towards the end of October, the Canadian Army Corps settled down for a long winter ahead, still covering the section of the front between Ploegsteert Wood and St. Eloi. The Van Doos returned to the trenches near the village of Kemmel, southwest of Ypres. *The fighting soon began to taper off except for sporadic minor skirmishes, so the days took on a monotonous routine. Uppermost in everyone's mind was the anticipation of the dreaded Flanders winter.*

Diary entry: Tuesday, 19 October

Today we are under continual bombardment by the Boche and there have been some losses. Several Allied aeroplanes and one German one have flown above us surveying our trenches. The German was chased away by one of our planes. Another of our pilots flew a superb complete reconnaissance of the German lines. He attracted attention from all sides, which he fortunately avoided. Shells exploded quite close to the plane. What bravado! Compared to the work that we are doing, these pilots are superhuman.

Flanders
21 October, 1915

My dearest Mater,
[...] A week ago I mailed some lace to you and to Eva: I trust you will receive it. I believe the two pieces complete one another — one being an "entre-deux", whatever that is. So make whatever combined use you like of both pieces and save a small portion for "Smink" [*Vanier's nickname for his sister Frances*].

At one of the convents near here, to be accurate (is the censor looking?)[1] at ——— [*Locre*], the girls make very pretty lace indeed: unfortunately they have orders that will keep them busy for months. In spite of that, I was so much impressed with the beauty of some of the samples that I ordered some for yourself, for Eva and for Frances. The three packages will not reach you before February but I am sure they will reach you eventually because I have implicit confidence in the nuns. The peculiar interest attached to the lace is that it is made within a radius of ten miles from where the 22nd are fighting. Someday, I shall tell you the exact spot in Flanders.

Father Gaume writes regularly, is very enthusiastic and wants to send me anything I may ask for. It is jolly gratifying to have so many friends thinking of you.

I came out of the trenches last night after the customary six days' stay. No untoward incident to report beyond the slight daily bombardment to which we are subjected and to which of course we reply. Our casualties have been light so far. It is not likely that we will be in a serious engagement for some months yet.

Diary entry: 16 October

[...] This morning there was some aerial combat: a Boche plane crashed between the 1st and 2nd German line. Success for the Allies. This afternoon, I launched a number of hand-grenades for the first time. It was a new sensation. I was rather nervous to begin with but then you get used to it, you calculate the time, and you throw it steadily. The grenades are the most effective way of capturing new trenches. Shells and bullets have too level a trajectory. A man lying flat in a trench is sheltered from them, but grenades can do a lot of damage when the trench is deep and very narrow.

Diary entry: 21 October

Radiant sun. The weather is beautiful and the air is fresh. After a stint in the trenches, the countryside looks even more beautiful, more comforting.

On October 27, the Van Doos celebrated the first anniversary of the founding of the 22nd Battalion at a dinner held at the Hospice of St. Antoine, an old Flemish convent in Locre. It was an impressive, yet sobering occasion that Georges described to his mother:

Flanders
27 October, 1915

My dearest Mater,

[...] This is the anniversary of the foundation of the Royal 22nd and to celebrate the event, we gave a dinner last night at the convent of ——— [*Locre*]. The General commanding the division and our Brigadier General were present. The occasion was impressive. Colonel Gaudet spoke feelingly of the death of Major Roy, the first officer of the 22nd to be killed in action and who, the General told us afterwards, has been recommended for the Victoria Cross. I am sure he will get this most coveted of decorations. As General Turner said, the V.C. will not give us back Major Roy but it will be a wonderful inspiration to the rest of us and a consolation to the family. He well deserves it. [*Major Roy did not receive the Victoria Cross.*]

I am going back to the trenches this afternoon for the customary six days. The weather has become a bit more damp and I fear we shall have a few months of wet and mud. With the care we have learned to take of ourselves, there is no danger of colds or rheumatism. The open air life is the best under all conditions, even the worst.

Diary entry: 27 October

4 p.m. Returned to the trenches. After two days of rain, they are in a deplorable state. There is mud and water up to our knees. The parapets have collapsed in several spots. The nights are frigid, our feet are cold and we have not yet received our supplies of wood and charcoal.

Diary or letter: 31 October

[In the trenches] we have two dugouts, underground of course, with an opening between them; one we use as a bedroom, the other as a dining room. Our batman found an old stove, complete in every respect, in a house which had been shelled to pieces not 100 yards from here and he carried out the stove one night. Now it is blazing away in our bedroom. In the worst weather we have dry socks, dry boots, hot coffee, bovril or cocoa.

"Oh, the Mud of Flanders" — October 1915

Diary entry: Monday, 1 November. Trenches near Vierstraat.

Major Dubuc has been wounded. A whizz-bang [*a high velocity shell*] exploded on the roof of a dugout and the roof collapsed, injuring Dubuc.

    A dismal morning. There are low clouds and the air is heavy. You feel oppressed and stifled: you paddle in a foot of mud and water. These are appropriate conditions for the Month of the Dead. The earth sweats and the departed return to us in a gust which is disconcerting and revealing also. We are ourselves the essential link between what is past and what is to come.

Diary entry: 2 November

The rain continues: the parapets are caving in. In certain spots, we have water and mud up to our knees. We made the change-over with the 26th this afternoon. In the communications trench there is five feet of water. We are forced to leave the trenches and go out in sight of the enemy. We are receiving a continuous shower of machine-gun fire which luckily has caused no losses.

Diary entry: 3 November

Back to our rest billets in Scherpenberg. Weather very bad. Rain and sleet.

Flanders
4 November, 1915

My dearest Mother,
[...] You will have heard from John and from Eva's letters that Adie [*Adrian McKenna, an old Loyola pal and close family friend*] was wounded in the shoulder. Nothing at all, only a flesh wound. I saw Ade a few times in the trenches and he looked splendid: very courageous soldier, I hear.

We are getting a specimen of Flanders weather just at present: I hope we will have a few intervals of sunshine because if we don't we will be cultivating a growth of mud. Of course we are so hardened to conditions of all kinds that we are not very much worried by rain and dirt. Oh, the mud of Flanders!

Just at present we are in rest camp after six pretty bad days in the trenches. As we left we were up to our knees in mud and jolly glad we were to get out too. We all have top boots and we manage to keep dry. You know how careful I am about my feet: this will give you an idea of the socks I make use of and the number of times I change a day. I am in the best of health and take very good care to throw myself on the ground when the bullets and shells start to fly about.

Out of the trenches we have a fairly decent time: of course the bath is a regular function: riding about the country is my favourite pastime. It's a wonderful life, Mater, the sort of thing I have always dreamt about and I would not exchange it for the matter-of-fact existence I led in Montreal.

Diary entry: 5 November. Scherpenberg.

[...] At night, about twelve of our aeroplanes rushed over to the German lines and received heavy shelling.

Diary entry: 7 November

Confession and communion this morning at the church in Locre. Mass at 8:15 a.m. In the afternoon, a horseback ride.

Diary entry: 8 November. Trenches near Vierstraat.

We returned to the trenches today — during the day because the communication trenches are blocked in several places and by night it is impossible to change-over. Often we are forced to leave the trenches: the Germans concentrated their fire-power and wounded several of our men. One of my section was wounded in the thigh. The trenches are filled with mud and more mud.

Diary entry: 9 November

The mud in the trenches is still up to our knees. Marching through the maze of the trenches is long and difficult. Occasionally, you must walk on and beside the parapet. A curious fact is that the Germans do not always fire on us when we expose ourselves. Perhaps they want a truce....

Diary entry: 10 November

A heavy rain continues to fall. The water rises, the tide of mud seems to flood us completely. I returned to my hut at 8 p.m. and found five inches of water and all my personal effects — sox, books, etc. — floating around.

Dans les tranchées
le 10 novembre 1915

Bien cher papa,
We returned to the trenches the day before yesterday. The sight was not very comforting. We stumble around in the mud up to our knees and the Boche artillery takes great pleasure in hurling shrapnel at us. A few men have been wounded. If you could see our men you would be pleased with them. They are splendidly daring. One of our machine-gunners was badly hit by a bullet in the thigh and somehow managed to get back up by himself. This is one incident out of many.

We have had the nuisance of mud and water for almost a week. Luckily, our rubber boots reach up to our hips so we can keep our feet dry. The nights are long and sometimes cold. A stove in our dugout gives off enough heat to warm the body and the heart. We do not suffer from cold, or from hunger or from thirst. Our orderlies are very devoted and are continuously looking after our comfort.

I believe that we will see some decisive events in the Balkans before long. Greece and Romania are lining up on our side and we will bring a strong blow to Turkey and Bulgaria.

To prove that I am not joking about our meals in the trenches, I will mention some of the dishes that we have tasted in the past two days — galantine de faisan [*pheasant*], riz de veau [*sweetbreads*], vegetable soup, lamb chops and, of course, coffee, cocoa or tea.

Diary entry: 12 November

Rained all day. The trenches are in an awful state, all nearly collapsing, and it is only with active work that we are able to save them.

In the trenches
12 November, 1915

My dearest Mater,

Flanders may be a beautiful country when the weather is fine, but when you are already wading in mud and water up to your knees and when you observe the rain steadily falling, your estimate of the historic land undergoes a change. One consolation is that we are not likely to have more than two and a half months of this climate.

I had managed to keep my dugout fairly dry until tonight: after spending a few hours with Captain Boyer in another part of the trench I returned to my dugout to find five inches of water on the ground and all my personal effects floating around merrily. This is not serious: I am an expert at drying out now.

We have been in four days and will have two more days of this before rest camp. All of us are in splendid shape and don't worry in the least about conditions. We always manage to have a fire of some kind and we keep our blood warm.

Germany will soon be thinking very hard of what a second winter campaign means with Russia. We have them on the hip now.

Diary entry: 14 November

We leave the trenches tonight after the most painful period I have experienced. I am filthy dirty but at least the cold I had when I entered the trenches is cured. My horse restored my morale. I can now sleep well after having looked after the comfort of the others, of their shelter, their food and their warmth.

During this period, another hazard entered their lives. A notice from a Lieutenant-Colonel Fotheringham dated November 16 advised that:

> One hundred tin atomizers have been procured by the Canadian Corps for the purpose of spraying coal oil about the dugouts in trenches and billets to clear them of vermin [lice], together with instructions for spraying the dugout, disinfecting clothing while having baths, cleaning and spraying billets before departure.
>
> This procedure, if faithfully carried out, and repeated for at least three times on coming out of the trenches, should free us from lice.

Diary entry: 17 November

Bath at the convent in Locre followed by tea with delicious cakes. The good sisters are very kind: we are always assured of a warm reception. In the evening, a dinner at Brigade Headquarters with guests of Lieutenant Watson, who was celebrating his birthday. Returned home by bright moonlight. Beautiful ride through the Flemish countryside.

Diary entry: 18 November

Began a new routine of four days in the trenches and four out. I believe in the winter it is better to relieve more often since your feet freeze and the men could catch pneumonia.

Diary entry: 19 November. Trenches near Vierstraat.

At 5 a.m., there was a violent gas attack on our left which we all felt. The men in the trenches used their gas masks for the first time.

The trenches are still in a deplorable state. It's impossible for me to make any sort of inspection of our emplacements without walking on the parapets which I manage to do during the night or just before dawn. There's been a curious transformation in the last two months: at first we would never dream of walking outside the trenches. Now it's become a regular habit: we no longer worry about errant bullets.

As the year 1915 drew to a close, gas attacks were becoming more frequent. In November, the men in the Van Doos used their gas masks for the first time.

Diary entry: 20 November

While returning from my rounds, I saw a poor devil who had just been wounded in the heart. I think he was dead.... *[Text faded.]*

In the trenches
20 November, 1915

"Oh, the Mud of Flanders" — October 1915

My dearest Mater,

I am afraid my supply of letters has fallen off during the last week. Please ascribe this to the rather bad weather conditions and not to any wilful neglect. Since writing you I have received your very cheery letters dated Oct. 28th, Oct. 31st and Nov. 4th and your two boxes of chocolates which were handed to me just before entering the trenches two days ago.

As you question me again as to what you can send to my men and to myself I answer most emphatically — SOCKS, all wool and as thick as you can find them. It amuses me to think that before the war I used to wear silk and cashmere socks during the winter. We should freeze out here without woollen goods: it is not so much from the cold that we suffer but from the humidity which will give you "trench feet" very quickly. Once you have "trench feet" it is very hard to navigate up and down the trenches in the cold water. At the slightest fall of rain or in temperature, the feet begin to swell and become numb. I am not telling you this from personal experience because I am taking jolly good care to avoid this malady. We grease our feet with a paste called <u>anti frost bite</u>: this combined with frequent washing and drying of the feet gives one reasonable protection against frost-bitten toes and heels.

[...] I told you in a previous letter not to worry about Adrian's [*McKenna's*] wound: it was only a flesh wound through the shoulder. Further details should have been cabled to Mrs. McKenna, it seems to me, in order to prevent her from imagining all sorts of wild possibilities. The boy will be perfectly well very shortly. But of course by this time, she must be "au fait".

The clipping you sent me with regard to Mr. McAllister's judgment gave me great pleasure. This is the most important case I have ever prepared. I took especial pains to have the pleadings in order and I trust the S.C. [*Supreme Court*] judgment will not be reversed. As a matter of fact Garneau [*one of Vanier's former law partners*] was never very sanguine about our chances of success and at one time we very nearly turned down the action. This of course is "entre nous".

Since the cold weather set in we have changed our mode of living in the trenches: we have four days in and four days out instead of six in and six out. This means besides that instead of getting a bath once every twelve days we get one every eight days. This applies to <u>every</u> man in the battalion. The bath is "de rigeur".

There are rumours to the effect that we will get leave in a month or so, not all the officers and men at once of course, but a small proportion at a time. I shall send you a cablegram the day my leave starts so that you may rest <u>absolutely</u> contented for the length of the leave — six or more days.

We are worrying through the wet weather as best we can: with top boots and many pairs of socks and gallons of boiling tea and coke braziers. I have had neither cold nor foot trouble nor fever so far and feel like congratulating myself. As some of us say — touch wood! Before we realize it the warm spring sun will be heating us again.

The Serbian question is most complicated and unfortunate: after the martyrdom of Belgium, the martyrdom of Serbia. The reckoning will be all the more serious for Germany. The horrible plight of Serbia will lengthen the war but will not change the issue. The Allies are going to win — if takes <u>ten years.</u>

I forgot to say in connection with our leave that I think it likely that we will be allowed to go to Paris. I should be delighted to see Father Gaume who writes to me very regularly. I have just received a small edition of the "Imitation" [*The Imitation of Christ*[2]] from him. It is extraordinary how one can find a sentence and a thought appropriate to any prevalent mood by simply opening the book haphazardly.

25 November 1915

My dearest Mater,
I have received your letter dated November 8th telling me that you had heard of Major Dubuc's wound. He has got over it already and is with us again. He was very fortunate to be so slightly injured: you know that he was buried under beams and sand bags after the collapse of his dugout which was struck at the corner by a shell (3 inch probably).

The weather has been very much better lately — colder and less rain. We expect to get a ten days' rest shortly and this coupled with our leave later on will carry us through the winter comfortably. Your socks reached me: many thanks. They are hardly thick enough: the kind I would like are the thick woollen ones worn by the shanty men and "habitants". The thicker the better and if possible <u>all wool.</u>

The officers in our hut found Page & Shaw's chocolates delicious: the brazil nuts in the centre were particularly good.

Diary entry: 29 November. Trenches near Vierstraat.

Very quiet day. A patrol was out last night and a message in German was sent to the German lines inviting them to surrender in small parties and telling them that we would take good care of them. But the message remained without an answer and the invitation does not seem to have been accepted.

Rest Camp (Scherpenberg)
1 December, 1915

My dearest Mater,
The news of Eva's engagement [*to Joseph Trudeau*[3]] surprised me of course, particularly as I do not remember ever having met her fiancé. I think that she is quite right to marry as soon as possible, if she has made up her mind. I know Eva well enough to be sure that her choice must be a sound one. There is no reason in the world for putting off her marriage: you are quite right to be opposed, as I am, to long engagements.

It is unfortunate that you should be left at home without Eva and without myself at the same time but you cannot forget that Eva sooner or later was almost sure to marry and that my absence is only temporary. Besides, you would not want to have me home when I would be unhappy at not being able to do my bit for the cause. Eva is taking the step she considers right and normal, just as I did almost a year ago and you still have both of us and I am jolly sure that when all this is over you will be glad we took the bull by the horns and decided to do what we considered to be our duty even at the risk, unfortunately, of giving you momentary pain. I am writing to Eva to offer my best wishes for the future.

At the front
4 December, 1915

My dearest Mater,
I have just received your Christmas package containing underwear, socks, cigarettes and chocolates. Be sure I appreciate very much indeed your kindness and thoughtfulness. You know of course that the greatest pleasure we have is receiving letters and gifts from home. The officers with whom I mess have asked me to thank you all for your Christmas presents. We share gifts and we are as happy as children when one of us, irrespective of whom it is, finds a package from home in his mail.

I checked the contents of the box with the enclosed list; not only is everything complete but I found moreover two boxes of cake. As everybody at home has had a hand in the making up of the box I wish you would tell each one of them that they have made a few officers in Flanders very happy indeed. The underwear is splendid, exactly what I needed. The socks however are not quite strong and thick enough. The "habitant" socks at Marché Bonsecours are the kind for the winter campaign in Flanders.

We have had a great deal of rain recently but curiously enough we do not seem to mind it. We are very careful about our socks and boots. You can get an idea of how particular we are when I tell you that I have not had a sore throat as yet.

In early December, Vanier received a letter from a first cousin, George Pelletier, who was then a second-year student at St. Anselm's College in Manchester, New Hampshire. Their sporadic correspondence continued for the duration of the war.

In the trenches, somewhere in Flanders
6 December, 1915

My dear George,
Your newsy letter gave me great pleasure indeed, specially as I did not expect it! And so you want me to give you a description of the

battlefields of Europe. I am afraid, my dear boy, that you are asking a great deal too much of me. All I can do is to give you an idea of trench life as we find it here in Flanders.

In the first place, we spend half our time in the front line trenches and half our time in reserve about three miles from the fighting line. At some points, our trenches are seventy-five yards from the Germans, at others three hundred yards. The distance varies from 50 to 500 yards, so you see we are never very far from the Boche whom we have to watch very closely.

We are all underground in holes called dugouts. Here we live, sleep when we can, fight and write sometimes, as I am to you tonight. In the daytime it is dangerous to show your head above the parapet: the German snipers have a good eye and unfortunately shoot some of our men through the head whenever they become careless.

At night however we come out into the open where we are not seen and where only stray bullets can harm us. After three months out here one learns to disregard stray shells and bullets of all kinds and we only worry about those that are aimed at us.

Some of the evening shells make a tremendous noise (you have heard them called "Black Marias", "Jack Johnsons", "Coal boxes") on explosion and send up a cloud of dirt and splinters fifty feet high. The detonation is terrific: besides the very large shells (5 to 12 inch), there are the field guns to be reckoned with (about 3 inch shells). These guns do most of the firing because the munitions are cheaper and because the guns can be more easily moved about. These guns fire shrapnel and high explosive shells. The shrapnel is set to explode in the air at a height of 30 or 50 feet. This shell after explosion scatters lead bullets and small pieces of steel and iron within a radius of about 75 yards. If you happen to be within this area your chances of receiving a small piece of metal are very good indeed.

Of course you know that our artillery and machine guns fire over the heads of our own troops: you see of course (from the drawing) how this is possible.

In this way our guns are always protected by our infantry and cannot be rushed by surprise by the enemy. No gun is ever left without protection of some kind: they are too precious to be abandoned in this fashion.

As I explained before, all our work is done underground: there is a long line of trenches running from the North Sea to Switzerland and in these trenches millions of men watch, wait and fight. Our quarters are pleasant and comfortable enough when the weather is fine but when it rains for days at a time, we wade in water and mud to our knees and higher.

We are very well fed in the trenches and we usually have enough left over for the thousands of rats and mice which invade our dugouts. Of course sometimes we witness disagreeable sights but one must get used to them.

You say that the Allies are bound to win: you are quite right. We cannot lose. It may take a few years yet, but in the long run Germany will be bled to death — in lives and money.

Diary entry: 6 December

The 22nd returned to the trenches. Machine gunners were relieved; all was completed by 4 p.m. No incident worth mentioning — a few bullets, some shells. A light rain falling. The weather is becoming bleak, the air is heavy. One must react in some way, so one dreams of the smiling spring and of friends far away.

Diary entry: 7 December

Went to bed at 4:30 in the morning. My bed consists of a number of planks with sand bags for blankets. But I managed to sleep for the next ten hours in spite of intermittent rain. The trench walls have turned into mud; the water in the trenches has risen. At 4 p.m., a serious bombardment of our position was launched by the Germans. More rain and how heavy it is! Impossible to work in the trenches. Everything has collapsed; fortunately we can presume that the Boche are suffering the same conditions. Miraculously the evening becomes quiet. The German artillery is silent. No flares to pierce the dark night. Major Dubuc and Captain Boyer are playing bridge. I pass the time reading, writing and watching the others playing cards.

"Oh, the Mud of Flanders" — October 1915

Flanders
16 December, 1915

My dearest Mater,

Your letters dated 21st November and 24th November (from the Hotel Lafayette, New York) have reached me. Thank you very much for your thoughtfulness in sending me news of home so regularly.

You were wise to go to New York at once, with Eva, to purchase her trousseau. As much as possible let Eva complete all arrangements for the wedding at least a few weeks before her marriage: most girls worry and work themselves to shadows before their wedding day and many remain nervous wrecks for some months after. My one piece of advice is — keep calm.

I am very glad indeed that you should be so well impressed with Mr. Trudeau and if you and the Governor are satisfied be sure that the rest of us are. All we want is that Eva should be happy. I am really delighted that she has the good sense to get married without unnecessary delay and without waiting for my return, the date of which is a bit uncertain.

On the 19th of this month I complete my third month in the trenches: I feel stronger, happier and more resolute than at the beginning. We know how to take care of ourselves in the trenches — dry feet, good braziers and wholesome food.

I am sending you some lace for Christmas. Will you buy something for Eva from me? The Governor is looking after my funds as you know. I wish you would ask him for $100 or $150 with which to buy a rather decent wedding present for Eva. Spend not less than $100 — I am enclosing a card. Besides this present I am sending Eva some lace which I trust will reach her.

Diary entry: 19 December. Trenches near Vierstraat.

At 5 a.m. I was on the point of catching some sleep after a night on watch when the German artillery started up on our left. It turned into a violent bombardment which lasted more than two hours. On the heels of this bombardment we received our first dose of German poison gas. In spite of the distance between us and the point being attacked, about 1$^{1/2}$ miles, the gas affected us in a surprising way: we wept like babies and the whites of our eyes became all red.

Vanier's first Christmas at the front focussed on the village of Locre, close to where the battalion was billeted. The highlight of the season was the Christmas Eve service in the village church presided over by Father Doyon. As Vanier notes in his diary, "all the men were present. All were covered with mud."

Christmas Day, 1915
At the front

My dearest Mater,
Today I have thought a great deal of home and of you all. I think it is the first Christmas I have spent away from the family circle and frankly I miss and regret the jolly Christmases of the past. In spite of my regrets, you know how I feel, Mater, and that I shouldn't wish to exchange my lot with those who have not had the privilege of coming out here.

We came out of the trenches last night after our customary six days' stay and very muddy and very wet we were: the men were, as ever, cheerful and despite the heavy accoutrements sang as they marched through the moonlit night to — — — [*Locre*], a village four miles from the front where we were billeted. Our quarters are a bit better than usual this week and for the first time since I entered the trenches I am billeted in a house with a watertight roof and real doors.

We reached our billets at eight o'clock Christmas eve, which gave us time to wash up before midnight Mass, which was said in the parish church of — — — [*Locre*]. I have attended midnight Masses when the singing was better, when the lighting was more brilliant, when the crowd was gayer and the clothes brighter. But never have I attended a more stirring or a more impressive Mass than last night's. The church is small and could not seat our whole battalion. The men stood, filling the church to the doors, and the officers occupied the sanctuary. We sang the old Christmas hymns in front of the Child Jesus lying with outstretched arms in his cradle of straw and the deep rough voices of the men stirred me to the soul and the sound was like the noise of the heavy sea breaking against the shore. Often I would take a surreptitious look back at the upturned faces of the soldiers; they were strong faces, with the straightforward look of the born fighter, of the man who will follow you anywhere.

After Mass we had a réveillon [*a traditional Christmas Eve party, popular in French Canada*] at the convent of which I have already spoken (I sent you the menu of the supper we had there) and we sang Canadian songs and ate Canadian dishes (pigs' feet etc.). We turned in at four o'clock.

Today, I distributed Christmas presents to my section. These consisted of cigarettes, stockings, magazines and chocolates which had been forwarded from all parts of Canada. The men were very happy.

I received yesterday and today a box from Miss and Dr. Gerard, a box of cigars from Mr. Trudeau, an electric light from Mr. Martin, a box of comforts from J.L. Vanier and two parcels from you. Really I have as many Xmas boxes as if I were at home and it makes our absence less painful.

On this night, of all nights, I wish I were with you in body as I am truly with you in spirit. To the Governor, to the children, to Sophie, to all my friends I wish every good thing that God's blessing can bring them.

Very devotedly your son, Georges

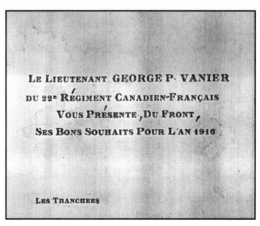

Vanier's greeting card sent from the trenches at Christmas, 1915.
It read "Lieutenant George P. Vanier of the 22nd French-Canadian Regiment brings you greetings from the front and his best wishes for 1916."

4

A "SPECIAL TASK"
JANUARY 1916

"In tonight's orders appeared my promotion to the rank of Captain. When someone calls me 'Captain', I smile: after seventeen months of 'Lieutenant,' I always imagine that when one addresses me as 'Captain', it could not possibly be me."
Georges Vanier in his diary,
18 January, 1916

"I will have myself photographed standing on my head before the Arc de Triomphe, galloping up the Bois de Boulogne, tearing around the Place de la Concorde wildly waving a sword and in all sorts of wonderful poses."
Georges Vanier to his sister, Frances,
18 January, 1916

As the New Year began, the Canadian Corps still held a six-mile tract of waterlogged mud stretching south from St. Eloi. A rest camp in Scherpenberg was the base for the Van Doos and they moved from there at regular intervals into the trenches near

Vierstraat. The raids and counter-raids continued while secret plans were being prepared for Vanier's first significant exploit.

In the trenches
1 January, 1916

My dearest Mater,
First, let me wish you all a very, very happy New Year and may we be united for New Year's 1917. We have been in the trenches since the 30th of December. Last night was fairly active and at eleven o'clock (our time) shouts and cheers, accompanied by bugle calls came from the German trenches. It was evidently a small celebration to usher the New Year in. There is I believe a difference of one hour between our time and Berlin time.

After midnight things were a bit quieter, and 1916 came in like a lamb. Will it go out like a lion? The boys are all very happy and enjoy the novelty of the New Year in the mud of Flanders.

How is everybody at home? I should have very much liked to be present at Eva's wedding, but under present circumstances, feeling as I do about questions of enlistment, I am frank in saying that I prefer to be there in spirit rather than in the flesh

Although Vanier assured his family that 1916 came in like a lamb, there were urgent matters unfolding that would indicate otherwise. On December 29, the battalion was back in the trenches near Vierstraat when Major Tremblay, now in command, sent Georges a handwritten message. It concerned a "special task" he had chosen Vanier to undertake. The message read:

> The General tells me that the special task you are on might have to be carried out tomorrow night, depending of course on the condition of weather, so I would advise you to hasten your preparations tonight in order to be ready tomorrow night.
>
> The men bringing up your rations tonight will also bring up for you four pairs of heavy wire cutters.

A "Special Task" — January 1916

You can send your men to York House for these.

If you are short of anything or want any information, let me know and I will do what I can to help you.

The "special task" was defined in a secret order dated December 30:

> A patrol under Lt. Vanier, consisting of one officer and five men, supported by a bombing party of one N.C.O. [*non-commissioned officer*] and ten men, will undertake the capture of a certain shack in front of the German lines opposite trench L-4 with the idea of seizing anything that the shack may contain and afterwards blow it up.

The following night, two patrols set out to reconnoitre, one of them under Vanier's command. On his return, it was decided that his operation would be carried out on the night of January 2. This allowed time to celebrate the New Year with a "petit réveillon" in Major Dubuc's dugout with the usual toasts to "a glorious peace and a happy homecoming."

Diary entry: Sunday, 2 January

My men are eager to attack the small hut opposite our trenches; I fervently hope that the weather will be favourable this evening — too long a delay gets on the nerves of the men....

8 p.m. Wind, rain, thick darkness — an ideal night for our little operation.

10 p.m. Received word that it is to go forward.

1:35 a.m. Order received to leave our trenches; two minutes later the patrol jumped over the parapet. I was accompanied by Sergeant Maurice Levin, Lance-Corporal L. Rancourt, private John Matt of the 22nd and Corporal P.E. Leclerc of the 5th Field Company of Canadian Engineers. Levin acted as guide, Rancourt carried the 15 lbs. of gun-cotton, and Leclerc the wire which he unrolled behind him. We easily got across our three lines of barbed wire, sometimes on our stomachs, and sometimes on our hands and knees, and made our way straight towards the German line with the intention of getting behind the right hand side of the hut. Levin and I were ahead of the others, who were slowed down by the weight of the gun-cotton and the unwinding of the electric wire. We reached the German barbed wire, four feet in depth, very thick and new, and three and a half feet high. We had to cut it in thirty places in order to get through. The Boche flares constantly illuminated the white hut against the dark background and could easily have spotted us. The bullets whistled in a normal way above our heads and on either side of us. We were thirty feet from the hut — was it occupied? In a few seconds we had crossed the barbed wire and were inside the hut. No one was there. There was a foot and a half of water in the hut and in the trench connecting it with the main trenches. Originally it was probably a machine-gun post. After placing the gun-cotton on the roof and joining the electric wire to the box containing the explosive, we left with a steel plate which served as a loophole.

2:25 a.m. The patrol returned without mishap. It was only at 5:30 a.m. that we were given permission to blow up the hut. A minute later the spark had done its work — a dull explosion, a very bright flash, a cloud of black smoke. The daylight showed us a hole where the hut had been: the gun-cotton had left nothing standing.

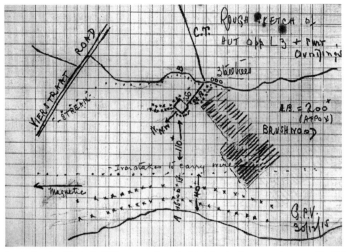

Sketched plan for Vanier's "little operation," which took place on January 2, 1916.

A "Special Task" — January 1916

Must write a report, send the loophole to H.Q., a piece of the Boche barbed wire, and a piece of tarred paper that covered the roof.

    To bed at 10 a.m. Very happy.

The following night, Vanier received this letter from Colonel Gaudet:

Au Lieut. G.P. Vanier:

Mon Cher Vanier,
It gave me great pleasure to draw the Brigadier's attention to the skillful and highly satisfactory manner in which you carried out the difficult task that you were entrusted with last night. I hope that the services which you rendered will be duly recognized.

With my most sincere congratulations,
Yours sincerely,
(signed) F.M. Gaudet, Colonel 22nd Battalion.

The same day, Major-General Turner sent his congratulations to Colonel Gaudet:

I wish to congratulate you on the successful manner in which the detachment from your battalion carried out their small enterprise last night.

    I regret to say it was the only success that we had.

And four days later, on January 6, Brigadier-General Watson, Commander of the 5th Infantry Brigade, added his own congratulations to the battalion:

With reference to the minor operation carried out by your Battalion on the night of the 2nd to the 3rd instant, I wish to take this opportunity of conveying to you my sincere thanks and appreciation at the manner in which the task was carried out on that occasion. This reflects great credit on your Battalion and I would particularly mention Lt. Vanier

and his party for the expeditious and efficient manner in which the work was performed.... I mention the specific case but it is typical of the manner in which your Battalion has acted in all its undertakings since arriving in this country. This has been noted and mentioned in my report which has been rendered to higher authorities.
Signed: D. Watson
Brigadier-General
Commander of the 5th Canadian Infantry Brigade

Trenches
4 January, 1916

My dearest Frances,
I should have answered your letter dated 21st November long before this. Were your holidays happy? Did you receive many presents from Santa Claus? Write me and tell me all about your Christmas and New Year: news from home always interests me.

I think, Frances, I must have been born for this life, because my health and spirits have never been so good before. I think the Germans are tiring and that we will beat them soon. Every time they send over a shell, we return two. Their guns are easy to silence.

You know dear that we are not doing very much open fighting but we hold a given line of trenches which are submitted to a systematic bombardment each day. They are knocked down and we build them up again and it keeps the men busy.

While we are in the trenches, we have little time for sleeping. Whenever we lie down we are disturbed by messages, by aeroplanes and by any abnormal condition — heavy firing for instance, artillery or rifle. When we come out however they let us rest up a bit and worry us only occasionally with fatigue parties and short marches.

And so you will be the big girl of the house when Eva marries, won't you? I wish I could be present with you at the marriage.

Your letters are always very well written. You are making wonderful progress at Convent [*Sacred Heart Convent*].

Flanders
7 January 1916

My dearest Mater,

I have received your letters dated December 12th and Dec. 16th, the former containing Mr. Martin's message which gave me great pleasure. The news of Major Tremblay's promotion to the command of the battalion and of Colonel Gaudet's illness is absolutely untrue. I cannot understand who spreads these rumours that do no one any good and that very often do a great deal of harm. Colonel Gaudet is still with us and I hope he will be with us until the end of the campaign.

I have received five pairs of <u>splendid</u> socks from you, exactly what I wanted — heavy, thick and strong. They are very much appreciated and will probably save me a cold. Quite a change from the silk stockings I used to wear in civil life!

There has been nothing of paramount importance in our sector: the same game of war still goes on and we are so used to it that any other mode of life would appear strange.

New Year's Day was spent in the trenches: it was relatively quiet, but there was nothing resembling a truce. Shells came over very much as they did in 1915.

Diary entry: Sunday, 9 January

Mass at 10 o'clock. At the beginning of Mass there was complete silence. During the reading of the gospel, you could hear the familiar sound of heavy artillery, the whistle of shells above our heads and the dull and distant explosions in the German lines. This accompaniment continued until the end of Mass. It was more impressive than the purest music. All one's soul was caught up in it and your heart ached. There, in front of us, was the symbol of charity — charity itself — and above us was the symbol of destruction and hate.

Trenches
12 January, 1916

My dearest Mater,
My orderly is about to leave for our battalion headquarters with the mail so this will explain the brevity of the note.

Your son is still able to sit up and take nourishment: the Boche have not yet succeeded in dampening my youthful enthusiasm.

I imagine you must be very busy with the wedding preparations. I wrote to Mr. Trudeau a few days ago. I know Eva will be very happy. Her choice, I think, is very good. And of course <u>he</u> is very fortunate to have such a splendid companion.

There is a glimpse of the more domestic concerns of trench life in these extracts from Messages and Signals, *a communiqué which Vanier appears to have sent to Major Dubuc:*

12 *January*: Could we possibly have the following? 1 dozen eggs, 1 box of Quaker Oats, 1 box of strawberries or mirabelles, 1 box of peaches or apricots, chicken (2 wings, 2 thighs) (oh! oh!) and all the breast (ah! ah!).... no stuffing. (Dupuy now tells me it is a turkey).

14 *January*: Have you one or two editions of The Times that you have read? If you have, the porter would be happy to bring them over, together with a bottle of Porto [*port-wine*]. Yours respectfully ...

Diary entry: 14 January

I returned from patrol at 3 a.m. and it seemed as if hundreds of bullets were whistling by tonight. It was the most beautiful night we have had for several weeks: the air is cold and clear and the full moon is brilliant making all sorts of strange shadows. It is a night made for lovers rather than for warriors. It is difficult to believe that only 200 yards away are men whose only desire is to kill us — and vice versa. Nature is so peaceful!

A "Special Task" — January 1916

Diary entry: 15 January

9 a.m. Captain Papineau [*E. Mackay Papineau*] came to wake me up saying "congratulations." Scarcely awake, I thought he was speaking about the "cabin operation" ... but he said it was something else: he came to tell me that the London Gazette of 12 January carried the news of my promotion to the rank of Captain effective 15 October, 1915.... I am a little sorry to give up the two stars which I have been wearing almost since the war began. Besides, my men will never get used to calling me "Captain".

At 4 p.m., I returned from a tour of cannons when Captain Plante shouted to me: "Major Dubuc is wounded".... On reaching Dubuc's hut, we found him with his head bandaged, stretched out on a bench. He was fully conscious. A grenade had exploded near where he was standing in the trench, wounding him in the head behind his ear. I accompanied him to the first-aid post where Doctor Prévost told me that the wound was only superficial. I sent a cablegram to Dr. Lesage, Major Dubuc's brother-in-law and wrote a long letter to Mme. Dubuc.

15 January 1916
TELEGRAM TO: Mr. and Mrs. Trudeau
LONG LIFE AND HAPPINESS
GEORGES

Flanders, 15 January, 1916

My dearest Mater,
This will be an unusually newsy letter. Some of the news is good and some of it is bad. Let me start with the bad news: Major Dubuc was wounded again today by the explosion of a rifle grenade which is a bomb shot from a rifle. The percussion grenade struck the sidewalk of the trench behind him, exploded on contact and burst into a thousand pieces. One of the pieces penetrated his scalp about two inches from the left ear. The major bled profusely, which I think is a very good sign but did not lose consciousness. In fact he even retained

his usual good humour. I accompanied him to the dressing station where I had a good look at the wound whilst being dressed by our doctor. If no complications set in, such as blood poisoning, he should be well in a month or so. The wound is very clean and as soon as the small piece which went through is removed (this is only done at the hospital where he is now), his recovery should be rapid. No fracture of the skull is apparent. The Major has had wonderful luck in each of his misfortunes. To be wounded twice in the head and to come through is simply marvellous.

Do you know that Major Dubuc and myself had both applied for leave to Paris from Jan. 24th to Feb. 1st and that we had very good hopes of success? Our little plan has been knocked on the head and I very much fear I shall have to go to Paris without him. I imagine he will be sent to England to recuperate. I am enclosing a letter for Mrs. Dubuc, his mother, whose address I do not have (Sherbrooke St. West, I think) and which I should like to have delivered as soon as possible.

My good news now. I was "gazetted" Captain in the London Gazette of January 12th, the promotion to date from Oct. 15th, which is the date on which it had been recommended. I have known about this change for some months now, but the process of gazetting is very slow and as "there is many a slip twixt the cup and the lip", I thought it wiser to keep counsel.

I cabled Eva for her wedding day [*17 January 1916*]: I trust the cable reached her.

You are quite right about my M.G. [*machine gunner's*] certificate. I carried it about with me in the trenches and it is Flanders rain that has put it in such a disgraceful state. Now I come to think of it, the certificate is almost illegible, is it not?

I have told you of course that I received your splendid Christmas boxes, but I should have made a special mention of Papa's "Rouge Quesnel" [*a top quality tobacco*] which was most popular with my men. It was quite some time since any had enjoyed any "R.Q."

[...] I shouldn't take Eva's marriage too much to heart. Sooner or later she had to marry: I know you are in favour of early marriages (by the way, to touch a personal note, at 28, I am getting on in years, eh?) and I think Eva's age an ideal one. Eva will be a capital wife loving home life as she does and I am firmly confident that she will be completely happy.

A "Special Task" — January 1916

Vanier accepted his promotion to Captain with typical modesty. He noted in his diary on January 18:

My promotion the rank of Captain appeared in tonight's orders. When someone calls me "Captain", I smile: after seventeen months of "Lieutenant", I always imagine that when one addresses me as "Captain", it could not possibly be me.

I am suffering from a headache, a head cold and a light fever. I spent the day writing to Maman, to Père Gaume, to my god-mother [*his aunt Josephine*] etc.

Georges Vanier, on receiving his promotion to "Captain."

Flanders
18 January, 1916

My dearest Frances,
I was very, very glad to receive the relic of St. Sebastian [*the patron saint of soldiers*] given to you by your mistress at Convent and I will always carry it with me. This relic, coupled with your prayers and those of my dear relatives and friends will protect me. I wish you would thank your mistress for me and tell her that I very deeply appreciate her kindness and generosity. I know how precious a thing a relic is. I shall carry it through the war with me and I hope to return it to the lender when the allies have won a victorious peace.

Are you angry with me for not having answered your letters sooner? It is not always easy to do one's duty as a correspondent: there are so many other things to attend to.

Now I am going to make a terrible admission that I have before me your unanswered letters dated Nov. 24, Dec. 1st and Dec. 20/15. You see how much I have taken heart from your order contained in the first letter and which I transcribe "P.S. Be as prudent in the trenches as you can for when you are careless for a moment it is just the time you may be hit with a SHARPEL. <u>Obey</u> me, eh? xxxx". No "<u>sharpel</u>" has hit me yet dear heart!

...I must tell you news that you already know, in our special language: "Me is awfuts person, horribits proud and terribits captain ... me wouldn't 'peak wif you!" The thing, you see, is very serious.

I hope to send you a little present from Paris — if my request for leave is granted.... I will have myself photographed standing on my head before the Arc de Triomphe, galloping up the Bois de Boulogne, tearing around the Place de la Concorde wildly waving a sword and in all sorts of wonderful poses.

A hug from your "big brother."

P.S. Be as prudent in the streets of Montreal as you can for when you are careless it is just the time you may be hit by a streetcar. Obey me eh? xxxxx G.

Diary entry: 19 January

My head is better. I got up for a few minutes today. However I still feel weak.

On January 21, Vanier received news that his old school friend Adrian McKenna, a corporal with the 24th Battalion, had been killed. It fell to Georges to inform the family.

TELEGRAM 21 January 1916
To: Frank McKenna, Dominion Express Bldg., Montreal
From: Georges Vanier

ADRIAN KILLED.

A "Special Task" — January 1916

Adrian McKenna, one of Georges' school friends, was killed on January 19, 1916. Vanier called him "an angel" and one who "had the cleanest mind and the best heart of any youth I have ever met...."

Flanders
21 January, 1916

My dearest Mater,
I have a very bad piece of news to give you: poor Adrian [*McKenna*] was killed in the early morning of January 19th, a bullet wound through the lungs. I am told he lived a very few minutes after the accident. It is only by the merest chance that I learned of his death from the bombing officer of the 5th Brigade whom I met last night. Poor chap, do you know I met him as recently as January 17th, not a mile from the firing line. Out of the darkness he came up to me saying "Hello George, Happy New Year. I am back from hospital". We spoke of Eva's marriage (strangely enough it was her wedding day) and hoped she would be very happy. He always had a very deep affection for Eva.

Barrack room life had not changed Adrian: he was an angel. Without exaggeration, he had the cleanest mind and the best heart of any youth I have ever met. He was unspoiled. He received communion on the morning of January 16th and of January 17th. He was buried January 20th in a little cemetery [*La Laiterie Military Cemetery at Kemmel, West-Vlaanderen, Belgium — south of Ypres*] within sound of the rifleshots. A white cross marks his grave, next to that of Lieutenant Buchanan, 24th Brigade, who was killed the day before.

I wrote a long letter to Mrs. McKenna giving her fuller details and asking her if there was anything I could do for her. Adrian's death gave me the worst shock I have had since I reached Flanders.

You have read in the casualty list the names of Major Dubuc and of Lieutenant Larocque, side by side, both as wounded. I had not spoken of Lieut. Larocque's accident in a preceding letter because I was not sure that he would be classed as "wounded" and I preferred to say nothing fearing that possibly you might speak of it before Lieut. Larocque wrote home.

The same rifle grenade caused both accidents: Lieut. Larocque was only a few feet from the explosion and instinctively threw himself backwards. He fell on a projecting iron bar and hurt himself how badly I do not know, but he has been in hospital ever since.

P.S. I had almost forgotten a most wonderful piece of news for the 22nd Battalion. Two men, A. Deblois (of "C" Company) and P.S. Lambert (Machine Gun Section) have been awarded the Distinguished Conduct Medal (D.C.M.). I am delighted to have a man of my section decorated. The act for which they received the D.C.M., in a few words, is this: in broad daylight they carried on their shoulders a man horribly wounded in the head, from an isolated trench. They were in full view of the enemy at 200 yards distance. It is extraordinary that they were not killed: needless to say they were fired at heavily. They brought the man safely to a support trench, where he was attended to but unfortunately died of his wounds.

The citation, identical for them both, read: "For conspicuous gallantry and devotion to duty. In the sector of Vierstraat, in November 1915, he carried in a severely wounded comrade under heavy fire. Having no stretcher, they carried him on their shoulders, and in doing so, had to cross barbed wire and several trenches. Their bravery and physical energy were most marked."

21/1/16
Memo to Major Gingras
Sir: I still feel very unwell. May I put my sergeant in charge of MG [*machine gun*] section? A slight attack of la grippe, I think.

When Colonel Gaudet was recalled to London at the end of January to work at the Ministry of Munitions, Lieutenant-Colonel Tremblay took over as Commander of the regiment. "Tommy" Tremblay was a modest

A "Special Task" — January 1916

and unassuming man who quickly proved to be a popular and highly successful military commander.

Meanwhile, Vanier was due for a week's leave and left for Paris on January 24.

Lieutenant-Colonel "Tommy" Tremblay took over as Commander of the regiment in January 1916. He was a popular and successful military commander — and was to be a life-long friend of Georges Vanier.

Grand Hotel, Paris
27 January, 1916

My dearest Mater,
My cablegram of course told you that I was in Paris — that I had obtained leave from January 24th to February 1st. I arrived at the Gare du Nord on the night of the 24th. Captain Prévost, our medical officer who accompanied me, wanted to spend his first night at the Grand Hotel so I followed him. This afternoon we are moving to the Regina where Major Hudon registered on January 25th and where the surroundings are a bit gayer and more homelike.

Paris is changed [*since a visit with his father in 1912*]. I had heard of the change but I could not have believed that it was so radical. The theatres are beginning to re-open but the audiences are a curious mixture — women mostly, officers and soldiers on leave, most of the former sporting a "Croix de Guerre" and the greater number of the latter with "la médaille militaire", men over the military age limit, many of them wounded. In all the plays I have seen — I think this applies equally to those I have not seen — there is a note of sobriety. The questionable cafés and theatres have been completely closed. There is no Montmartre, needless to say. At night the boulevards are quite dark and <u>no</u> café or restaurant is open after 9 o'clock. The number of women in mourning is most striking and very touching.

I have seen Father Gaume, who looks very well indeed, and who thought I had got broader and stouter. My appearance, he said, was a great surprise to him. I brought a bag full of souvenirs from the front with me and I am leaving them with Father Gaume until I can find some way of sending them to Canada. At present it is very hard indeed to get anything through.

Well, Mater, one of the dreams of my life has been realized. If four years ago someone had foretold what has happened to me, I should have thought he was mad. Ah, the sheer joy of it — to visit Paris on leave from the trenches where we are all trying to do our bit for the triumph of civilization — and to avenge 1870 [*Prussia's successful invasion of France which was compelled to hand over Alsace-Lorraine to the new German Empire*].

Hotel Regina, Paris
31 January, 1916.

My dearest Mater,
Tomorrow morning, I leave for the trenches, after having spent a very pleasant week here. Curiously enough during my stay the Zeppelins, after having ignored Paris since March 1915, paid two visits to the Metropolis, one on Saturday night and again last night. Many bombs were dropped — I do not know exactly how many — and as a result nearly fifty people, among them women and children, were killed and a great number were wounded. Today, I visited the spots where the gigantic bombs or shells fell: the side of a house was completely sliced off by one bomb, ten people being killed. Some distance from this house, a shell struck the centre of a boulevard and went through to the metro cutting away pavement, macadam and vault and making a hole fifteen feet in diameter. The bombs used must be tremendously destructive to give such results.

Last night I happened to be on the boulevards when the air raid alarm was given. The firemen raced furiously through the streets ringing "Garde à vous" ["*Be careful*"]: none of the boulevardiers paid any attention to the warning: they stared into the clouds looking for signs of the Zeppelins. Paris at that moment was practically in pitch darkness.

This morning I served Mass for Father Gaume at Notre Dame des Victoires. Then we both went to a photographer's (Pierre Petit):

Father Gaume was very anxious to have me photographed. If the result is good, will you please destroy the two Elliott & Fry horrors I sent you. I look like a blinking cat in E & F's pictures and I cannot understand why I did not destroy them on receipt.

I spent an interesting half-hour at the Les Invalides museum examining the trench mortars, the machine guns etc. taken from the Germans in September 1915 in the Champagne drive.

1e février 1916
Postcard from Calais

Bien cher papa: Warmest greetings from Calais. How the Boche would love to capture it!

There were by now fifty thousand Canadian troops in the field. The Canadian Corps, as part of the Second Division, was still holding a six-mile front south of the Ypres Salient, from Ploegsteert to north of Kemmel.

Vanier returned to his battalion on February 3, in time for the change-over — and a new job.

Diary entry: 3 February

I am leaving the machine-gun section to become second-in-command of "C" Company, replacing Captain Chassé who is taking over command of "D" Company. Major Hudon becomes my commander again as he was in the early days of the 22nd.

Flanders
4 February, 1916

Dearest Mater,
A number of friends have sent me clippings dealing with the little affair of the 2nd/3rd January [*Vanier's midnight raid across No Man's*

Land to destroy an enemy gun position]. A great deal of prominence has been given to something that all of us in the ordinary course of events must do.

Whom do you think I met in the railway carriage from Paris to Calais on my way back to the front? His Eminence Cardinal Bégin [*a Roman Catholic cardinal who had become Archbishop of Quebec in 1898*] who was most cordial to me and who spoke in very flattering terms of the Royal 22nd and with whom I conversed during the whole trip.

Tell me, will you, how Mrs. McKenna was affected by poor Adrian's death?

No sooner had the battalion returned to the trenches than a German attack was expected and Tremblay issued the following communiqué:

> I am confident that the French-Canadians will defend all their trenches with a desperate vigour and will hold firm at whatever cost, even to death. Let us not forget that we represent an entire race, and that a great deal — even the honour of French Canada — depends on the way we conduct ourselves. Our forebears have left us a brave and glorious past which we must respect and emulate. Let us continue in the ancient and fine traditions.

Flanders
7 February, 1916

My dearest Mater,
[...] The leap from Paris to the trenches was a bit quick and disconcerting but by this time I have quite regained my former spirit of indifference to the little inconveniences of Flanders. I was fortunate enough to be in Paris on the nights of the Zeppelin attacks: the scene was impressive, the city was in total darkness but there was no panic. The boulevardiers were interested and gazed into the blackness of the sky, utterly disregarding the warning of the firemen to take refuge in the cellars. With Father Gaume I visited

two of the places where the Zepps did some damage. Curiously enough both of these spots have been photographed and reproduced in the newspapers.

I called on Mme. A.V. Roy who has a small apartment on rue Pierre Charlin. The poor woman is very much cut up by her husband's death in action.

Trenches
8 February, 1916

My dearest Mater,
Father Gaume has forwarded the photographs I had taken at Pierre Petit's in Paris. I find them very good indeed. You will see that I have got no thinner and that, if anything, I have broadened a trifle. I wish you would destroy Elliott & Fry photographs which were very badly taken, in a blinding sun: I may not be an Adonis but I hope I don't look quite as ridiculous as E & F would have us believe. Of course since the tiring training of England I have become stouter, but my nerves certainly are very much steadier than they have ever been before. I ascribe this state of affairs to the sane, broad open-air life.

Though I say little in my letters of the mode of warfare we carry on at present (because it hardly varies from week to week), I might repeat the old, old story of a daily bombardment, of continual watchfulness, of unfortunate casualties and of wonderful escapes, of the long nights with an occasional patrol to enliven things....

My trip to Paris has been a tonic. It has burnished up my ideas and has shown me that when we are through with the mud of Flanders, the normal life of other days will be very pleasant and because of our little trip to Flanders it will be possible to look honest people in the eyes.

Diary entry: 9 February

The Boche have bombarded our lines furiously.... Several pieces of shrapnel fell all around me.

Flanders,
15 February, 1916

My dearest Goo [*sister Frances*]
This is in answer to your delightful letter of Jan. 11th in which you tell me not to be <u>too brave</u>. Have no fear on that score, "smink!"

Well I have been to "froyebits" in Paris and now I am back in the grey mud of Belgium. My holidays were long enough to make me forget what a trench looked like or how a bursting shell impressed one.

The Boche are becoming more active around here and I think we will have to thrash them one of these days — if it is not in 1916 it will be in 1920.

Things are shaping splendidly for us. We are very well organized and if ever the Huns try to smash the line — me thinks it will be "awfuts" for them! Don't tell them this!

All sorts of good wishes, dearest.

Flanders
18 February, 1916

My dearest Mater,
[...] I am sorry my cable from Paris caused such a commotion. I cannot understand how you could have thought, from the wording of the message, that I was returning to Canada. Ce sera pour la fin de la guerre. [*That will have to wait for the end of the war.*]

Winter is waning and we are all jolly glad of it. What I feared most of all, for my men and for myself, was trench foot, the result of cold, of rain and of a run down constitution. There is hardly any danger of that now. Each day the sun is getting warmer: warmth you know is the most important factor in the open air life we lead.

...The 22nd is still hanging on to a line of trenches, without any great difficulty: it is not likely that we can do much until the great advance comes, or until we bear the brunt of an important attack.

Flandres
le 25 février 1916

A "Special Task" — January 1916

Bien cher Papa,

I was very happy to receive your long letter giving me all the news of Eva's wedding. It is clear that her choice pleases you.

...The Boche are becoming more and more active on the Western front. At the moment I am writing, the Germans are attacking furiously at Verdun. They are desperate strikes: the Huns are at the end of their tether.

5

THE BIG PUSH
FEBRUARY 1916

"The Germans are giving a last desperate kick at Verdun.... What they have gained hardly justifies the awful losses sustained."
        Georges Vanier to his sister, Frances,
        2 March, 1916

"It is comforting to hear the birds sing again, to see the grass turn green and to see the flowers beginning to bud and what is more wonderful and surprising still to see the mud slowly but surely drying. The hardship of winter is over and most of us feel that there will not be another winter campaign...."
        Georges Vanier to his mother,
        21 March, 1916

The situation in early 1916 was hardly encouraging for the Allies. Large areas of France and Belgium were still in German hands and the German offensive at Ypres left the Allies holding only a part of the Salient.

The Allied plan for 1916 was to launch simultaneous offensives on the Western, Eastern and Italian fronts. On the Western front, they chose the region of the Somme and planned an assault for mid-year.

However, the Germans jumped in first and thwarted the scheme. Quite unexpectedly, on February 21, the German army launched a massive attack on the French city of Verdun. The German barrage — known as the Battle of Verdun — struck with an intensity and firepower unprecedented to that date. It ground on until the end of June, by which time casualties on both sides had soared dramatically, the French spirit was shattered and the French Army hung on the verge of mutiny.

Other smaller battles followed that spring, most notably the Battle of the Craters of St. Eloi in March and April and the Battle of Mont Sorrel in June.

Meanwhile, as February drew to a close, the Van Doos returned to the trenches near the village of St. Eloi, an area that was quickly becoming the focus of continuous bombing attacks. Lieutenant-Colonel Tremblay was officially named their new commander on February 26. In accepting the position, he said "I fully understand all the responsibility that this position carries.... All my actions will be guided by our beautiful motto 'Je Me Souviens.'"

At the front.
1 March, 1916

My dearest Mater,
I was delighted to hear in your letter of Feb. 3rd that Frances had received her lace collar and cuffs ordered from the sisters of L— — — [*Locre*] Convent. I think I told you some months ago that I had chosen lace for you and Eva from the same nuns: the parcels will probably be forwarded separately.

I should be very glad to have Mr. Pierce call at the Canadian Commissioner's office, Blvd. des Capucines [*Paris*], where he will find a parcel of small souvenirs (mostly fuses, etc.) I would advise giving him one of the fuses as a memento. When mounted, they make splendid paper-weights. I wish you would keep them for me in their natural state and when I return, we will decide what to do with them.

I am sending under separate cover, by mail, two small statues in a souvenir box of biscuits. The box is one of a great number distributed to the troops through the kindness of the people of Toronto. Will you put both box and statues aside for me? The statues have no intrinsic value but have a very peculiar interest for me.

In the trenches,
2 March, 1916

My dearest Frances,
[...] Lately things have been much livelier than formerly: the bombardments have become a bit stiffer and we may see some real fighting one of these days. The Germans are giving a last desperate kick at Verdun: what they have gained hardly justifies the awful losses sustained.

Tell Eva I slept over a piece of her wedding cake three nights in succession without any results. I could dream of nothing and of nobody. I am afraid I shall remain a bachelor. Curiously enough other officers had no better luck. There is not much chance for us poor soldiers, is there?

13 March, 1916

My dearest Mater,
Your letter of February 17th gave me great pleasure. I am glad indeed that you have met Mrs. Dubuc, who is a charming woman. She was kind enough to write me a letter of thanks for the little I was able to do for Major Dubuc.

Winter set in here two weeks ago and we have had rather a harder time than usual: in the front line trenches keeping warm has been a difficult matter. Although March came in like a lion, judging from the warm sun of yesterday and today, it will go out like a lamb, and once again we will enjoy the bright warm scenery of Flanders. And it is beautiful when the fields are green and the hedges thick and the trees in blossom. Really in summer and in spring our life out here is a glorious holiday.

Lieut. Grothé was wounded a few days ago and a most fortunate wound it was, in the fat and muscles of the back. An inch to one side and poor Grothé would have been killed. As it is the muscles of his neck will be affected for some time. I don't think Grothé will come back to us.

Poor Papineau was struck by a piece of shrapnel near the eye and has been sent back for examination. His eye <u>I think</u> will be affected at least temporarily. He was a remarkable officer and I trust we will not lose him.

In the trenches,
Flanders' front
21 March, 1916

My dear George [*Pelletier, Vanier's cousin*],
[...] Here things have not changed materially on our front ... except that in all artillery duels we easily have the upper hand and when the time comes to go through the line this superiority will be of the utmost importance.

We are more confident than ever of final victory, since the Verdun affair where the Germans have weakened themselves to such an extent that it is doubtful if they will ever attempt an attack of that kind again.

Flanders
21 March, 1916

My dearest Mater,
[...] I have been transferred from second-in-command of "C" Company to temporary officer commanding "A" Company. I was sorry to leave Major Hudon a second time. I was appointed to replace Captain Papineau wounded near the eye who may not return to the battalion. Another officer, Lieut. Dorval, one of the St. Johns' crowd, has been wounded (you have probably seen the notice in the newspapers) by a bullet through the jaw and face. Latest reports are that he is doing very well indeed. We have had rather hard luck lately but we have not fared worse than the 25th & 26th Battalions, as the casualty lists show.

It is comforting to hear the birds sing again, to see the grass turn green and to see the flowers beginning to bud and what is more wonderful and surprising still to see the mud slowly but surely drying. The hardship of winter is over and most of us feel that there will not be another winter campaign. Nobody knows of course but the Mark [*German currency*] is falling very rapidly and one of these days Germany will wake up to discover that she is strangling.

Verdun may serve as an eye-opener to the people of Germany. The Huns will never get through; even if they did they would be so weakened that they could not put their victory to permanent use. They would have to dig themselves in once again.

Flanders
le 22 mars 1916

Mon bien cher papa,
For several days ... I have been commanding officer of "A" Company replacing Capt. Papineau who was wounded in the eye. Capt. Papineau has left for hospital and we do not know to what degree his eye is affected.

[...] We are entering into our seventh month in the trenches — it is still something. The future might hold some surprises which could be a little more violent — who knows?

Flanders
24 March, 1916

My dearest Mater,
I was overjoyed to receive four letters from you last night. It was jolly of you to send me a home reminder each day.

The first instalment of Trudeau's Joffre tobacco reached me last night together with cigarettes and chocolate. Will you thank Eva and her husband for me?

I shall be pleased to receive the maple sugar and maple syrup you speak of: it will be a rare delicacy here where such things are unknown. Don't worry, Mater, about the German drive: they will never get through. As you say, the Huns are becoming desperate. Bear in mind that the oftener and the sooner they attack the better for the Allies. Such attack means a great loss of life to both of us of course but more particularly to the attacking troops.

My writing is a bit erratic today because I am penning this on my knee in the Company cook house. The weather has grown chilly again, snow having fallen all night and this morning and I find the atmosphere of the cook house the most comfortable.

Flanders
28 March, 1916

My dearest Mater,
On coming out of the trenches I found four parcels from you. The first parcel contained candy, cake, sardines, chicken, ham, and tongue and milk, the second Sunday papers from the Governor, Quesnel tobacco, the third Joffre tobacco from Trudeau and the fourth tobacco, sardines and "Mutt & Jeff" clippings from the Governor. I am very grateful to you all for your thoughtfulness.

The weather still remains cold, I am beginning to think that we will not have spring until the month of May. However, the real winter is over — thank heaven.

Flanders
4 April, 1916

My dearest Mater,
[...] I had a letter from Ernie [*McKenna, brother of Adrian*] yesterday from somewhere in Flanders. He is with the 14th Battalion, as you have heard probably from Mrs. McKenna. I have been told on excellent authority that Fred Shaughnessy[1] was killed a few days ago. Please say nothing about it to anyone should his name not appear in the casualty list as it is always possible for the informant to be mistaken. Should it be true, I can imagine what a stir it will make in Montreal, particularly after his father's baronetcy.

Since I wrote you last I have been through an inoculation

against typhoid and paratyphoid. I have come through the always unpleasant ordeal very well indeed.

I am in splendid health and spirits. The weather is helping us out now. It is becoming fine and warm. In some other respects, things may become a bit hotter as clement weather is ideal for attacks. The ground is hard, the roads in good shape, the fields dry....

Flanders
5 April, 1916

My dearest Mater,
I have just received your letter dated March 18th giving me the ever welcome home news. I am always very glad to see your well known handwriting on an envelope. It means getting in touch with the things which remain dearest to me. So Anthony is in long trousers; it is a rather trying time at College. One feels like a fish out of water. I am afraid he will have a few fights before he has been in long trousers over a few weeks.

As you say, the snapshots I had taken in Paris are very clear. They were taken with my small Kodak which of course is <u>taboo</u> at the front....

I am awaiting the arrival of the maple syrup: it will be a splendid treat. You ask me if "Le Reveil" and "l'Action" come regularly. Yes ... and "l'Action" particularly is always interesting.

Flanders
8 April, 1916

My dearest Mater,
Many thanks for your birthday wishes which will, I trust, come true. I quite agree with you that we little thought that this birthday would not be spent in Montreal. Let us confidently trust the next will.

Without being able to give you any definite information I can say that we are having a much more lively time than formerly and that we are now seeing some real fighting.

6

TRENCH WARFARE INTENSIFIES
APRIL 1916

"At the first glimmer of dawn in the east, I heard a cock crow once, twice, and then a third time. I remembered that it was Good Friday. Who is now denying the Lord? Alas, we all are."
            Georges Vanier in his diary,
            21 April, 1916

"These instruments of torture are not so bad when studied a bit: one usually has time to see what the general direction of the bomb will be and to run ... in the opposite direction. I have never done 50 yards in quicker time, the end being a dive onto the trench mat and a painful wait for the hellish explosion. Enfin, c'est la guerre."
            Georges Vanier to his mother,
            17 May, 1916

April began a period of intense activity for Vanier's battalion. On April 1, the Canadian Corps returned to the Ypres Salient to take over a stretch running from outside the village of St.

Eloi to around Hooge on the Menin Road. Four days earlier, the British had blown up six large mines beneath the German line at St. Eloi. The explosion was so intense the sound could be heard as far as Folkestone in England — about seventy miles away.

The Canadians, including the Van Doos, stepped into a completely water-logged battlefield. Shell holes and giant mine craters had turned into ponds and the trenches were nothing more than drainage ditches. It was under these conditions that they waited for the Battle of the Craters of St. Eloi.

The battle began on April 6. The first few days saw heavy German shelling and a non-stop bombardment of artillery fire resulting in many cases of shellshock (a condition which we now would call post traumatic stress). The exchange of artillery rarely let up for most of the month and throughout it all, the rain continued to drench the battlefields.

Diary entry: 9 April

Instead of hearing Mass at Reninghelst, I left with Captain Chassé on a reconnaissance mission to Voormezele, near St. Eloi. Since the English attack, the area is very violent. The communication trench which leads from Voo to St. Eloi is in such a dreadful state that it is impossible to go any further. On our return, we had an excellent meal in Dikkebus: this village has been bombarded every day. In spite of that, the Flemish women and children continue to live in houses that are partly destroyed by shells. They sell eggs, jams, coffee — a veritable Godsend for the soldiers.

Diary entry: 10 April

Made a hasty departure from our camp for Dikkebus by way of Reninghelst, Leveloten, Ouderdom, Hallebast. The Boche bombarded the village on our arrival. The whole battalion broke up into three fields to avoid losses.

8 p.m. "A" and "D" companies received orders to return to Scottish Wood to serve as emergency reserves.

Trench Warfare Intensifies — April 1916

Diary entry: 11 April

During the night there was intermittent artillery fire. At 5 p.m., heavy and intense bombardment began.... Superb moonlight.

On April 12, sobered perhaps by the relentless bombardments the battalion had faced in the previous few days, Vanier took the time to write his will, penned in French in firm clear handwriting and tucked into a small envelope labelled "Mon testament" ("My will").

Flanders
12 April, 1916

My will

I believe in God and in the holy Catholic church.

I believe in eternal rest and in the divine mercy. Without fear I entrust my soul to our Lord Jesus Christ. I renew all the promises and vows made at my baptism and at my confirmation.

I believe in the sanctity of our cause and in the triumph of justice.

I believe in the future of French Canada.

All my possessions at the time of my death I leave to those whom I love the most: Maman, Papa, Marie Eva, John, Antony and Frances to be divided equally among them.

I name my father my executor with full powers and no obligations to report. I entrust my father to act at the time he alone considers opportune.

Pray for me.

Georges P. Vanier

Capitaine au 22e bataillon Canadien français.

Diary entry: 20 April

I have been designated to command a fatigue-party of 400 men who will work repairing the trenches [*probably draining trenches and rebuilding damaged parapets etc.*] near St. Eloi. In the afternoon, drove by London bus to Dikkebus to the quarters of the 4th Canadian Field Company Engineers to see to details of the organisation.... At 6:45 p.m., we left for Reninghelst where we boarded another bus for Hallebast. From here, we continued by foot to Dikkebus and Tranchief. Worked in the trenches from 10 p.m. until 2 a.m.

Diary entry: Good Friday, 21 April

Returned to camp on foot at 4:30 a.m. Needless to say I was dead tired.

At the first glimmer of dawn in the east, I heard a cock crow once, twice, and then a third time. I remembered that it was Good Friday....

Trench Warfare Intensifies — April 1916

Repairing the sodden trenches was a never-ending chore. Here, members of the 22nd Battalion pause for a break.

Who is now denying the Lord? Alas, we all are. Really you would never believe that it was Good Friday — there was no religious service.

At the front
21 April, 1916, Good Friday

My dearest Mater,
Lately I have written less often — you have not been worried, have you? There have been very serious reasons for my apparent neglect. During the last month I have had very much less time for letter-writing than during the preceding months. We are waging a different kind of warfare — one that requires undivided attention. This said let us proceed.

I have received birthday presents [*for his birthday on April 23*] from all of you and from the bottom of my heart I thank you. I have told you before — but repeating does no harm — gifts which come to us in Flanders give us a thousand-fold more pleasure than those received in Canada. Your maple syrup and maple sugar were particularly delicious: it was a splendid idea to send peanuts, almonds (Bernie Languedoc has a special liking for them and includes his thanks), raisins and dates. These are delicacies we do not pick up with ease in this (as we term it when it has rained for 48 hours at a stretch) God-forsaken country. Needless to say, I have not waited until my birthday to open the packages and to sample (and in some cases completely consume) the contents. I will say however that the provision will last me until some time after the 23rd.

It is consoling to know (it gives one courage and strength) that you are all praying for me and that you are asking for St. Anthony's intercession through the devotion of the Thirteen Tuesdays.[1] Your prayers so far have carried me through and I wish in the future and in the Virgin Mary's protection.

Captain Papineau is coming back to us in a few days. I am afraid this news will not be very welcome to Miss Rodier [*the girlfriend of Papineau*]: you can tell her that Papineau is a hero — one of the most efficient officers in the 22nd. He is returning to active service only because he is anxious to do so and unwilling to be invalided home....

This is the anniversary of the Ypres trouble [*the second battle of Ypres*] last year. If the Germans decide to celebrate the event, they will find us ready — more prepared than in 1915. I doubt however if they wish to go through a second Verdun — which by the way, has been a French victory of the first magnitude [*but which was still far from over*].

Diary entry: 22 April

The anniversary of the Battle of Ypres. We expect a Boche attack. All day long, a heavy rain has been falling and soaking everything. The time is not favourable for an advance.

Frightening bombardment from 10:30 p.m. until 3 a.m. All night long, we were on "Standby". Little artillery during the day....

Diary entry: Easter Sunday, 23 April

Twenty-eight years old today! Beautiful weather, hot sun. At 9 a.m.,

Mass at Reninghelst in an old parish church that dates from the 17th century. Took Holy Communion with many of my men....

Flanders
23 April 1916

My dearest Mater,
Today, Easter Sunday, is my 28th birthday. I received two letters from you and jolly welcome they were, bringing me news of home. Your letter dated April 7th contained a note from the Governor telling me of Martin's victory[2] and that he had managed to obtain some new maple syrup. The old syrup (I have received two cans in perfect condition) was delicious.

So the Governor worked for a defeated candidate again! I am beginning to think that my distinguished father is a sort of hoodoo.

Captain Papineau came back to us today. By looking at his eye you cannot tell that it is sightless. It appears that it is an affliction of the retina and that it will not affect the other eye.

Lieutenant Browne [*Peter S. Browne of the 22nd*] has returned from leave in England. Did I tell you, in a former letter, that this young officer had helped to repulse a Boche attack, of which the papers have spoken and that he had been mentioned for a decoration? I jolly well hope he receives it, as he deserves it as much as anyone I know. [*He did receive the Military Cross.*]

Diary entry: 25 April

Left camp "B" at 3 p.m. for Dikkebus where we spent the afternoon and the night. I am in quarters with the officers at no. 88 on the "Grand Rue".... We go into the trenches tomorrow night.

Diary entry: 26 April

Summer weather, radiant sun.... The village of Dikkebus is deserted: the houses are half demolished and the church is perforated with shell holes. It brings us back to reality.... Several Boche planes tried without success to approach Dikkebus.

Diary entry: 27 April

Last night, the 22nd relieved the 20th Battalion in the trenches. During the changeover, a fight with hand-grenades broke out on our left. This was followed by a severe bombardment which lasted an hour. All day long, the Boche bombarded the woods next to where I am.... The papers are announcing a rebellion in Dublin.[3] Regrettable....

Diary entry: 28 April

At noon, I received a telephone call from crater no. 1 (Lieut. Pelletier in command) when a shell hit the lip of the crater, killed four men and wounded six others. This was a rather tough initiation for Lieut. Pelletier who had just arrived.

Weather superb — sun hot — summer temperature.... The night is quiet, the sky starry. Lieut. Pelletier returned from the crater and told me that the bodies of two of the dead were so slashed into pieces that the remains had to be carried away in sacks.

Diary entry: 29 April

Still summer weather. The sector seems very quiet. Fewer high calibre shells. Tonight I am going to the front line with my company. (For three days I have been in the trenches with the 2nd company reserves.) The birds sing to us before dawn: at the "stand-to" we can hear their sweet music.... It is all so restful I feel as if I am on holiday.

Midnight: The whole front line has completely changed over. At 1 a.m., there was rapid and violent gunfire and intense bombardment, accompanied by gas on our right flank — apparently no more than a mile or so. The din lasted an hour and a half. Our sector suffered little.

Trench Warfare Intensifies — April 1916

This morning I am told that the Boche launched a gas attack and added another which also failed to cause much distress with the 50th English division.

The situation in Ireland is regrettable — without significant importance perhaps but it will carry a moral lesson to neutral countries.

Radiant sun, superb weather and a tranquil night. No mail from Canada....

Flanders
1 May, 1916

My dearest Mater,
The Canadian mail must have taken a roundabout course lately: the life of the sergeant-major is becoming less and less bearable as each time, on his return with rations, he informs me that there are no letters from Canada. We have daily English and French mails of course but this is not what we look forward to.

It is hard to realize that the month of May is at hand and that we are well into our eight month of mud-life.

I should like to spend one of these weekends in Magog, doing nothing in particular except lying on my back on our broad veranda.

Diary entry: Monday, 1 May

The Canadian mail has finally arrived. Two letters from Maman and a box of maple syrup, maple sugar and chocolate.

Diary entry: 2 May

The night passed without incident. At dawn, the Boche launched a series of grenades ("sausages"). We replied in kind with some success.... This afternoon, there was a big storm and the first thunder and lightening. What a curious mixture of sounds and noises — the carbines, the cannons, shrapnel, the grenades and the thunder. We are counting on being relieved this evening. It may be just an illusion....

Flanders
2 May, 1916

My dearest Mater,
[...] After the spell of fine weather, rain has set in again — this time rain with fireworks — a regular thunderstorm. I don't remember having heard thunder before in Belgium.

A rather amusing thing happened today in connection with the electric storm. I was in the trench and by chance was looking at the dark rolling clouds. Suddenly I saw a flash of lightning and knew that the sound of thunder would follow. Before the crash I looked down the trench at the unsuspecting men who had not seen the flash. Then came the violent thunderclap: the men, who are used to the sounds of rifle grenades, shrapnel, percussion shells, trench mortars, sausages, machine-gun fire, kerosene tin bombs and what not, looked at one another in amazement. They expected some sort of unusual occurrence after this new explosion. It was quite interesting to watch the men's expression change from consternation to broad smiles. They had not recognized the erstwhile familiar sound of thunder.

Poor Mrs. McKenna's wish to have Ernie back in Canada with the Irish Rangers has not been fulfilled. I hope he will have good luck and come through it to console his mother for the great loss sustained.

Diary entry: 3 May

7 a.m. The Boche have relaunched their noisy din with grenades and mortars. An efficient reply on our part. From 1 to 2 p.m., the Boche let loose an intense bombardment. Lieutenant Bauset was wounded in his left hand by an exploding shell the same moment that Colonel Tremblay and Colonel de Lanaudière were passing by. Their wounds are not serious. We are counting on being relieved tonight.

Diary entry: 4 May

I left the trenches at midnight and walked to Dikkebus, then by bus (a double-decker bus) to Reninghelst — a curious trip. I thought I was in London. A starry night.... Slept until noon.

Flanders
6 May, 1916

My dearest Mater,
A few days ago I received two packages, one containing tobacco (Joffre very much appreciated), chocolates and cigarettes, the other containing maple syrup (ever welcome) in perfect condition, tobacco and chocolates. Today another parcel arrived with maple syrup, maple sugar and chocolates. Need I say how grateful I am to you for your thoughtfulness?

By the merest chance, I met Ernie [*McKenna*]: he looks splendid and expects to be recalled to the 199th Battalion shortly! I am very glad indeed for the sake of his mother that he will return to Canada. His friend, Gordon Ross [*an old friend from Loyola days*], whom I knew very well, was killed only a few days ago, together with Johnny Howe, another Loyola boy.

Life has been running on very much as usual. The weather remains fine. The countryside really is beautiful: under different circumstances we might have an opportunity of appreciating it still more.

Diary entry: 12 May

Rode on horseback to Reninghelst where I saw Captain Briggs, the dentist. I have a crown that is in need of repair. Intermittent bombardment on both sides.

Flanders
13 May, 1916

My dear Frances,
...You are becoming a great reader: I suffered from the same complaint myself. It will probably do you more good than harm, even if occasionally you neglect your studies. You had better not let Mother know I gave you this advice. During the summer months you will have time to get through quite a number of books.

You have heard of course of the fighting in our sector. So far I have been fortunate to come through alive. Perhaps your devotion to Saint Anthony has helped me.

Flanders
15 May, 1916

My dearest Mater,
I don't think I have ever written a letter in such a cramped position. I am in a dugout two and one half feet high. The floor is too muddy to sit on, so I am perched on a small arm [sic] ammunition box which means that my head is continually banging against the corrugated iron roof.

Last night when your letter, dated April 30th, reached me, I was in very much the same position and prospects for a change are not very bright for a few days. Tant pis — c'est la guerre!

Yes, quite a few of our officers have returned to take up new commands but I see by the Gazette that an end is to be put to these transfers. In some cases it is a splendid thing for an officer to return after eight months in the trenches: it clears his head of cobwebs, so to speak.

I am very glad indeed that these officers have managed to obtain a Canadian command but I cannot say that I envy them exactly. Lately the Germans have got into the very bad habit of chucking over kerosene tins very much of the following design: these contain three hand grenades and a good sized trench mortar, probably thrown in for luck. The noise they make is deafening! If the censor were not looking I would tell you what effect they have.

There are all sorts of little incidents — pleasant and unpleasant — to vary the monotony of trench warfare.

Flanders
17 May, 1916

My dearest Mater,
Still in the trenches but this time I am not writing from a two foot high dugout but from a fire-step with nothing above but a sheet of corrugated iron which is rainproof, not <u>bomb</u> proof. The reason for the change is that the Boche took it into their heads to demolish the parapet by means of kerosene tins in front of the aforesaid dugout and I thought it wise to move with my blanket and shaving articles. These instruments (not shaving articles) of torture are not so bad when studied a bit: one usually has time to see what the general direction of the bomb will be and to run ... in the opposite direction. I have never done 50 yards in quicker time, the end being a dive onto the trench mat and a painful wait for the hellish explosion. Enfin, c'est la guerre.

Flanders
19 May, 1916

My dearest Mater,
Your letter of May 1st reached me last night: it was most welcome after the rather hard days in the trenches. I think I told you that I had abandoned my dugout for the firestep because of unpleasant visitors (rats). Curiously enough the dugout, the next day, was struck by a .77 shell. So once again, I have been fortunate.

Flanders
27 May 1916

My dearest Mater,
Your newsy letter of May 20th reached me last night. I was quite surprised to hear of John's proposed engagement as I was to hear of

Eva's some time ago. I am afraid the officers of the 22nd had better marry abroad: the Montreal girls — and who can blame them? — do not appear disposed to wait. I am very glad indeed that John has decided to marry. Considering his character and habits, he is quite old enough. I congratulate him and in a way envy him.

We have had a slightly better time during the last week and with some sort of luck Canadian casualties should soon become normal. Major Hudon is in England, on his way to Canada: his health was not very good during the last month of his stay with us: his spirits however were always splendid.

Flanders
29 May, 1916

My dearest Mater,
The weather is still astonishingly fine — fine weather in Flanders is always astonishing. The days are very long which means that the hours of bombardment have increased and that the chances of night attacks have diminished. One always finds some kind of compensation in everything that happens.

Today we witnessed a daily occurrence — a combat in the air between German and English aeroplanes whose occupants used machine-guns on one another. They were 5,000 or 6,000 feet up and one could hear distinctly the sound of the machine-guns whilst pieces of shells sent up by the land anti-aircraft guns fell about us. I can imagine how delighted and interested Anthony would have been to witness the sight which to us is very commonplace.

I wish you would let me know when John becomes officially engaged. Judging from Eva and John, I am afraid that I am a bit of a laggard. What do you think?

Flanders
3 June, 1916

My dearest Mater,
Today is our King's birthday but nothing very unusual has occurred

Trench Warfare Intensifies — April 1916

on our front as yet. Curious how on a day like this, one always expects something to turn up. Is it because we become superstitious, through the inactivity of the brain brought about by lying for days in a low dugout?

Diary entry: 4 June

3:00 p.m. Colonel Tremblay called me on the telephone to inform me that my name appeared in the "Times" of 3 June as among those who have received the Military Cross.

Indeed, Vanier was awarded the Military Cross for his role in blowing up the enemy hut. He was the first in the regiment to receive this important distinction. The citation read: "His courage, his example and his desire to conquer instilled in those under his command the most noble spirit of combat."

But the thrill of receiving such an honour was dimmed by more bad news:

Diary entry: 6 June

Poor Beaubien [*Captain Antonio*] was killed in the trenches. Another of my old friends has gone. Tony was an excellent boy and a good company commander. I loved him very much and his death has struck me hard.

Captain Antonio Beaubien, a close friend of Vanier's, was killed by a piece of schrapnel on June 6, 1916. On hearing the news, Vanier noted in his diary: "Another of my old friends has gone.... I loved him very much and his death has struck me hard."

Trenches,
6 June, 1916

My dearest Frances,
[...] Today, dearest, one of our officers, Captain Beaubien, was killed. This is the first death among officers since Major Roy. Captain Beaubien was a splendid chap, a sterling officer and I can assure you that we all feel his loss keenly. He was one of the "old guard" at St. Johns barracks.

Mother tells me that I will hardly recognize you when I return, that you have grown in wisdom and in body.

Here life is as exciting as ever — and the Canadians are not in the quietest sector either.

Flanders
7 June, 1916

My dearest Mater,
This morning I received your cablegram of congratulations for which I thank you most heartily.

You know by this time that the Canadians have again suffered heavily: our luck has been against us lately. Captain Beaubien, poor chap, was killed a few days ago by a piece of shrapnel which went clean through his body. I have had no news from Ernie McKenna for two or three weeks: the 14th Battalion I am afraid has seen some sharp fighting. The weather still remains fine, which helps us to take things cheerfully.

In spite of taking things cheerfully, there was more bad news ahead. On June 7, the 22nd Battalion returned to the trenches, this time in the sector of Zillebeke in the Ypres Salient. Lieutenant-General Sir Julian Byng,[4] a British aristocrat and cavalry officer, had just taken over as Commander of the Canadian Corps and was planning an attack to win back Mont Sorrel and Hill 62. On June 9, during what became known as the Battle of Mont Sorrel, Vanier was commanding a company at the front line when a shell exploded three feet away from where he was standing.

Trench Warfare Intensifies — April 1916

Diary entry: 9 June

8 a.m. A shell exploded a few feet away, deafening and shaking me and knocking me out completely. If the earth hadn't been soft, I would have been killed. I was forced to leave ... and was sent via Dikkebus to Reninghelst where I spent the night.

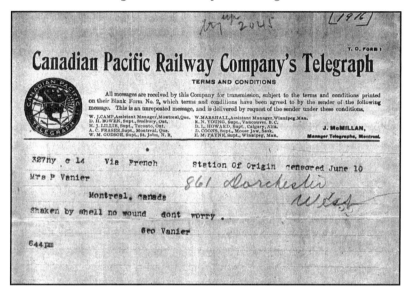

Canadian Pacific Railway Company's Telegraph
June 10 (1916) 6:44 p.m.

To: Mrs. P. Vanier, Montreal, Canada

SHAKEN BY SHELL NO WOUND DONT WORRY

GEO VANIER

The impact of the explosion knocked Vanier out, but luckily it did not injure him. Nonetheless, the shellshock and its aftermath required immediate evacuation.

An article in La Patrie, preserved in Vanier's War Album, cites his wounding and that of his fellow-officer, Captain Henri Chassé.

7

CONVALESCENCE IN BRITAIN
JUNE 1916

"I appreciate very much what all my friends in Canada have done for me, but somehow I can't go back. I must be at the front so long as I am fit. I should be unhappy anywhere else."
            Georges Vanier to his mother,
            25 July, 1916

"I feel that it is my duty to see this sacred war through and with God's help I shall."
            Georges Vanier to his mother,
            16 August, 1916

The explosion Vanier experienced on June 9 left him suffering from intense shellshock. The next morning, he was taken to a rest hospital at Mont des Cats, one of the highest points of northeastern France, overlooking the Flanders plain with a view north to the sea and east to the trenches. The hospital had taken over a Trappist monastery and Vanier later recalled the small chapel where "every night at 2 a.m., the old monks would chant their offices." By coincidence, some forty years later, Vanier's eldest son, Benedict, chose to join the same order of Trappist monks in Oka, Quebec.

Mont des Cats
10 June, 1916

My dearest Mater,
[...] I am now in a rest hospital, not by any means in the best of condition but I expect to recuperate shortly.

I hope you received my cablegram telling you not to worry in case you saw my name in the list of casualties. Two days before my little accident I was to have gone to London on leave, but all leave was cancelled at the last moment.

Mont des Cats
11 June, 1916

My dearest Mater,
The night before I left the trenches I received your three letters dated May 22nd, May 23rd and May 26th. I had to wait until dawn to read them as I was in a "rat-hole" where even candle-light would have been a danger.

At present I am stationed in an old monastery which has been turned into a hospital for officers and other ranks. I am receiving the best of treatment and I am getting what I need more than anything else — complete rest. The surroundings are very beautiful. This morning I heard mass in the old chapel which the monks still use.

I have heard that Ernie [*McKenna*] is not seriously wounded. In fact he has returned to duty but I cannot altogether vouch for this.

By this time I presume you are enjoying the fresh, bracing air of the lake.... I think it is splendid of John to get married at once. Why should he wait? The Governor must be particularly delighted. I know his views on late marriages.

Mont des Cats
13 June, 1916

My dearest Mater,
I am still resting in hospital. Everybody here is very kind to us and

we are made comfortable and happy. Fortunately we are out of sound of the artillery which I could not stand just now. One reaches a point sometimes where one feels that one cannot stand very much more. And I am beginning to get over that feeling.

Mont des Cats
June 14th, 1916

My dearest Mater,
I am resting still and picking up steadily. Of course I walk about and read and write and take an interest in things generally. These are moments of work and of trial for Canadians but when the work and the trials are over you will find I think that another not inglorious page has been written in Canadian history. The casualty lists unfortunately speak for themselves.

[...] Did I tell you I had met Canon Frederick George Scott[1] [*a Canadian army chaplain*] in hospital? He has written some very good war poems a few of which I have already sent home. He is a delightful speaker and a very fine type of Canadian. I knew his son William in Montreal very well. We are both members of the Junior Bar.

You know that I expected to be in London by this time on leave, but at the last moment leave was cancelled and I remained in Flanders to be sent to hospital. The official name of the hospital is "North Midland Divisional Casualty Clearing Station" (N.M.D.C.S.S.) [*sic*] and it is not twenty miles from the front. Still it is as quiet as if we were in England: at least we are not troubled with Zepps.

Mont des Cats,
15 June, 1916

My dearest Mater,
I am still enjoying the quiet life of the very high spot chosen as a rest hospital by people who understand the importance of beautiful surroundings and of soothing solitude. In the valley, or rather on the plains, far below, villages here and there dot the ground and the bricks of the buildings look like red spots against the green of the fields of the

hedges of the woods. From the centre of each spot of red a spire protrudes and one is reminded of the village churches of Quebec.

I am beginning to wonder if it is always cold up here. Since my arrival five days ago, we have had almost winter weather. Of course this helps one to sleep. I have as many as four or five blankets on me at night.

There are beautiful walks and gardens about the monastery and I stroll through these in spite of the wind and cold, because I do not wish to lose my taste for open-air life. The war is not by any means over and a great deal of fighting remains to be done yet.

I attended a concert last night given by the sick and wounded soldiers of the institution. It was very lively and it did one good to see the cheerful faces of the men who have been fighting and who expect to return to the front shortly. They appeared not to have a care.

I am very happy here. Why shouldn't I be? I am going through one of the periods not unusual in a soldier's career, and I am very fortunate that I have not been maimed for life instead of having received only a severe shaking up.

Mont des Cats.
18 June, 1916. Your birthday

My dearest Mater,
I have been thinking of you this morning and I have been praying at Mass that you may live to see very many more birthdays. You are so necessary to us all — especially to the younger ones.

It is only late in life that one understands the importance of a mother. If I may recall something that hurts both of us, I may say that years ago when poor Wilfrid [*a younger brother who died at infancy*] died and you were dangerously ill, Aunt Kate tried to make me realize what I realize now. She said "How much worse it would be if it had been mother." And looking back I see how right she was, because I cannot conceive how we could have lived without you.

I heard last night through Canon Scott that Jacques Brosseau had been <u>seriously</u> wounded. Canon Scott had seen him when he was half delirious and was being rushed to a clearing hospital. I do not know the extent of his injuries and I wish you would say not a word to his mother. The Colonel will probably send her a cablegram with definite news. My information is too vague, but there is no question about his being badly wounded.

While Vanier was still convalescing, the Battle of Mont Sorrel continued, with casualties among the 22nd Battalion rising daily.

Diary entry: 19 June

Lapointe informs me that Lieut. Brosseau is dead, that Major Laflèche has been seriously wounded and that Captain Chassé has had his foot pierced by a bullet. What terrible losses!

Diary entry: 22 June

I slept badly last night... an exceptional thing for me. The weather is heavy, and depressing....

Diary entry: 23 June

I am waiting for news of my leave. Another bad night — didn't sleep until the dawn. Leave has been granted from 27 June.

No. 12 Casualty Clearing Station
A little further from the front
23 June, 1916

My dearest Mater,
The day before yesterday I was moved here from the North Midland Casualty Clearing Station [*at Mont des Cats*]. I feel very much better. In fact I expect to get my leave warrant today or tomorrow. This will give me a further rest in London before I return to the battalion.

Poor Jacques Brosseau died of wounds. When I wrote you that I had heard he was seriously wounded, I had heard that he had died of his wounds but as the informant had not seen him dead, I would not and could not believe the horrible news. Poor Jacques. It is impossible to believe! When I look back over the two years we have lived together and played together and fought together it is almost as if I had lost a brother. I knew no one so devoted to and thoughtful of his mother. He wrote to her each day and numbered his letters, which had reached, I believe, the five hundred mark. I have reason to believe that this awful blow will kill his mother.

I received definite news of his wounding yesterday. His company was in the front line and went through a three hour bombardment with heavy casualties. Towards the end of the bombardment, almost the last shell burst near Jacques fracturing a leg (I was not told which) in three places and practically severing it below the knee. His wounds were bound up, stretcher-bearers took him out and he lived over a day in hospital. I don't think he can have suffered much. The injuries were so great that the nerves must have been numbed. He did not complain very much, it appears. All this happened while I was at the Clearing Station. I am sorry I cannot speak from personal experiences and observation: if I could I would write his mother a detailed account of the sad circumstances. As it is, I can only write her a note of condolence. De Martigny, who was with Jacques at the time, is sending all particulars to the family.

le 24 juin 1916
Bien cher papa,

I am feeling better little by little. I should be completely recovered in a few days.

I am here in France and that is no small consolation. Much that I admire and respect Belgium where I spent the winter, it is France that I love.

I think often of the travels we made together here and promise myself that we shall repeat them after the war is over.

British Officers' Club, Boulogne
26 June, 1916

My dearest Mater,
I reached Boulogne last night, too late to catch the leave boat for England.

I was forced to stay overnight, which means that I shall be in London a day after my legitimate expectations.

I feel very much better: my rest in hospital benefitted me very greatly. I have not received my mail for some days. As I have asked the battalion to forward it to the Savoy Hotel, I expect to have news from you in London.

It has rained here all morning: most unpleasant hanging about until tonight with nothing to do except to walk the quays and to go to a cinema show this afternoon. I console myself however when I think of the worse things that I might be doing.

Diary entry: 26 June

Visited the city of Boulogne. Rained all day. At 7:30 p.m., left for England.

Arrived at Folkestone at 9:40 p.m. and London at midnight. Staying at the Savoy.

Diary entry: 27 June

In the morning, visited the Canadian Commission and the Commission of Quebec. In the afternoon, Half-Past Eight at the Comedy Theatre.... In the evening, Mr. Manhattan at the Prince of Wales.

Savoy Hotel, London
29 June, 1916

My dearest Mater,

I took a trip to Bramshott Camp (where the 4th Canadian Division is stationed) yesterday afternoon. I saw General Watson who was most kind to me. I motored back to London this morning: it is a beautiful drive which only takes an hour and a half in a fast motorcar. Captain Boyer you know is aide-de-camp to General Watson and Camp Commandant of Bramshott. It is a splendid position and one which he fills to perfection.

I have received letters from a number of friends who have been thoughtful and very good to me. It cheers one up wonderfully to be remembered in this way.

Vanier was still recuperating in London when the Somme offensive, conceived months earlier as "the Big Push," moved ahead. On July 1, 100,000 men advanced across No Man's Land but encountered a firmly entrenched and well-prepared phalanx of heavily armed German troops. The result was a slaughter of horrendous proportions: over 57,000 British soldiers killed, wounded and missing on the first day alone and another half million by the end of November.

Vanier remained in London but moved to the Perkins Bull Hospital in the London suburb of Putney.

The Perkins Bull Hospital for Convalescent Canadian Officers,
Putney Heath, S.W., London
2 July, 1916

My dearest Mater,
When I was in hospital in France I thought that I was well enough to proceed on leave and later to return to the battalion. However two days after my arrival in London, I discovered that I had not completely recovered from the effects of the shock. I reported at once to the medical authorities in London and I was sent to this hospital which is really not a hospital but a home. Mr. Perkins Bull, advocate of Toronto, is the founder of the "home" and has provided the officers with every comfort and every convenience. He is a charming man who lives with his family only a few doors from here. His house is open to us at all times. He has a splendid tennis court

where I have played a few times. My hand is rather out, as it is some time since I handled a racquet.

Today I saw Capt. Chassé who is in hospital with a bullet wound in the foot and Captain Routier whose ears and general health are giving him trouble. I have no idea of what my stay in hospital will be: I will keep you informed of any change in my movements.

Perkins Bull Hospital
4 July, 1916

My dearest Mater,
My cablegram has already informed you that I appeared before a medical board and was given six weeks' sick leave. I expect to remain a few days here, then to be sent to the country where I can more easily rest. I should be quite well — better than before the accident — in six weeks' time.

I see Captain Chassé very often: his bullet wound is healing rapidly. I have told you already, I think, that I have received perfect treatment in every hospital in which I have been. When the war is over it will be hard for me to retain the same dread of hospitals that I used to have. The Canadian women are doing a great and a good work in looking after the incapacitated. In this hospital girls belonging to the best Canadian families attend to the cooking and to the serving of the meals, to the rooms, to the beds — in a word do everything. It is splendid and we appreciate it.

Savoy Hotel, London
8 July, 1916

My dearest Mater,
I have not moved from the hospital to the Savoy, as you might suppose. I am only waiting for Captain Boyer with whom I have an engagement. Putney is only three quarters of an hour's ride from the heart of London which makes staying there very pleasant as I can run in to a matinée when I have nothing better to do. I play quite a bit of tennis which helps to get me fit.

The Allied offensive is taking satisfactory proportions. The

Germans, I imagine, must be getting anxious.

I still receive no mail: it is not your fault of course but the battalion's. But mail is a wonderful consolation. I am getting along splendidly.

Savoy Hotel, London.
13 July, 1916. 7 p.m..

My dearest Mater,
You will think that I am always at the Savoy but I am not really. I have come in from Putney Heath to dine with Colonel Gaudet and I have an hour to while away because we are dining at 8.

I am getting along splendidly. I am quite as well, in fact, as I have ever been before. It is advisable, however, for me to get as fit as possible before returning — to store up a reserve of energy, so to speak.

Everybody in England is delightfully kind to all of us so-called invalids (because I look very healthy you know) and we are received very cordially — as of the family.

Tomorrow is France's day, in more senses than one. A tag-day collection will be taken up throughout England for the "Croix Rouge Française" [*French Red Cross*]. Englishmen have the most extraordinary admiration for France and her fighters — and by Jove, they deserve the admiration. Those who think the war will <u>soon</u> be over are very much mistaken. Germany has not begun to be beaten yet!

On July 24, Vanier received word that, because of his health, he was authorized to return to Canada if he wished. But he had other plans, which he shared with his mother.

Savoy Hotel, London
25 July, 1916

My dearest Mater,
[...] Today I received a notification from H.Q. Shorncliffe telling me

that authorization had been received for my return to Canada, if I wished it. I appreciate very much what all my friends in Canada have done for me, but somehow I can't go back. I must be at the front so long as I am fit. I should be unhappy anywhere else. Of course if I am offered an appointment where the work is less trying than in an infantry company, it is possible that I may accept it. However I shall be very sorry to leave the 22nd where so many of my friends are.

A score of people have written notes of congratulations and of sympathy. Some of those from whom I hear had not written since the beginning of the war. My sick leave expires August 12 when normally I should return to Shorncliffe and in due course (four or five days) back to the Battalion. I shall inform you, by cable, of my movements.

Latterly things have been taking a very good turn for the Allies and I think that continued pressure applied will have far-reaching effects.

The Perkins Bull Hospital
Putney Heath, S.W.
1 August, 1916

My dearest Mater,
[...] I am quite well again. My sick leave is up August 15th. If by that time I have not secured a combatant position with the 4th Canadian Division (a little less trying than infantry work), I shall return to the 22nd Battalion which has kept up its very good work. I can't go back to Canada now, with the boys fighting in France. I should be as unhappy as I was in the early months of the war before I enlisted. Please do not think that I am ungrateful for all you and the dear Governor and Major Hudon and Pierre Casgrain have been doing for me.

[...] In two weeks my sick leave will be up. I shall let you know by cable of any move I may make. A cablegram "Happy Birthday" will mean that I am leaving for the front.

The Perkins Bull Hospital
Le 1e aout 1916

Mon bien cher Papa,

[...] As you know, I have received two letters from Canadian headquarters in Shorncliffe telling me that they would return me to Canada, if I wished. Unfortunately, I cannot accept this offer. Please understand that my place is at the front with those who are fighting. If they offer me a position with the 4th Division, where the work would be a little less arduous, I would accept. If not, then I will return to the 22nd, which has not lost its excellent reputation.

This hospital is founded by a Torontonian, Mr. Perkins Bull. He lives with his family a few steps from here. He is a charming man who keeps an open house. All the wounded and the sick are received here at all hours. All his children are too young to enlist, so this is his way of doing his part.

The military situation is becoming more clear. It is clear that we will win, but slowly. Certain things are reassuring — the nightmare of German domination no longer obsesses us. Some day we will grasp the ferocity of the wild beast we have been facing. History will recount that during the months of August and September 1914, humanity came very close to virtual collapse.

The Perkins Bull Hospital
1 August, 1916

My dearest Mater,

[...] I have not spoken to you of Magog have I? But I am delighted that you have decided to go back to the lake, which is one of the prettiest spots God made. I am afraid I shall not be with you this summer: I hope to in 1917.

The Perkins Bull Hospital
7 August, 1916

My dearest Mater,

[...] I have no definite news to give you yet but it is very probable that after my medical board, which takes place August 15th, I shall be sent to the 69th Battalion, which is at the 22nd base battalion, Shorncliffe and in the course of a week or ten days, I would be sent on to the 22nd. Captain Chassé and Captain Routier are still at this convalescent home with me.

I have seen Captain Papineau who is in hospital with a sprained leg caused by a fall when playing indoor baseball. Major Laflèche is in bad shape: I don't mean that he is in any danger of death but he is dreadfully mutilated. I think his recovery will take years.

I was most fortunate in being sent to this home, where all the work is done by girls known as V.A.D.'s (Voluntary Aid Detachment). They are charming and very obliging. It is splendid to see them do menial work, often of a very unpleasant character as if they had done it all their lives, whereas they have always been used to having maids and cooks of their own. It is a substantial way of "doing your bit" and they do it cheerfully.

Each day sees me a fitter man.

Diary entry: 9 August

Met with Boyer at 11:30 a.m. at the Savoy. Boyer informs me that General Watson is offering me the position of pay officer in the battalion of the 4th Division. Since I do not want to leave the fighting troops, I refused the offer.

The Perkins Bull Hospital,
14 August, 1916

My dearest Mater,
[...] I cabled you today to address mail, for the immediate future "c/o Bank of Montreal, Waterloo Place, London". I do not know as yet where I shall go after August 15. If I obtain a combatant appointment with the fourth division, I shall probably accept: otherwise, I shall refuse.

Meanwhile my very pleasant sojourn in this home (it is hard to call it a hospital) continues to make me fit and fat.

[...] When is John going to marry — in September or October? I regret very much that I shall be unable to attend the marriage.

Isn't it extraordinary that I should be away for both marriages? And it is such a long time to wait for Anthony's!

CANADIAN PACIFIC TELEGRAPH
To: Vanier, Magog; Quebec.

MONEY RECEIVED. THANKS. MEDICAL BOARD TODAY EXTENDED SICK LEAVE TO SEPTEMBER FOURTEENTH. TRUST IN MY JUDGEMENT. VANIER

The Perkins Bull Hospital
16 August, 1916

My dearest Mater,
[...] The 4th Canadian Division has left for France and it is just possible that I shall join them when my sick leave expires. If I do not go to the fourth division (this depends of course upon the wishes of General Watson, who has been most kind and who has given me unmistakable proof of his interest in me), I shall return to my old battalion.

The authorities in London, acting under instructions, I suppose, from Canada have been very obliging and have formally offered to return me to Canada. I hope you are not angry that I refused. It isn't that I am not anxious to see you all, dear, but I feel that it is my duty to see this sacred war through and with God's help I shall. The further I get from the firing line, the more unhappy I am. I don't mean that I revel in the noise of bursting steel, because I don't, but there's the tremendous consolation of being in the thick of it, of the biggest fight that has ever taken place for the triumph of liberty. At some time or other we have all wished that we had lived in Napoleonic days, but the present days are fuller of romance, of high deeds and of noble sacrifices.

Diary entry: 24 August

Tennis in the morning and again in the afternoon. Went to see a slide show of the Battle of the Somme. Heartbreakingly realistic! It should be shown in all the neutral countries.

The Perkins Bull Hospital
30 August, 1916

My dearest Mater,
I am glad you are all having a good rest at Magog. By this time you are probably thinking of a return to Montreal.

My health improves each day: really I feel better than when I left for France last September. Unfortunately I am unable to give you news of my future plans because I do not know myself what I shall do.

Did you see that another Loyola boy, Capt. J.P. Walsh, had been killed at the front?

Until recently, the weather has been delightful: now we are beginning to taste the joys of rain. Heaven knows when it will cease. I have received a command to be present at Windsor Castle, next Friday, to receive the Military Cross, which I will send on to you as soon as I can.

The Perkins Bull Hospital
1 September, 1916

My dearest Mater,
I had the honour of receiving the Military Cross from the King at Windsor Castle today. There were about twenty-five recipients of decorations. What impressed me most was the simplicity of the whole ceremony. Each officer was presented to the King who shook hands and spoke with him for a few minutes. He questioned me about my nationality and appeared surprised when I told him I was a French-Canadian. He was most gracious in his manner.

After the presentation we were invited to lunch. The dining room overlooks the beautiful gardens of the castle: as the weather was delightful our short stay was most enjoyable in every way.

I shall forward the cross to you as soon as I can.

Vanier had already turned down the offer to spend his leave in Canada but this did not stop his parents from using what influence they had to have their son returned permanently to Canada. They felt that with his decoration and wartime experience, his services would be valuable as a recruiting agent in Quebec at a time when enlisting new recruits for war service was becoming increasingly difficult. Vanier was not to be persuaded.

The Perkins Bull Hospital
le 3 Septembre 1916

Bien cher Papa,
I am glad that you have seen Major Hudon and that you have found him likeable. He is a charming man who at the front has always been a sincere friend and an enthusiastic companion. He is one who I find completely likeable. I am going to write to thank him for all the trouble he has gone to to obtain a holiday in Canada for me.

[...] You know, Papa, that I appreciate, more than I can say, all the efforts you have made on this subject [*of returning home to help recruitment*]. You must not think me ungrateful if I do not return to Canada. I feel that my work at the front is not yet finished. If I dared to think that my efforts in Canada would help in the recruiting of new volunteers, I would return at once. Unfortunately, I am convinced that no one would listen to me: after all, Sir Wilfrid Laurier[2] and Sir Rodolph Lemieux[3] have both failed in their attempts.

The Perkins Bull Hospital
17 September, 1916

My dearest Mater,
[...] I appeared before a medical board Thursday last (September 14th) when I was declared "fit for general service" and was given instructions to report to the 69th Reserve Battalion, Shorncliffe, pending my return to France. General Watson has been most kind in every way: he has written to General Carson [*special representative in England of the Canadian Minister of Militia*] asking for my

services. It may interest you to see a few extracts from his letters: "I wrote to General Carson yesterday asking him to have you transferred over to me at once. Will you see him at once and arrange to have your transfer effected with the least delay. As you know I am only too pleased to help you out or do anything I can for you or any of our friends and it will be a great pleasure indeed to have you along with us." You see how cordial General Watson's attitude is. He says little however concerning the sort of position he would give me. In spite of this, I think I shall go to his division as I have absolute confidence in him. He is most sincerely anxious to do anything he can for me. Be sure that I shall cable definite news of any kind. Will you please say nothing of all this, except to the Governor?

My intention is to leave Shorncliffe as soon as I can for the front.... I applied for leave yesterday as I had a few purchases to make in London and because I wanted to see Ernie McKenna who is over on leave and is staying at the Hotel Cecil.

Mr. Bull, the president of the Perkins Bull Hospital, is most gracious and has asked me, whenever I come to London, to stay here. I have accepted his invitation. I told you in a former letter that I would cable "Happy Birthday" the day on which I sailed for France. If I go to the 4th Division, I shall add the word "Watson"; if to the 2nd Division (22nd Battalion), I shall add the word "Turner".

The Perkins Bull Hospital
19 September, 1916

My dearest Mater,
Yesterday I wired for three days extension of leave which was granted. I have already told you I believe that I propose to spend as little time as possible in Shorncliffe. One never knows how long it will take to get to France — it depends upon the request from officers from the front. It may take two weeks or one month.

[...] Captain Boyer has written to me from the front. He tells me that he would be glad if I joined the 4th Division. He is a very lovable sort of chap and I like him. The fourth division, as far as I can make out, is in our old sector, not many miles south of Ypres.

I saw Ernie McKenna yesterday. He is in London on leave. His appearance is splendid: he has not got any stouter and looks absolutely fit. Mrs. McKenna wrote me a long letter which gave me great pleasure. It is a satisfaction to get news and inspiration from such old friends who mean so much to us and who conjure up the past full of happy memories.

Will you please buy something for Jeanne and John and ask the Governor to give you the money — should I have any in the bank. It is practically impossible for me to make the purchase here and send the gift to Canada. I am enclosing a card which you might place with the present. You do not know how sorry I am to be absent for John's wedding. It is a great sacrifice.

The Battle of the Somme raged on. Vanier was still recuperating in England when the Van Doos took part in one of their most heroic encounters to date, the battle of Flers-Courcelette. This was the first use of tanks — the new "wonders of the war." It was also the first major engagement undertaken by the Van Doos. The three-day battle, begun on September 15, ended victoriously in the capture of the village of Courcelette and won praise from The Times *of London which carried a banner headline reading: "Canadians' Day of Glory." But the devastation in human terms was huge: out of the twenty-three Van Doos officers who took part in the action, seventeen were killed or wounded along with nearly seven hundred NCO's and soldiers. "If hell is as bad as what I have seen at Courcelette," wrote their Commanding Officer, Lieutenant-Colonel Tremblay, "I would not wish my worst enemy to go there."*

Back in London, Vanier was exhilarated by the news of his battalion's successes but devastated by the human toll it took. He noted in his diary on September 21:

I read, with tears in my eyes, the communiqué from Philip Gibbs[4] regarding the exploits of the 22nd at Courcelette. It is clear that the French-Canadians were superb in terms of daring and initiative. I am proud of the old battalion.

The Perkins Bull Hospital
20 September, 1916

My dearest Mater,
[...] By this time, I am afraid you will have read an appalling list of casualties. I have heard unofficially that the 22nd Battalion has suffered greatly but I have received no names yet.

The tragedy of war was brought home to me today when the news came that Mrs. Willison's husband had been killed in action. You will have seen her in snapshots I sent you of the Perkins Bull hospital V.A.Ds. The poor little woman won't believe that her husband is really dead. It may be that one becomes callous at the front. However that may be, nothing in the trenches has affected me so much as the sight of this heartbroken wife. In this war, a woman's lot is the most terrible. She has neither the excitement nor the glory but only the awful suspense.

The Perkins Bull Hospital
21 September, 1916

My dearest Mater,
I am enclosing a clipping from the "Daily Chronicle." What a splendid consolation it is to know that the French-Canadians did so well in action! Unfortunately I do not know how many and who paid the awful penalty, as glorious as it is terrible. I am very much afraid that some of my friends have made the supreme sacrifice.

Thank God the 22nd has upheld its record. It will be a lifelong sorrow to me that I was not able to be with my beloved battalion when it made its first glorious charge.

Diary entry: 23 September

Leaving London for Shorncliffe at 11 a.m. Zeppelin raid: I very clearly heard the explosion of bombs even though I had nothing to drink!

Upper Debgate Plain, Kent
69th Battalion (Canadian)
Sunday 24 September, 1916. 11 a.m.

My dearest Mater,
You have heard, by this time, of the terrible losses of the 22nd Battalion on the Somme. I am told on excellent authority that Major Renaud, Captain Bauset and Lieutenants Binet, Beaudry and Lavoie have been killed and that Captains Lefebvre, Chaballe and Languedoc and Lieutenants Belzile and Falardeau have all been wounded. There are other names not included in this list, but I give you these so that one can get an idea of the severity of the fighting. The English papers speak very highly of the work of the French-Canadians and all of us here are very proud of our battalion.

I had lunch with Colonel Gaudet on Friday and he was most enthusiastic. Major Gingras, who was blown up by a shell, is in London. I had a long talk with him and he gave me some of his impressions of the battle. He was not in the attack itself but had to go through a barrage of artillery fire the intensity of which was terrific. Colonel Tremblay, I am told, went through everything, not receiving a scratch. He is a splendid soldier and led his men most gallantly. In large measure the success of the attack was due to his splendid example. I feel sure that his valor will not go unrewarded.

Officers' Club Rooms,
Hotel Cecil, London W.C.
25 September, 1916

My dearest Mater,
[...] I cabled you this morning "Leaving for France Friday 29th. Please cable forty pounds." I am not absolutely without funds but because of the additional expenses incidental to my departure, I thought it wiser to cable for money. You will think, I am sure, that I have got to be a great spendthrift. But you will be glad to know that the money sent me from Canada has enabled me to have a very comfortable and enjoyable time during my convalescence. And I knew you would not want me to deprive myself of comforts.

Upper Debgate Plain
69th Reserve Battalion.
30 September, 1916

My dearest Mater,
I expected to leave for France yesterday but our departure, in some way, has been delayed. I am almost sure now of going to the 22nd Battalion; after its brilliant dash at Courcelette, it is an honour to return to such a unit.

You will find under cover some interesting snap-shots taken at the 69th Reserve Battalion where Lieut. Col. Dansereau is officer commanding. I was most cordially received by everyone here. This makes things easier when being attached to a new unit.

Will you forgive the pencil? The ink has run out.

Diary entry: 3 October

The papers have announced the death of Réné Lefebvre of the 22nd. He was a veteran of the battalion and one of my good friends! He was very brave. Colonel Tremblay told me that under machine-gun fire he led his men with a whistle. He should certainly be decorated for his work in the capture of Courcelette.

69th Battalion (Canadians)
Upper Debgate Plain
3 October, 1916

Dearest Mater,
[...] I am still in Shorncliffe without any definite news of my sailing for the front. It is only a question of days now however.

Most of the 22nd officers wounded in the recent fighting have been transferred to England. I had a letter from Bernie Languedoc but he does not say how seriously he is wounded.

I should like to write a letter of condolence to Maurice Bauset's mother but I do not know whether she is living or not. Will you let me know in your next letter whether Mme. Bauset is alive and what her address is? Maurice died splendidly, fighting for the honour of his race. His family can be proud of him, although I can understand what a blow his death is to his relatives.

Upper Debgate Plain,
Shorncliffe
4 October, 1916

My dearest Mater,
[...] 9 p.m. I sent a cable this afternoon to say that I was still in England. This evening however, Colonel Dansereau informed us that those chosen for service in France would leave tomorrow at 7:30 a.m. I am most certainly going back to the 22nd Battalion. All my friends are there and my men are there and it is perhaps the best place for me. The Battalion has been doing such big things lately that we who have not been with it are a bit ashamed of ourselves.

5 October 1916

My dearest Mater,
[...] I left Shorncliffe at 5:03 this afternoon. In all fourteen officers are going to the 22nd and I presume my destination is the same in view of General Watson's letter to General Carson. I am going to find out for certain tomorrow whether I am being sent to my old Battalion or to the 4th Division. In any case I will advise you by cable of any future development in my plans.

[...] Poor Bauset's death grieved me very much. He was most courageous and had a very level head. I received a letter from him dated 12 September, three or four days before his death. The last sentences of the letter (written in French) in the light of later events are very touching. "...It is not the B.T.C. (Back to Canada) that attracts me. It is rather a change of scene and command that will heal my nervous system. I will perhaps be in the next offensive. Regards to you, Maurice." Elsewhere in the letter he says (still in French) "You know that we are now on a new front, which you have guessed. We will do something very big before long...." He was right. He died, only a few days after. The greatest and the grandest thing any man can do, he laid down his life for his fellow men. He will live on in the minds and in the hearts of all who knew him.

Diary entry: 5 October

7:30 p.m. Lieut. Col. Dansereau has announced that we leave tomorrow morning at 7:30 a.m. for the front — at last!

8

RETURN TO THE BATTLEFIELD
OCTOBER 1916

> *"The battalion is very much changed since I left it: most of the officers and men have either been killed or wounded. It is hard to be very merry under these circumstances but it is necessary not to be downhearted, so we try to think of the present and of the living and not of the past and of the dead."*
>
> Georges Vanier to his sister, Frances,
> 15 October, 1916

Vanier left Shorncliffe for Southampton on October 5 and headed back to France aboard the S.S. King Edward. He reached Le Havre on October 7, dined at the Hotel Tortoni, then joined up with his old battalion. It was now under the temporary command of Major Dubuc and they were billeted near Brigade Headquarters in the French village of Bully-Grenay, not far from a dangerous part of the front.

The Battle of the Somme, begun over three months earlier, continued to rage on....

France
9 October, 1916

My dearest Mater,
[...] With Captain Chassé, I reached my old battalion last night and everybody appeared to be glad to see us among others Major Dubuc, Captain de Martigny, Captain Archambault and the old officers who remain. The saddest part of our return was the absence of so many dear comrades, such as Captains Lefebvre, Bauset and Sylvestre to mention only a few of those who have fallen.

We are now stationed in a small French village not many miles from a very violent sector. I think we will have a quieter time for a month or so and tomorrow we start marching.

The battalion set out on a series of route marches, designed to keep the men fit and train the new troops. They stopped only at night. Vanier spent the first night in l'Hôpital Bonnières where he slept in a small grocery shop. The second night, he was in Dieval and slept in a tavern called "Au Chat Rond."

France
12 October, 1916

My dearest Mater,
I am enclosing two snapshots for my scrapbook and a one mark [*German currency*] bill taken at Courcelette.

We are still on the march: if I were not mounted, I would be very tired probably. As it is the horse is a bit tired and I am quite fresh. It is unlikely that I will be under fire for two or three more days yet.

I am jolly glad to be back with my men — it is true that most of them have been killed or wounded but those who remain gave me a hearty welcome.

I have been most fortunate so far with billets when on the march. I have always managed to get a clean bed in a house whose inmates receive one most cordially. The French peasants are very kind to us.

They reached their final billets in Hersin, a small village south of Bethune and west of Lens where they remained on reserve for the next six days. Brigade Headquarters was in the nearby village of Bully-Grenay, also west of Lens.

France
14 October, 1916

My dearest Mater,
[...] We are about at the end of our marching now and very shortly, we should be not many hundred yards from the Boche. I rather expect that our sector will be fairly quiet, though it is unwise to boast of such things beforehand. I am in the best of health and spirits.

Please excuse pencil and writing. I am a bit tired and I am writing this on my knee in bed.

France
15 October, 1916

My dearest Frances,
[...] How are you getting on at Convent this year? If the war lasts very much longer, you will have graduated before I get back. As you say, the family circle has dwindled down — only four of you left. It must make a difference. But Georges will be back soon to even matters up.

The Battalion is very much changed since I left it in June: most of the officers and men have been either killed or wounded. It is hard to be very merry under these circumstances but it is <u>necessary</u> not to be downhearted, so we try to think of the present and of the living and not of the past and of the dead.

France
16 October, 1917

My dearest Frances,
[...] You ask me if I still had the relic you sent me. Of course and I always carry it with me together with your letter in which you say "keep it on you always. Your loving sister Goo" [*Vanier's pet name for his sister Frances*].

Be sure that I will not part with this relic, unless through some misfortune I lose it.

France
19 October, 1916

My dearest Mater,
I have just had the privilege of spending the whole day in the pouring rain! Needless to say, I was soaked to the skin, but I rather enjoyed the experience. As a matter of fact, I have always liked the rain and I remember very well when I was at college taking long walks in a heavy downpour. I was able to get beside a fire afterwards and dry properly. I am beginning to think that the weather here will not be very much better than in Belgium.

Did I tell you that I was in command of "A" Company? We are still short of officers, but expect a draft of twelve tomorrow or the day after. With a great number of officers life is more comfortable since it is possible to relieve one another.

The battalion has changed to such an extent that one would hardly recognize it. I miss the cheery faces of those who had been with us from the start and who gave up their lives at Courcelette.

Colonel Tremblay is in London still and is not expected for a month or so yet. Meanwhile Major Dubuc (who is temporarily commanding the battalion) carries on to everybody's satisfaction. Four Military Crosses have been awarded to officers of the 22nd, to Captains Fontaine and Chaballe, and to Lieutenants Dupuy (not Romeo who is in England) and Greffard. This gives you an idea of what the authorities thought of the work done by the battalion. I can speak freely and with admiration of what took place at

Courcelette because I had not the honour of being there.

P.S. There is nothing to indicate that our work this fall and winter will be different to that of last winter so there is no cause for abnormal anxiety.

France
22 October, 1916

My dearest Mater,
[...] After a three months' absence, I am once more in the trenches and I am settling down to my old mode of existence. The sector is not particularly lively but we manage to have a comfortable time.
    I can understand the Ostell and the Bauset families being cut up over Maurice's death. He proved to be a very good soldier and he led his men splendidly. They have every reason to be proud of him. It's unfortunate however that the dead receive no decorations other than the V.C. Otherwise Maurice would certainly have been decorated.

France
25 October, 1916

My dearest Mater,
I was very glad to hear that Mr. Browne had called and had left my Military Cross. I am sorry you did not meet him. He is a splendid chap, a mining engineer who overworked himself out here and strained his heart. I do not think that he will come back to the line.
    It was very thoughtful of you to send Mr. Martin a birthday present in my name. I am most grateful for what you have done. I read with interest the Gazette clipping with respect to the chemical body shield: I have heard of these shields before and their usefulness is questionable. Sometimes they deflect a bullet and sometimes a bullet or a piece of shrapnel which would not kill otherwise makes a fatal wound after going through the shield. It is largely a question of luck. Besides, these shields are most

inconvenient and worry the spirits. If I thought they would be of unquestionable service in saving life, I should buy one at once. In any case I shall consider the matter.

Did I ever tell you that I met Charlie Sullivan [*an old friend from Loyola*] when on the march through France? Our battalion had halted on the side of the road when the unit to which he belongs passed through and I saw Charlie Sullivan, not in the least changed, coming towards me on horseback. He saw me first and called out "Hello Mr. George". I just had time to shake hands with him.

P.S. You can be quite sure that I will not fail to make a promise to my patron saint.

Diary entry: 25 October

Telegram from headquarters announcing that the French have taken Douaumont [*one of the ring of forts protecting Verdun which had fallen to the Germans in February. Its recapture by the French was regarded as a great achievement*]. They captured 3000 prisoners. They saw this as their revenge for their defeat by the Prussians in 1870....

Diary entry: 27 October

Came out of the trenches at 2:30 p.m. Billeted in Bully-Grenay with Mme. Caillières-Lecomté, a very kind woman. She prepared a hot bath, a fire and coffee for us.

Diary entry: 2 November

7:30 a.m. Confession and communion and Mass. Left Bully-Grenay for the trenches. Relieved Company "C" on the front line.

Trenches
3 November, 1916

My dearest Mater,
Yesterday being "All Souls Day" I went to confession in the village of B——— (*Bully-Grenay*) before entering the danger zone. The sector is still quiet but we had the great misfortune today to lose another officer, Lieutenant Hudon, a splendid little chap who had been in the trenches only a few days.

I should be grateful if you would send me socks (very heavy all wool), Woodbury's soap (impossible to procure it in Europe) and a pair of boots from Dangerfields. I should like the boots one size larger than my measure, heavy soles, hob-nailed, as waterproof as possible and two inches higher than the ordinary ankle boot. In other words very much like one of the pairs you sent me last year.

It was during this period that Vanier was temporarily appointed adjutant. This was an important job that involved long hours assisting the commanding officer with various duties concerning administration, logistics, personnel and discipline problems. "He's a right-hand person who should know everything that is going on," explained a former officer of the Van Doos. "It's an important and a delicate position. And it's usually a twenty-four hour a day job."

Vanier accepted the new position with some scepticism but he carried out his duties in an exemplary fashion. Almost at once, he became what his fellow officer, Joseph Chaballe[1] *called "a model adjutant-major — one of the few officers who know how to keep friends in spite of his rather delicate duties and who represents politeness and courtesy in uniform and still remains a very brave soldier and a strict and efficient officer."*

France
13 November, 1916

My dearest Mater,
For some time now I have been extremely busy and I regret that my

correspondence has suffered. I had no idea until I assumed them that an adjutant's duties are so onerous. You know of course that Major Gingras is still in London and that (perhaps you do not know this) Captain de Martigny has obtained two month's sick leave. He was really unwell and was forced to leave.

Major Dubuc is on leave in London and Captain Chassé is in command of the battalion. I have been appointed — temporarily — adjutant. There is a great deal of office work — some compensations of course besides — and I cannot tell how long I will like the work. I am in the best of health and spirits. The 22nd is still in good form.

Major Dubuc returned from London on November 25 to take over command of the battalion in place of Lieutenant-Colonel Tremblay, who was invalided a month earlier.

In the field
27 November, 1916

My dearest Mater,
I am still very busy, too busy as a matter of fact. I suppose somehow that the work will keep my brain active and prevent me from falling into a state of partial mental paralysis.

[...] Our front is still very calm although I am not inclined to proclaim it from the housetops because one never can tell....

Is recruiting any better than it was? It might be possible to get together a brigade if everybody would lend a helping hand.

In the field
29 November, 1916

My dearest Mater,
I fear this Christmas will not see us united: let us hope it will be the last before our union. I can only repeat that the sector is very quiet, you can see that from the last of our casualties. The battalion is shaping splendidly after the arrival of so much new material: the

spirit is the same spirit that has always reigned here. The men are anxious to get into serious action once again. We have received some very good officers who are anxious to live up to the example set them by those who have made the great sacrifice, that their loss may not be in vain.

18 December, 1916

My dearest Mater,
[...] There is a possibility of my getting leave before the New Year which would be splendid wouldn't it? I have not decided whether I shall go to London or to Paris. I have made so many friends in London that I am tempted to return. In any case I will advise you by cablegram of my movements.

We are all looking forward to Christmas. It is curious how everybody does, even those in extraordinary circumstances.

I trust you will all have a very happy Christmas and a merry New Year. I wish I were with you.

Very devotedly Georges

Diary entry: 23 December

We captured a Boche this afternoon. It wasn't too difficult; the Boche seemed happy to surrender. He was a thin chap, and well clad. He complained about the food and the officers. He claimed that the Boche do not have any desire to attack....

Diary entry: 31 December

Midnight mass in the village chapel.

9

THE CAMPAIGN HEATS UP
SPRING 1917

"The more I see of the peasant class ... the greater is my admiration for the French nation and the greater is my faith in the triumph of Latin civilization. It is a great consolation and a great privilege to be able to work, in some measure, for the attainment of this triumph."
        Georges Vanier to his mother,
            14 January, 1918

"I thank God every day for the opportunity and the strength he has given me to assert my conviction of the righteousness of the great cause."
        Georges Vanier to his mother,
            14 January, 1918

As the New Year of 1917 dawned, a war that many expected to be over in four months had now dragged on for a seemingly endless twenty-eight months. Not only was there no end in sight to the conflict but 1917 also ushered in one of the harshest winters in living memory. When the frost finally eased up, the rains came — in torrents — turning the battlefields into the worst mud soldiers had ever seen.

Undaunted by the weather, the general of the Second Division advised Vanier, as adjutant, that he planned to inspect the battalion on the 2nd or 3rd of January. The men were still recuperating from the excesses of New Year's celebrations so Vanier feared the worst. In a speech to the Friends of the Royal 22nd in Montreal in 1955, he recalled the inauspicious event:

> As adjutant, I was responsible for the training and turn-out of the men, and I nearly went sick when I realized that an inspection so soon after New Year's Day would leave much to be desired. When the tragic morning arrived and the battalion lined up, I noticed with dismay that some of our men gave the impression of having celebrated the New Year with too much enthusiasm. My presentiment was confirmed when I saw that both the General and Colonel Tremblay were displeased so I decided to move away from the Colonel (where the adjutant usually stands) during the inspection so I could became slightly invisible and thus avoid the General's wrath. After the General had left, Colonel Tremblay said to me in that voice that some of you know so well: "Vanier, I order you, at any future inspection, to stay beside me the whole time."

Soon after this occasion, Vanier received ten days' leave and travelled to London with Colonel Dubuc.

Savoy Hotel, London
13th January, 1917

My dearest Mater,
I reached London last night with Lieut. Col. Dubuc. We are both

on ten days' leave and are staying at the Savoy. It is possible that I may go out to Mr. Bull's in Putney Heath. Mrs. Bull has been very kind as usual and has asked me to stay with them.

I cabled you today, telling you of my arrival. In one of your letters you mentioned that Mrs. McKeown had come over: I will inquire if she is still in London and if she is, I will look her up.

Before I left France, I was very <u>very</u> busy with courts martial besides the ordinary duties of an adjutant and I apologize for an apparent carelessness in my correspondence. I am afraid you have not received during the last month the proper proportion of letters. You know of course that I was quite well — didn't you from the cablegram I sent at Christmas.

Before leaving the front I received five or six boxes from you containing nuts, socks (the right kind) candy, maple syrup, chocolate, Woodbury's soap (will you send a few more bars?) and other most useful gifts. I believe most of the packages you send reach me eventually.

Savoy Hotel, London
21 January, 1917

My dearest Mater,
My leave is coming to an end and it has passed quickly and pleasantly. I have had a jolly time, and I have been to a few of the theatres. I have spent some time at Mr. Bull's house seeing my old friends who were so kind to me last summer. I have seen Colonel Tremblay and some other officers of the 22nd Battalion on sick leave and altogether I feel that I have benefited by the vacation. I am returning to the battalion quite happy.

I have been receiving letters from you very regularly and I am resolved when I return to the unit to write to you at least three times a week. You will forgive me won't you for not writing more often when in London?

Opinion over here is most optimistic about the end of the war and I must say that I share it to a certain extent. We feel that perhaps for Christmas 1917, we will all be back in our happy homes....

Hotel Folkestone,
Boulogne-sur-Mer
23 January, 1917

My dearest Mater,
I reached Boulogne yesterday afternoon on my way to the front and I expect to be with the battalion tonight or tomorrow morning. I had my usual luck in crossing the channel — a bit of wind but no tossing or pitching.

Colonel Dubuc remained on in London for his investiture on 24 January. He is to receive the D.S.O.

I have an idea that Colonel Tremblay is returning to the battalion. We are not very sanguine about a French Canadian Brigade <u>at the front</u> although it might be possible to form one in England. We will still carry on with what we have here, trusting that the future will hatch out a F.C. Brigade. It would be a tremendous thing for French Canada to have a brigade in the field.

[...] I am afraid I have not answered letters from Frances and Anthony as regularly as I should have, but will you ask them to write because their letters refresh me wonderfully.

Vanier returned to the battalion, which was undergoing a non-stop succession of route marches, inspections, drills and lectures.

At the front,
28 January, 1917

My dearest Mater,
I have been really worked off my feet since my return to the battalion and I am afraid my correspondence is beginning to suffer. You will pardon me won't you if my letters are short? I have taken up the duties of adjutant: once one understands the routine, the work is simple but the hours are long.

My health has never been so good and my spirits are absolutely "top hole".

On February 14, the Van Doos relieved the 42nd Battalion on the front line, moving to the sector north of Neuville-St. Vaast between Arras and Lens and within sight of Vimy Ridge — a target that would soon be of great significance for the Canadian troops.

15 February, 1917

My dearest Mater,
I am resolved from now on to answer your dear splendid letters each day as they arrive, even if the answer is a very short one. It is the only way that I shall ever manage to keep you properly informed of my doings. I am still doing the adjutant's work although I have not been appointed officially. The responsibility is great and the hours long but the work is most interesting and I rather think I shall end up by becoming a full-fledged adjutant.

Your boxes have arrived at short intervals and each time the headquarter mess has been happy making merry with maple syrup, gum, chocolate and various other sweets and comforts. I received the Dangerfield boots ten days ago. They are a perfect fit, splendidly turned out and very comfortable. After a ten mile walk my feet are quite rested. Other boots would have raised blisters and other unpleasant things.

You cannot know how your letters buck me up: I always look forward to the mail hour and it's always a happy evening that brings me news of home.

15 February, 1917

My dearest Mater,
[...] Fortunately this month we have not been having the very cold weather you speak of: if we had, we should have suffered a bit.

As a matter of fact, life has been much more comfortable this winter than last and we have no complaints to make. Of course I managed to work in a leave to England in January, which makes a difference.

We are very optimistic about the end of the war and we all

expect to be in Canada for Christmas next. In the next great offensive, the Huns should be pushed back.

On February 15, Vanier finally received confirmation of his position as adjutant, a job he had filled in a temporary capacity since the previous November. He took up his duties with enthusiasm. To his, and the soldiers' delight, Lieutenant-Colonel Tremblay returned in February to lead the battalion once again. "How good it feels after four months to be back among my brave men," Tremblay wrote in his diary. "And with much joy I rejoin my old friends, Major Dubuc who led the battalion in my absence and Major Vanier, the adjutant."

Au front,
le 16 février, 1917

Mon bien cher papa,
Your letter from Atlantic City and your card from Philadelphia gave me great pleasure. I was happy to hear that occasionally you do decide to take a holiday. I can give you a good example of travelling. In the past five years, I have spent at least half my time in a foreign country. You could say that I am on a perpetual holiday!
   My health is excellent and my morale is too. The general impression here is that we are going to finish up this year.

25 February, 1917

My dearest Mater,
[...] Today we received the splendid news of the withdrawal of the Germans on a part of the Somme front. The information has bucked us up wonderfully.

At the front
9 March, 1917

The Campaign Heats Up — Spring 1917

My dearest Mater,

I received yesterday your two letters dated 6 February and 14th February and they cheered me up as all your letters do. I am still very chirpy and always in the best of health and spirits. Major Asselin is at present with us, for how long I cannot say: you have all heard of course of Asselin formerly of "l'Action." He is a splendid sort and should show fighting qualities in the field if he lives up to his reputation as a journalist. Lt. Col. Dansereau of the 69th battalion is also with us for purposes of instruction, probably for a period of ten days.

How is the Governor and the dear children?

During the spring of 1917, Allied leaders, including US President Woodrow Wilson, were busy trying to negotiate various peace offers, but they all failed. News from Russia was equally destabilizing: in early March, Russia's Czar Nicholas II was forced to abdicate. Later that autumn, the Red Guards would storm Leningrad's Winter Palace, paving the way for the Bolshevik Revolution.

On the Western front, also in March, the Germans quietly withdrew to the Hindenburg Line, strong new defences south of Arras, thus exchanging a long, bulging line for a shorter straighter one which they fortified heavily.

In early April, the Allies prepared to launch another massive offensive, one that would have important implications for the Canadians. Plans called for a French attack in the south, along the Chemin des Dames between Reims and Soissons, preceded by British attacks around Arras. The Canadian share of the British assault was to be the seizure of Vimy Ridge, north of Arras. A preliminary bombardment, designed to conceal the exact time and extent of their proposed attack, had already begun on March 20. It was intensified from April 2 with such crushing destruction that the Germans called the period "the week of suffering."

The Van Doos returned to the trenches on April 4, relieving the 29th Battalion in the region of Neuville-Saint Vaast. Companies "A" and "C" occupied the front line while "B" was in the support position and "D" remained in reserve. On the right was the 4th Brigade and on the left was the 3rd Canadian Division. Everyone was considerably bucked by President Wilson's announcement that, as of April 6, the United States had entered the war. Until now, the Americans had been reluctant to take part, preferring to remain neutral, but with this move many hoped they would bring new and vitally needed resources to the Allied side.

Diary entry: 6 April

Enemy bombarded continuously. Our bombardment more and more intense.

Diary entry: 7 April

Our bombardment increases in intensity. Operation which was to take place in morning of 8 April is delayed 24 hours.

On the night of April 8, the infantry moved into prepared positions. The attack itself was under the command of Lieutenant-General Julian Byng, with General Arthur Currie,[1] a former real estate agent from Victoria, B.C., acting as his senior divisional commander. The operation, involving some 40,000 men, began in very bad weather at dawn on Easter Monday, April 9.

Diary entry: 9 April

At zero hour (5:30 a.m. on 9 April), the artillery barrage started on the German front line and the infantry jumped over the parapet.

It was April 9, Easter Monday, when all four divisions of the Canadian Corps, operating as a unit for the first time, moved forward together and swept up Vimy Ridge in the midst of driving wind, snow and sleet. The position of honour was assigned to the 5th Brigade. The Van Doos, part of the Second Division, supported the 24th, 25th and 26th battalions. By mid-afternoon, they had managed to take

The Campaign Heats Up — Spring 1917

Lieutenant-General Sir Julian Byng, a British aristrocrat and cavalry officer, was appointed commander of the Canadian Corps in June 1916. It was he who would lead the Canadians to victory at Vimy Ridge. He would also become a life-long friend of Georges Vanier.

A Canadian bunker, marked "Canadian Front Line," near Vimy.

command of the whole crest of the ridge with the exception of Hill 145, the highest point of Vimy Ridge, and the Pimple, a grassy mound at the north edge of the ridge. Three days later, they also took these.

The victory at Vimy Ridge, which the French called "an Easter gift from Canada to France," was above all a victory for the Canadians. "Crest of Vimy Ridge taken. Canadians Lead in Triumph" noted a banner headline in the Toronto Globe, while Philip Gibbs, the well-known war correspondent, hailed Vimy Ridge as "the Canadians' greatest day in the war since the capture of Courcelette." British historian John Keegan was equally euphoric in his book The First World War, calling Vimy "the first major offensive effort by a Dominion contingent on the Western front.... The success of the Canadians was sensational."

The triumph at Vimy provided a well-needed boost to everyone — including Vanier, who wrote to his mother on April 14:

At the front

My dearest Mater,
Today brought me your two letters dated 19th and 22nd March. I have been receiving your boxes regularly and each time we have a splendid feed.

You know of course that things are going with a tremendous swing and that we are pursuing the Boche. The morale of our troops is magnificent. We cannot lose — what is more we are winning quickly and the war will be over within six months.

Curiously enough the weather here has been very cold — with a great deal of snow which is extraordinary for this part of the country in April.

You will probably hear from us within the next two or three months. Already our casualty list of officers will give you an idea of the work already begun.

I am in the very best of spirits. My health has never been so good and I am happy.

P.S. It's a wonderful consolation to be driving the Boche out of France.

The Canadians' victory at Vimy meant far more than the capture of a strategic landmark: the event was seen by many as the true coming of age of their country. "No matter what the constitutional historians may say," wrote historian D.J. Goodspeed in his book The Road Past Vimy, *"it was on Easter Monday, April 9, 1917, and not on any other date, that Canada became a nation."*

Nowhere is this new-found national pride more strikingly portrayed than in the Canadian National Memorial erected nineteen years later on 250 acres of land donated by France at Hill 145. It is an impressive structure: two massive spires of white Adriatic marble surrounded by twenty carved stone figures honouring the more than six thousand Canadians who died in the battle.

The Canadian National Memorial at Vimy, dedicated in 1936 to those who lost their lives in that battle. The war correspondent Philip Gibbs hailed Vimy Ridge as "the Canadians' greatest day in the war since the capture of Courcelette," while historian D.J. Goodspeed wrote "it was on Easter Monday, April 9, 1917 ... that Canada became a nation."

At the front
15 April, 1917

My dearest Mater,
Cold and rainy. The countryside looks bleak. But however bleak the countryside, the spirit is bright because we are winning. We are going on. My health has never been better.

The battalion was relieved two days later, and marched to billets at Aux-Rietz. On re-entering the line, they spent the next two months in the area in front of Vimy Ridge preparing for what would be another Canadian triumph, the capture of Hill 70.

At the front
Letter undated

My dearest Mater,
Will you pardon me if I have not written as often during the last three weeks as I should have done. I have really been overwhelmed and usually in spite of my good intentions I have been a bit tired when bedtime comes — a curious sort of bedtime which varies between the hours of 8 a.m. and 8 p.m.

We all feel very bucked up over the Hun retirement which in spite of all sorts of assurances from the German press remains nevertheless a victory for us. It was not we but they who decided to straighten the line. There is no doubt of course that temporarily it strengthens their position: their front is materially shortened which means more men and more guns to the mile.

I have not heard from any of you for quite ten days but the fault I am sure is with the mails which have been more erratic. Will you tell Anthony and Frances that a letter <u>always</u> makes a difference however short it may be.

5/5/17

My dearest Mater,
Last night your letter dated 15 March reached me. Need I say that it cheered me up?

Today I heard — quite unofficially that the United States had declared war on Germany. [*This actually happened on April 6.*] The morale effect should be very great ...

P.S. Health splendid and spirits.

The Campaign Heats Up — Spring 1917

In the field,
14 May, 1917

My dear Frances

Many thanks for your delightful letter containing your birthday greetings. I spent a very happy birthday in spite of my surroundings. Birthdays are beginning to frighten me however — my next one will take me out of my twenties. It will be an ominous date.

If you have a photograph or snapshot of yourself taken recently I should be pleased to receive it.... I have been very chirpy since my return to the trenches. I am now in the best of health and spirits. We are all hoping to be able to do something worthwhile before long and we may be given the opportunity soon.

In the field
14 May, 1917

My dearest Mater,
[...] It is not always easy to get into a "letter writing" frame of mind particularly when it is almost impossible to give you an idea of one's life and doings without overstepping the bounds set by the censorship regulations. As a matter of fact, the daily papers keep you perfectly acquainted with movements of the Canadians.

Diary entry: 15 May

Still in quarries. Less shelling today. Weather fine. We hear that Roeux has fallen. There are rumours that the French are coming to take Lens. Black night.

On June 6, Lieutenant-General Byng, Commander of the Canadian Corps since June 1916, stepped down and Lieutenant-General Sir Arthur Currie took over as Commander of the Corps. He thus became the first Canadian to hold the position.

A month later, on July 9, Vanier accompanied Lieutenant-Colonel

Tremblay to Belgium for a ceremony in which the French Minister for War, M. Paul Painlevé, presented Tremblay with the French Legion of Honour and Georges Vanier with the Cross of the Legion of Honour.[2] *The honour conferred by the French government was "for services rendered to France as one of the organizers of the first French-Canadian unit to fight on French soil since the passing of French Canada to England in 1760." Vanier wrote to his mother about the occasion on July 12:*

A few days ago I had the privilege of receiving the cross of the Legion of Honour from the hands of the French Minister for War, M. Painlevé. It was one of the proudest moments of my life. To a French Canadian, a decoration awarded by France has a two-fold significance. I will forward my cross to you as soon as I find a suitable occasion.

Anthony has spoken to me of the Loyola College Review and of his published story. I should very much like to read his story.

Your letters always reach me very regularly and are one of the sources of real pleasure that I have in France.

My spirits and health remain perfect. I feel much better than when I returned to France in October last.

At the front
17 July, 1917

My dearest Mater,
[...] Although my time has come for leave, I have been unable to make up my mind whether I wish to go to London or to Paris. Possibly I may go to neither but to some watering place. As a matter of fact, I feel in no way in need of a change again.

You asked me in a recent letter if I should like a large photograph of Frances. I think it would be better to send nothing larger than 4" x 5" as it will be very difficult for me to carry it about. If you have been photographed yourself I should be delighted to have one of your pictures.

I was greatly surprised and shocked to hear of Frank McKenna's death. How did it affect poor Mrs. McKenna? She has had rather a hard time within the last two years. I am writing to her today. I sometimes envy you all the delightful breaks at Lake Magog although the weather has been most pleasant and quite warm out here.

My health and spirits are always extraordinarily good.

Diary entry: 21 July

Late at night, I received Eva's cablegram telling me about her baby girl [*born July 16, 1917 and named Madeleine*].

On July 22, the Battalion moved to Marqueffles Farm, near Lens, where they were based until mid-August.

In the field
10 August, 1917

My dearest Mater,
You say in your last letter that brother Anthony did very poorly. There is hardly any excuse. 334 marks out of 900. I can understand 550 or 600 marks but not 334. I am afraid he will have to "buck up". Then if he did not work very hard during the year, with a little "cramming" (of which I do not, of course, approve) he could have done very much better and I would have imagined that his sense of pride would have helped him. I would certainly not try St. Laurent however. Perhaps an altogether different atmosphere would be better for him and if I were not away from home I might suggest a Jesuit College in England where he would get away from his numerous friends and where he would get a solid training physical and moral. What do you think?

14 August, 1917

My dearest Mater,
It is just possible that I may be in something worthwhile before long and I want you to know that I feel very confident and very happy and I should not want to be elsewhere.

"*Before long*" was an understatement. The next morning at dawn, the Van Doos, with Lieutenant-Colonel Tremblay in command and Georges Vanier acting as his adjutant, joined the other Canadian forces in the Battle of Hill 70, a point overlooking the Flemish city of Lens. Not only were they successful in capturing this strategic position on the northern approach to Lens, but they also managed to secure the western part of the city as well.

Captain Henri Chassé was also involved in the campaign and recalled the part played by the Van Doos in this assault when he addressed the Académie Commerciale in Montreal on February 5, 1920:

> The 22nd had as their objective a German trench — "Catapult" — stretching in a north-easterly direction, and crossing the miners' houses in St. Emile, a suburb of Lens. It was difficult work, because the Boche had nests of machine-guns hidden in many of the houses, and these only stopped firing when the men of the 22nd could grip them by hand.
>
> The 22nd had completed its preparations for this attack at the farm of Marqueffles. We had left the farm — about six miles from the line of fire — the evening of the day before. In the driving rain ... we passed through Bully-Grenay where the population, hearing that we were about to attack the enemy, gave us a magnificent ovation. Our men were in great spirits and sang as they went along. Our own songs blended with the acclamations of the French in Bully-Grenay. "Vivent les Canadiens" cried the good peasants; "Vive la Canadienne et ses jolis yeux doux" intoned one of our foot-soldiers, and his comrades took up the refrain "et ses j-o-lis yeux doux." Sometimes women and children would interrupt one of our singers with a kiss.
>
> It was a magnificent sight to see the old France applauding the young France which was on its way to die for her.

The Campaign Heats Up — Spring 1917

Georges Vanier spoke of the same occasion in a speech he gave in Montreal on February 16, 1928.

> One evening in August 1917, at Marqueffles, in the region of Lens, the battalion was lined up ready to leave the farm [*for the assault on Hill 70*]. It was raining. Our Chaplain [*l'Abbé Crochetière*] gave absolution to the men as they stood in line under the weeping sky and the battalion set off on the march to Bully-Grenay. One by one the platoons disappeared over the crest of the hill and disappeared. In spite of the rain the men were singing. Would they have sung in the same way without the great peace that the blessing of the priest had given them?

On August 22, still advancing toward Leus, the battalion stopped at Petit Servins.

Diary entry: Sunday, 2 September

Mass in village church at Petit Servins with our new padre, l'Abbé Crochetière.

Diary entry: 3 September

Paid a visit to the village curé and paid for some broken champagne glasses.

On September 15, the battalion gathered for a special dinner to commemorate the second anniversary of the Van Doos' landing in France and the first anniversary of the Battle of Courcelette. The following week, Vanier attended Mass at the YMCA hut near Hosselines, then boarded the train for Boulogne to begin his leave.

Diary entry: 24 September

Reached Boulogne at 7 a.m. Breakfast at the Officers Club in Boulogne. Sent illustrated post cards to the family. Embarked for Folkestone at 1 p.m. Delightful crossing.... Reached Folkestone at 3 p.m. and London a few hours later. No taxis at Victoria so took the tube to Charing Cross and walked to the Savoy by the light of a beautiful half-moon.

Savoy Hotel, London
25 September, 1917

My dearest Mater,
You know of course that I am in London on twelve days' leave. I cabled you today. I reached London yesterday afternoon and I had rather hoped that I should be free from gunfire for some time. My hopes were unfounded. During the performance of Cheep at the Vaudeville, it was announced that Hun aeroplanes were about. Shortly after heavy anti-aircraft gun fire was heard. There was no respite for over an hour. Bombs were dropped, but casualties were slight. Six killed and 20 wounded. It is very probable that nightly raids on London will take place during the coming week at least. There is an early moon and the light and weather are ideal for raiders. Do you remember that in January 1916 when I had leave in Paris, there were two air-raids during my short stay there? I seem to be followed about by this sort of unpleasantness.

Diary entry: 25 September

The Pall Mall Gazette reports casualties [*from the bombing raid*] as six killed and 20 injured. Shopped all morning — Burberrys etc.... Saw Berry in The Boy at the Adelphi.

The Campaign Heats Up — Spring 1917

Diary entry: 26 September

As expected, another air raid last night. Two bombs dropped on London. Twenty casualties. Monday's amended casualty return given fifteen killed, seventy wounded.

Diary entry: 27 September

Lunch with Miss Doris Robson. Before lunch saw Jack Manson and his wife (née Marjorie Starr). Tea with Miss Elsie Moore. Dinner very much alone at Simpson's [*a well-known restaurant in the Strand*].

Savoy Hotel, London
27 September, 1917

My dearest Mater,
I spent the greater part of yesterday with Mr. Bull and his charming family. I had lunch with Mr. Bull at the Union Club, dinner with the patients of the Perkins Bull Hospital and the taxi-service being hopeless, I slept at Putney Heath. Mr. Bull is carrying on the same good work as before. He is going to Canada next month and has been kind enough to offer to take back some things for me. I am getting together a few souvenirs which I shall send you for safe keeping.

Mr. Bull will be in Montreal between trains and will send you a wire from his port of debarkation. As he will be but a short time in the city he will probably ask you, in the wire, to meet him at his hotel for dinner. He is a charming man and outside of the battalion, has seen more of me than anyone else during the last two years.

Did I tell you that quite a few of our officers, NCO's and men had been decorated recently? Major Chassé received the Military Cross, as did Lieutenants Guay, Lamothe, Coté, Morgan and Payette. When I left France, Bauset [*Lieut. Maurice, who had been wounded in his hand*] was in very good health and spirits. He came through the last attack like a veteran. The battalion has never been in such a good position — discipline, officers, men and morale. Lt. Col. Tremblay is still in command and Major Dubuc is second-in-command.

Diary entry: 30 September

Brighton. Put up at the Metropole. Lieut. Dupuy took me in his side car from the Metropole Hotel to Shoreham Camp. 9:40 p.m. Left for London. Air raid.

Savoy Hotel, London
2 October, 1917

My dearest Mater,
As you will see from the clipping enclosed, there have been raids each night since my arrival here in London. It's a bit of a nuisance: there are a great number of people who take very badly to the raids and who in theatres and other public places make scenes that are far from soothing. Generally speaking, however, the conduct of the civilians is splendid: when the official air-raid warning is given, they take cover quietly and remain in places of relative safety until the ALL CLEAR signal is given.

[...] I have been fortunate enough to meet Lieut. Guillon, formerly of the 22nd Battalion and now attached to the R.F.C. [*Royal Flying Corps*]. He is a member of a tennis club in Wimbledon and I have been out two or three times in an attempt to keep fit.

As a matter of fact, I am in splendid health and I am getting heavier each month. I shan't be sorry, however, to get back to France: it is there really that I have the best time, with friends of three years' standing. I shall be leaving London on the morning of the 6th October.

Diary entry: 2 October

Tennis in the morning at Wimbledon with Georges Guillon and the ladies.

Vanier returned to France on October 7 to join the battalion in the area west of Méharicourt, southeast of Amiens, and was writing to his mother two days later.

France
9 October, 1917

My dearest Mater,
I returned from leave 7 October and on arrival, I found your three letters dated 5th, 9th and 11th September. I am very glad indeed that the packet containing the L. of H. [*Legion of Honour*] reached you.

My leave rested me completely. The weather during the crossing and the weather in England were both delightful. The only drawback was the air raids. Almost every night German aeroplanes came over and dropped bombs with varying results. The defensive guns made a deafening noise and one would have imagined oneself at the front. Fortunately no bombs dropped near me to spoil my holiday.

Mr. Perkins Bull will probably bring you a trunk containing souvenirs and some belongings I have no further use for. I would suggest that you have all rust removed from metal objects. The revolvers are not loaded, but as there is ammunition for them it would be well to be very careful. If Ernie [*McKenna*] is still in Montreal when you receive the trunk, he might explain the working of the revolvers. He knows the types in the trunk.

I am pleased to learn that Eva and the baby are so well.

Vanier's busy job left him little time for writing home. But others filled that gap. A compatriot, Bernard Brady, wrote to Mrs. Vanier on October 15, 1917:

> (Georges) is quite the tallest and largest of the Officers and is quite stout. You would have to look twice to be sure it was he. He has filled out and says that he enjoys his life here. Certainly he looks as if he did. His Military Cross colours look quite as if they ought to be there and he seems to be a general

favourite with the other Officers, notwithstanding the fact of his being Adjutant, which appointment requires endless tact and diplomacy to fill properly.

France
30 October, 1917

My dearest Mater,
A few days ago, I received your letter dated 23 October. I am glad that the "Daily Mirror" arrives regularly. It will make a most interesting review of the war in later years.

We had some very well known visitors a few days ago — the Honorable L.E. Blondin, the Hon. Mr. Turpen of Alberta and Capt. the Hon. K.J. Shaughnessy. Capt. Shaughnessy whom I saw in London when on leave looks very fit. He expects to return to England in a few weeks to become staff captain at Canadian Hq. London.

Captain Doyon, our old Chaplain, is at present in London and he says he hopes to return to the front. Did he look you up in Montreal? I rather expected he would.

Major Dubuc is on leave in London and returns in a few days. I am always as fit as ever and quite happy with my open air existence.

The battalion moved on to the area around Neuville-St. Vaast and for the rest of the month were continuously on the move until they reached Borre. Before long they were recruited to participate in the latter part of another campaign: the capture of a small Flemish town called Passchendaele — a name which now, like the Somme, has come to evoke the horrors of the Western front. From their base near the village of St. Eloi, they were among some twenty thousand men whom General Currie ordered, on October 26, to inch their way across the muddy terrain from one shell-crater to another while constantly under heavy fire.

The Canadians joined two British divisions for the assault on Passchendaele. In spite of a violent rainstorm they managed to gain the outskirts of the village and for five days, often slogging through No Man's Land waist-deep in mud and exposed to a hail of shelling from the Germans, they held on resolutely.

The Campaign Heats Up — Spring 1917

Soldiers of the 22nd Battalion resting in a crater before the assault on Passchendaele. One man scans the skies, presumably for approaching aircraft.

Their meagre victory came at a horrendous cost: in this one battle, seven thousand Canadians died. The Van Doos alone lost ninety officers and men.

Captain Chassé, in his speech of February 5, 1920 to the Académie Commerciale in Montreal, described the ordeal of the battalion:

Canadians carrying the wounded during the battle of Passchendaele. Vanier later said that "this battle remains for me the most haunting of the war."

We had been ordered to rest our right flank close to the church at Passchendaele, but when we arrived there after a night of marching through the mud the village no longer even existed. That march was the most painful of all our adventures. To begin with we had to follow a little pavement of trenches, three feet wide, for more than six miles in order to reach the reserve line. This pavement was a landmark for the German batteries. We were forced to follow it as best we could, although in certain places it was partially demolished, so you risked death by submersion in the mud if you put your foot to one side. Unfortunately a number of our comrades met their end in this dreadful way.

The officers, who led the march, had never known such difficulties. At last we came to what had once been the village of Passchendaele. The enemy, supposing that there was still a wall left standing, continued its bombardment. We spent twenty-four hours in this hell before we were relieved.... We returned to the rear, marching in mud up to our waists under the fire of an unrelenting bombardment. Surely Napoleon's veterans of one hundred years ago could not have been more miserable than we were.

Georges Vanier was also haunted by memories of that occasion. In a speech on September 26, 1964 marking the fiftieth anniversary of the founding of the 22nd Regiment, he recalled that bleak day:

On 14 November, we were in Passchendaele. This battle remains for me the most haunting of the war. In the evening, the regiment climbed up the ridge on a footpath, very straight and slippery from where you could see from each side those who had fallen along the road and who were sleeping with no other shroud than the mud of Flanders. Outside the narrow road, not one greeting. A quagmire barely visible had swallowed up an unfortunate soldier that a bullet or a false step had discharged on the path.

On November 11, the battalion returned to the line near Méharicourt and would remain there for the next three months.

At the front
16 November, 1917

My dearest Mater,
Today I received two letters from you containing clippings relating to Stuart MacDougall's [*a family friend*] wedding and Harding's [*a business associate*] new field of activity. There were also very cheerful tidings of Xmas gifts, puddings and all sorts of holiday sweets. In advance ... many thanks.

I trust the Hun submarine campaign will take a much needed rest and not sink the eatables. You can be assured that all Christmas boxes will receive a cordial welcome.

I am very sorry that my photographs have not reached you. I know of no other reason than loss in transit. They were certainly sent from the battalion. It is not worth worrying about however.

[...] I am very sorry indeed (to take up a matter touched upon by you in a letter received almost a week ago) that Father Doyon should have left you under the impression that my intention, after the war, was to settle down in Europe. I cannot understand where he obtained his information — certainly not from me. As a matter of fact I have never discussed the question of beginning life over again in Europe. I have been too busy with taking care of the present to think very much of the future. So please don't think of the matter any further. Between ourselves, Father Doyon's statement was hardly warranted.

In the field
9 December, 1917

My dearest Mater,
[...] I am very glad indeed that you received Major Redmond's book

and the rest of my photographs and the packages of the "London Gazettes."³ What pleases me most is that the trunk containing so many war souvenirs has reached you. I am writing to Mr. Bull to thank him for his extraordinary kindness. This is only one more instance of the interest Mr. Bull takes not only in me but in all Canadian officers. It is easy enough to be hospitable, it is easy enough to help in a monetary way but what is more difficult is to carry on one's graciousness to the point of being inconvenienced with packages and trunks.

I have mailed a number of Christmas cards to the family — one to each of you because I know that they will be interesting souvenirs now and after the war. I am only sorry that the third page of the Christmas card was not engraved according to the instructions given by us.

I regret we will be separated once more during the coming holiday season. Let us hope however that 1918 will bring decisive victory and with it the reunion of so many who have borne with patience the long separation.

From the bottom of my heart and soul, I wish you a very Happy Christmas and best of health during 1918.

Vanier also sent a small greeting card with an embossed emblem of the 22nd Battalion and along the edge, he wrote simply "France 6th December 1917."

To my dearest Mother,
From the bottom of a loving heart I wish you all at home a very happy Christmas.

Try to remember that my Christmas will not be altogether unhappy: given conditions as they are, I do not think I would wish to be elsewhere.

God grant that we may be united in 1918.

Your most devoted son

George

The battalion spent Christmas 1917 in Ligny-les-Aire. After Midnight Mass in the village church on Christmas Eve, Georges wrote again to both his parents.

La veille de Noel

Mon cher Papa,
Tonight, all my thoughts are with you, mother and the children. I wish you a very happy Christmas. I want you to know that my happiness here is very real; besides, in times of war, it would be incomplete if I were anywhere else. I will spend the last minutes of Christmas Eve in a listening post close to the Boshe. You will give me, I know, your blessing on New Year's Day. It will sustain me, as it has in the past.

From the bottom of my heart, I wish you a new year of health and of happiness.

Christmas Eve, 1917

My dearest Mater,
I received the finest Christmas box I could wish for tonight of all nights — three letters from you. Be sure that I am thinking of you and the letters seem to bring you nearer.

I trust the happy season will give you peace of mind. There is no cause for worry. I am in splendid health and spirits. I intend to go through the line to-night with a sandbag containing cake, sucreà-la crème and cigars, all gifts from Canada, and to act as Santa Claus to the company officers. As I go down the deep dugouts, I will feel like St. Nicholas in his chimney.

After Passchendaele, the Canadian Corps spent a relatively quiet winter during which an uneasy calm spread along most of the Western front. Vanier and the rest of the Van Doos remained in the region of Méharicourt, near Neuville-St. Vaast. During this period, Vanier began to take a keen interest in politics.

In France
14 January, 1918

My dearest Mater,
Within the last week I have received parcels from you, from Papa, from Eva and Joe, from Anthony and Frances. These little messages from home are always greeted with cries of appreciation when brought into the mess (which is sometimes a hole in the ground). In spite of what returned officers may say about our being able to obtain everything we wish for at the front, be sure that whatever we buy here has not the flavour (perhaps sentimental) of what loving hands have packed. Your weekly parcel which comes with a certain (or uncertain) regularity is looked forward to.

I have been interesting myself in things political recently and have subscribed to Le Temps and L'Homme Libre (Clemenceau's[4] paper) which I receive quite regularly in the trenches. Besides these The Daily Mail, The Sketch and The Times reach me each day.

The political situation, in France particularly, is intensely interesting. The power of Clemenceau is enormous and rests unquestionably on the good sense and patriotism of the French people. The Socialists (whether "United" or "Radical") are losing their hold on the common people, who perceive the wide gulf which exists between the Dreyfus[5] and the Caillaux[6] matters and who insist upon the nation as a whole preparing peace and not a mere fraction (one might say faction), such as the proposed international convention of socialists. The more I see of the peasant class, and it is the class I see most often, the greater is my admiration for the French nation and the greater is my faith in the triumph of Latin civilization. It is a great consolation and a great privilege to be able to work, in some measure, for the attainment of this triumph.

This letter has taken a serious turn which I did not mean it to take but it is right that you should know my deep feelings on the question. I thank God every day for the opportunity and the strength he has given me to assert my conviction of the righteousness of the great cause.

In mid-February, Georges left camp and his afternoon rides on his horse, Queenie, to accompany a group of visitors to Paris.

Hôtel Meurice, Paris
18 February, 1918

My dearest Mater,
I reached Paris this morning at 2 a.m. and had the good fortune to be motored from our battalion headquarters near the line to the door of the Hôtel Meurice. Sherif Lemieux, Major Grothé and Major Chaballe both formerly of the 22nd Battalion and the other Canadian scrutineers [*probably investigators or inspectors*] paid us a visit on the day on which I was to proceed on leave. It is seldom that one has the extraordinary good fortune to be motored from the front to Paris. It is just possible that I may have the same luck when returning as Major Chaballe says he is arranging a visit for French officers to the Canadian front and of course to the 22nd Battalion where French officers are welcomed with open arms.

Hôtel Meurice, Paris
19 February, 1918

My dearest Mater,
Today I saw Father Gaume who was most cordial and most generous in his reception. He accepted — or rather refused to entertain — my

apologies, saying that he quite understood the peculiar conditions under which one worked at the front. He was charming. His health, I think, has improved. He spoke to me about you all and was particularly interested in the marriages of John and of Eva.

This afternoon a splendid film of the visit of the Canadian scrutineers to the French front was shown at "La Section Cinématographique des Armées." One sees the scrutineers, and very clearly, at Reims and at Verdun, piloted about by French officers. It will be a living and a most precious souvenir of their visit to the French front. You will see it in Montreal as Sherif Lemieux means to lend the film to the Red Cross Society for exhibition purposes.

Did I ever tell you that I had received your cablegram at New Year's with your greetings and best wishes? It came at a very opportune moment and helped to keep me as cheerful as the occasion warranted when so far from home.

Hôtel Meurice, Paris
20 February, 1918

My dearest Mater,
Today, under the guidance of Lieut. Jean Dreyfous, I visited the Palais de Justice. Lieut. Dreyfous is a lawyer and son of a very well known Paris lawyer, Georges Dreyfous... I visited the courts "cassation" [*in France, the highest court of appeal*], "d'appel" and "correctionnelle" and was presented also to a "juge d'instruction." I was very fortunate in having Lieut. Dreyfous to guide me.

Tonight I expect to dine with Lieut. Col. de Lanaudière and Major Grothé. Colonel de Lanaudière is always the same delightful companion. He is one of our best types of French Canadians.

Hôtel Meurice, Paris
21 February 1918

My dearest Mater
I spent a most interesting day with Father Gaume. First I lunched with him after which I visited the institution where we distributed candies

and "sous" to the orphans, listened to very good piano playing by a blind artist who gave selections from Chopin and who played the inspiring marches Sambre & Meuse [*later adopted as the regimental march by the Van Doos*] and Lorraine. I also attended a demonstration of X-rays which I have never seen. It was almost like being present at the realization of a miracle.

We then went together to the St. Charles Orphanage where I saw more than a hundred boy orphans, quite happy and comfortable and overjoyed to receive each a handful of candy. It gave me unalloyed pleasure to give them one moment of unusual and unexpected happiness (because they are not unhappy really). They promised to pray for me and they shouted "Vive le Canada" .

The visit to St. Charles Orphanage made a marked impression on Vanier. He mentioned it further in his diary.

Diary entry: 21 February

This afternoon, I visited the St. Charles Orphanage.... At each place I saw a hundred orphans to whom I distributed candy and a few coins. They were so pleased that their whole faces lit up. What a great joy for me, who am so fond of children and have seen so few of them for more than two and a half years. This was such a great joy. Many of them are crippled and walk with crutches. They were all grateful and gay.

One case was particularly sad, that of seven children whose mother is dead and whose father is a prisoner in Germany. The youngest was three years old and he called me "Papa".

Paris
22 February, 1918

My dearest Mater,
Today I visited "L'Ecole Polytechnique" with M. Maurice Roy, a young friend of Father Gaume. He works very hard and is one of the most brilliant students there. France's greatest soldiers have gone through the Polytechnique since the days of Napoleon.

Diary entry: 23 February

Visited Notre Dame Cathedral with Major Grothé. We walked around the portals of Notre Dame and looked at the sculptures.

Vanier took advantage of a few more days' leave to travel to the south of France and explore some of the favourite corners he had last seen with his father six years earlier.

Hôtel Westminster, Nice
23 February, 1918

My dearest Mater,
I left Paris at 8:15 p.m. the 23 February and travelled from Paris to Nice (approx. 22 hours) seated in a <u>first class seat</u>. Impossible to obtain a berth (as they are reserved 1 <u>month</u> ahead) and very hard even to obtain a seat! I am not too tired after the long journey. Reached Nice 7 p.m., the day after leaving Paris.

You had not told me that Jean Désy[7] [*an old friend attached to the Canadian Commission in Paris*] was studying in Paris. I was very much surprised when he came to see me at my hotel. He looks very well and appears to be working hard. The two years' solid work in Paris will be of incalculable value to him and will give him a foundation upon which he will be able to build later on. He seems to be very much in earnest, he takes very careful notes and, I believe, should be in a position to be a lecturer at Laval University when he returns. He is very fortunate indeed. When you see Mme. Désy and Dr. Désy will you tell them what a very good impression Jean gave me. I expect to see him again when passing through Paris en route for the front.

They did meet again and soon after, Jean Désy sent the following message in French, dated March 11, to Vanier's parents.

We were both delighted at the chance which brought us together again. Georges has changed physically. He is far more robust and vigorous than when he was practising law. The handling of arms has made of him a strapping fellow and he bears himself splendidly.... He has kept intact the sincere enthusiasm of his early campaigning days, still the same smile and warmth, the same unshakable confidence.

Hôtel Westminster, Nice.
24 February, 1918

My dearest Mater,
I received your letter containing the Sacred Heart medal given you by a sister of the Precious Blood. Thank her for me and tell her I will always carry it with me and that I feel sure that the medal and her prayers will protect me.

Hôtel Westminster, Nice
25 février 1918

Mon bien cher papa,
I should long since have acknowledged your letter of mid-January. Was the Canadian election result[8] a surprise for you? Well, here I am in Nice after a train trip of 22 hours from Paris. The difference with Paris is striking....

The war situation has become difficult to forecast. The Germans have succeeded in disarming the Russians and in making them accept positions as virtual allies. The situation thus bodes ill for the "Western" Allies. The Americans have been obliged to accept a bitter blow.

Diary entry: 25 February

Cloudy morning but without rain: the sky is heavy. A hundred metres from my window, the sea rolls up in long waves, blue and frothy and the beach withdraws silently. The outdoors, in spite of the closeness, is exhilarating. At two o'clock, the sun draws pictures and appears radiant. I took a long walk along the seaside.

Hôtel Westminster, Nice
26 February, 1918

My dearest Mater,
Today I took a very long and a very delightful tram ride. I saw most of the Mediterranean coast from Nice to the Italian frontier. The tramway follows the coast except here and there where the land juts out and where following the coast line exactly would mean making the journey too long to be pleasant. As it is, it takes one hour and a half to go from Nice to Monte Carlo and almost one hour from Monte Carlo to the Italian frontier. There are innumerable turnings and the small trams (very much like Montreal's first trams) convey every vibration, every twist to the body. If the surroundings and the sun and the wonderful sea were not above consideration of fatigue and of ennui and of personal comfort, the trip might even be called tiresome. But one soon forgets the jolts and the hard seats.

Passing through Mont Boron, Villefranche (where the Franconia dropped anchor in 1912), Beaulieu, St. Laurent, La Turbie, St. Antoine and Monaco I made a stop at Monte Carlo, where I lunched. Monaco and Monte Carlo touch one another, each built on a point of land with the "Rade de Monaco" in the centre thus:

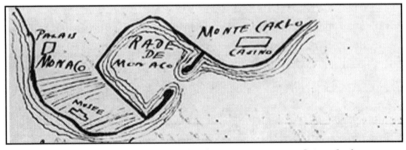

I visited the Casino, with the exception of (and the most important part) the gaming tables. Men in uniform are not allowed to enter. Civilians however continue to gamble but I am told that there is very much less gambling than before the war.

[...] After lunch I boarded another tramway and continued the journey almost to the Italian frontier, passing through Saint Roman, Roquebrune, la Plage, Menton and Menton Garavan (really a continuation of Menton). The coastline from Nice to the Italian border is most uneven and rugged and each bay and each peninsula presents a different aspect of beauty and of grace. The sea here does not frighten but it rather attracts and comforts. The waves creep up the shore with the sound of a lullaby and do not crash with the roar of guns.

Hôtel Westminster, Nice
27 February, 1918

My dearest Mater,
This morning sun and wind.... I took a long walk by the sea (when I say long walk I do not mean in the same directions because the boardwalk is relatively short but I mean now East now West and vice versa).

In the afternoon I went to a cinema performance in the Jetée-Promenade (called in America PIER). In the evening I heard Mignon [*a light opera by Ambroise Thomas*], at the Théâtre des Variétiés. The roles of Mignon and of Philine were very well sung and that of Meister very badly (I hear Eva saying "What does <u>he</u> know about singing and how does <u>he</u> know Meister sang badly?"). Meister was amusing, played by a man at least six foot six and weighing 300 pounds, with enormous feet and enormous hands which were always in the way. He strutted about the stage saying "Ah vraiment?" (or words to that effect because he mouthed his words continually and one did not know whether he was talking, singing or simply gesticulating). To complete the tragedy he wore really fine clothes and considered himself a "lion". If I were wealthy I would settle him down in the butcher business. He should be able to fell an ox, <u>perhaps</u> with an axe, <u>certainly</u> with his voice.

The air and the sun are doing me good. I needed this change after the tiring winter months. I will go back to my work with a reserve of energy and of buoyant spirits.

Diary entry: 6 March

Leave Paris by train from the Gare du Nord at 9 a.m. for Amiens. Visited the beautiful Cathedral and bought a book on Rodin [*the famous French sculptor*] in a little bookstore. On to Arras and arrived a little before 9 p.m. Walked as far as Carency [?] where the battalion was in reserve. Happy to see all my old friends again but sad to hear that poor Côté died from his wounds.

Vanier rejoined his battalion at the front just in time to march with them to Auchel, west of Lens, where they were billeted. Their days were filled with a rigorous training program — four hours of military exercises in the morning and organized sports all afternoon.

It was a period of intense activity with a massive German offensive expected any moment. Barely a week before this decisive challenge, it was Vanier's sad duty to witness the execution of one of his men who had been found guilty of thirteen convictions of desertion and two of drunkenness. He had been tried by a military court martial on February 26 and the verdict was unanimous. Referring to the event, Vanier made this sombre entry in his diary:

Diary entry: 14 March

At 4:30 p.m., I officially announced to the condemned man that the Court Martial has found him guilty and has sentenced him to death. His attitude was calm and I left him with the Chaplain. I have been put in charge of the troops that will take part at the execution tomorrow morning. A sad task, a sad command.

Diary entry: Friday, 15 March. Auchel.

Up at 5 a.m. The dawn has not yet broken. A platoon from each company, 20 men from Company Headquarters and all the detainees from the guard room lined up on the square in front of the church. In silence, I led them to the site of the execution. At 6:30, the condemned man arrived, his eyes blindfolded.... The Chaplain recited prayers and I heard the man say "Padre, padre" twice, then the sharp and clear sounds of the rifle shots, followed by silence. We all filed out past the body.

At 8:30 p.m., German planes dropped bombs and torpedos. One bomb fell thirty metres from the Divisional Headquarters. The house was hit and collapsed. Two young children who were sleeping there didn't receive a scratch. The tenacious Boche returned three times. Our planes at the Auchel airport took off on patrol. While the bombs were exploding, you could hear the roar of the plane's motors and the sounds of the destruction they were causing.

Diary entry: 17 March

Mass in the parish church. Captain Crochetière read a very moving farewell letter from the executed man.

In the afternoon, we played baseball against the officers of the 25th Battalion. The officers of the 22nd won 3–2. I played first base — the first time in ages. In the evening, the weather was clear — excellent for the German planes which were not coming yet. Air patrol on our side.

Diary entry: 18 March. Auchel.

General Ross [*Brigadier-General J.M., Commander of the 5th Brigade*] came to visit us. All the men of the battalion have been inoculated against typhoid and paratyphoid.... Meanwhile, the roar of the German planes drones on and on....

Movements of the 22ⁿᵈ Battalion from March to April 1918

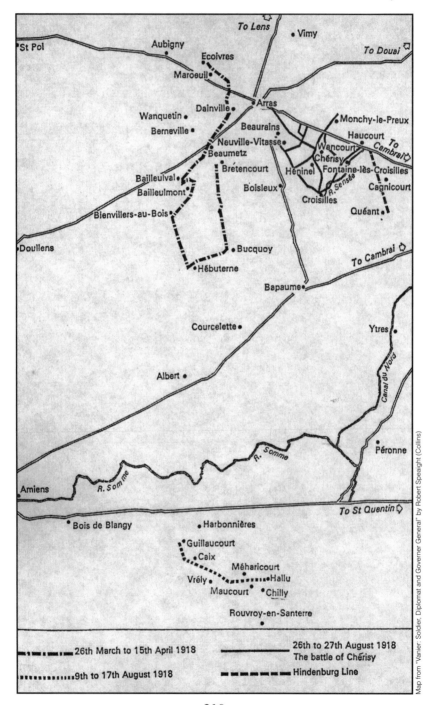

10

"SUCH FRIGHTFUL CARNAGE"
MARCH 1918

"Oh God of battles. One would like to think that this is your cause as well as ours, and one thinks that it is."
　　　　　Georges Vanier in his diary,
　　　　　27 March, 1918

"At last I felt that I am doing something useful — the war that I have experienced up to now has been so impersonal, an affair of metal and gas and barbed wire.... Contact with these poor folk fleeing from the barbarian is far from depressing. It is exalting — and you feel it a great privilege to contribute, even in the smallest degree, to the defeat and rejection of the savages."
　　　　　Georges Vanier in his diary,
　　　　　27 March, 1918

In March 1918, the military situation was grave with the German High Command planning a grand offensive to try to break the Allied front and end the war. Their plan was to separate the Allied armies and force a decision in the West before the *full potential of the newly arrived American troops could be realized. It very nearly succeeded.*

On March 21, the might of the whole German army was thrown upon the British front between St. Quentin and Arras. Exhausted Allied troops reeled and retreated but the front did not collapse. The Allies finally achieved military unity with the appointment, on March 26, of Marshal Foch[1] as Supreme Commander and with badly needed reserves provided by the American troops.

The 22nd Battalion was billeted at Ecoivres, waiting on "stand-by" for orders to move. It was a moment of great anxiety, with the Germans advancing quickly towards Amiens and cutting communications between the British and French armies. As Tremblay noted in his diary on March 25: "The situation is very grave."

Diary entry: 26 March. Ecoivres.

The general situation here is serious: there are rumours that the Boche will attack from Arras to Bapaume. The Brigade is still in reserve ready to go anywhere. At 6:00 p.m., we received orders that the battalion will leave at 11 p.m. for Bienvillers-au-Bois. We marched all night along the road from Maroeuil, Louez, Dainville, Beaumez, Bailleulval, Berles au Bois and finally to Bienvillers-au-Bois. The moonlight was magnificent.

As a boost to his troops at this critical time, Lieutenant-General Sir Arthur Currie, Commander of the Canadian Corps, sent out this order on March 27, 1918:

> ...Looking back with pride on the unbroken record of your glorious achievements, asking you to realize that today the fate of the British Empire hangs in the balance, I place my trust in the Canadian Corps, knowing that where Canadians are engaged there can be no giving way.
>
> Under the orders of your devoted officers in the coming battle, you will advance or fall where you

stand facing the enemy. To those who will fall I say "You will not die but step into immortality. Your mothers will not lament your fate but will be proud to have borne such sons. Your names will be revered for ever and ever by your grateful country and God will take you all to Himself."

Canadians, in this fateful hour, I command you and I trust you to fight as you have ever fought with all your strength, with all your determination, with all your courage. On many a hard fought field of battle you have overcome the enemy. With God's help you will achieve victory once more.

Diary entry: 27 March. Bienvillers-au-Bois.

Arrived at Bienvillers-au-Bois very tired after marching all night, about 30 miles. The men are lodged in an enormous factory that is no longer in use. The proprietor, Monsieur Beudin, is an old man who does not want to leave his village. We stayed with him sleeping on the stone floor. For dinner, we had jugged hare with prunes prepared by Monsieur Beudin's maid. M. Beudin has already been badly wounded and his house has been hit several times.

11:30 p.m. The Brigade announced that the Boche is on the edge of the Bois de Quesnoy, 6300 yards from here. Alert! — everyone is ready to march.

It was a cold and moonlit night when the battalion began its march southward. Vanier noted in his diary:

There was the constant noise of enemy aircraft — a bomb exploded in the distance....

The moon was up. At the turning of the road leading to Maroeuil, [*three miles northwest of Arras*] an enormous crucifix threw a shadow which we crossed silently — shadow and reality — without any sense of blasphemy, each one of us seemed to make a comparison. The great Apostle of civilization and of love inspired the humble disciples. Oh God of battles, one would like to think that this is your cause as well as ours, and one thinks that it is.

The men marched a little heavily, weighed down with all their equipment. The night was cold and it warmed them to be kept on the move. When we halted, some of them fell asleep. No one faltered — that would be a moral and physical failure, and the soldier's honour lifted him above his own strength and gave him fresh resources.

We were obliged to halt for an hour on the Doullens-Arras road between Dainville and Beaumetz. Lorries, ambulances, motor vehicles of every sort follow one after another. An incident: we met a cart driven by a young girl, accompanied by her brother — even younger. We asked her where she was going. "I don't know, sir," she said. "My father was killed this morning and I was left in charge of the cart with hay for the horse. I have brought all the bread and meat we had left, and my brother and I are getting away." They went off into the night — it was sad to watch them, and significant too. I could have wished that certain young girls I know could have seen them ... but would they have understood?

At last I feel that I am doing something useful — the war that I have experienced up to now has been so impersonal, an affair of metal and gas and barbed wire ... so that I sometimes forgot that I was not a cog in a huge machine. Contact with these poor folk fleeing from the barbarian is far from depressing. It's exalting — and you feel it a great privilege to contribute, even in the smallest degree, to the defeat and rejection of the savages.

An announcement the next morning brought news that the enemy's assault had been contained. But not before there were more casualties. Out of "C" Company, forty men were killed or wounded. Among the fallen was the battalion's much-loved chaplain, Father Rosaire Crochetière from Nicolet, Quebec, who died when a bomb hit a first-aid post where he was helping to care for the wounded. Vanier called him a "saint" and a "martyr" and later, on April 8, wrote to his mother about the loss:

"Such Frightful Carnage" — March 1918

Father Rosaire Crochetière, the much-loved chaplain of the 22nd Battalion, died on April 2, 1918 when a bomb hit a first-aid post where he was caring for the wounded. Vanier spoke of him as a "saint" and a "martyr."

Father Crochetière was buried in the communal cemetery in Bailleulmont, south of Arras. "Many of the men could not keep back their tears," noted Vanier. "He was a man of peace, not of war, which he hated with all his heart and soul."

We had the terrible misfortune to lose our chaplain Father Crochetière of Nicolet, who was killed by a shell on the 2nd April. We buried him in a little village [*in the Communal Cemetery in Bailleulmont, five miles southwest of Arras*], not many miles from the front, after a funeral service in the parish church at which Father Fortier[2] of Ottawa officiated. The priest's death had a marked effect on the men, whose friend he was. Many of the men could not keep back their tears. It is particularly unfortunate because he was the last man in the world who should have been killed — he was a man of peace, not of war, which he hated with all his heart and soul. He was a very saintly man and I am sure he looks down and protects the 22nd Battalion from on high.

En France
3 avril 1918

Mon cher papa,
[...] Last month was an exciting one, but the worst is over. The element of surprise which the Huns counted on has failed. We now know all we need to know about the configuration of their front lines, their methods of attack, their paucity of reserves. The Germans played for big stakes and lost. We no longer have anything to fear.

Thank you for your good wishes on my 30th birthday. My how the time flies!

Diary entry: 5 April. Bailleulmont.

5 a.m. We left again for the trenches. An hour before our departure, a dozen shells fell around our village but there were no losses. Our departure point was the little chapel on the road from Bailleulmont to Bailleulval. As we marched through Basseux, Grosville, Wailly, Agny, several shells exploded between Bailleulment and Basseux. The horses were very nervous — they do not like these explosions....

Diary entry: 6 April. In the trenches south of Agny-Beaurains, just south of Arras.

Visited Companies "A" and "B" which are the furthest advanced and under observation from Neuville-Vitasse.... All the men were in excellent humour and very anxious for action. The defensive suits them less than the attack.

Diary entry: 7 April. In the trenches south of Agny-Beaurains.

The Boche bombarded the left of "B" Company. Several losses. The weather is cold. The men suffer a little from the lack of a fire and of hot food. Apart from that, they are happy.

France
8 April, 1918

My dearest Mater,
[...] There has been a break in my letters which I will not attempt to explain. The reason is not a military secret and I may say without danger of criticism that we have been very busy for some time....

You have read of course of the German advance on the Western front. We are all very glad that at last the enemy has struck his great blow: from now on he becomes weaker and will be unable to continue his smashing tactics. He needs a decision at once; we do not, we can wait if needs be several years more.

The most complete confidence reigns everywhere. The Hun will not get through.

Vanier's optimism may have been a "front" to assuage his family since few others shared his confidence at the time. In fact, it was on April 11 that General Haig[3] felt sufficiently threatened to issue his famous order of the day: "Many amongst us now are tired. To those I would say that victory will belong to the side which holds out the longest.... There is no other course open to us but to fight it out!

Every position must be held to the last man: there must be no retirement. With our backs to the wall ... each one of us must fight on to the end."

Diary entry: 11 April. In the trenches facing Neuville-Vitasse (south of Arras).

6:30 a.m. Intense bombardment on the front lines and on our reserve lines. The Boche attacked the right front of Company "A". Gélineau gave a good example of determination and initiative.... All night long, the Boche continued to bombard the roads, the trenches, the villages....

Diary entry: 13 April

News from the north is not good. Luckily, the French army is still intact. We will know the secret of the Boche in good time. One thing is certain — if anyone can save us, it is Foch. Every soldier believes in his judgement and in his genius.

On the 15th of April, the battalion left Bailleulmont for Brétencourt, headquarters of the 2nd British Division.

Diary entry: 15 April. Brétencourt.

Weather is warm and fresh. Our billets are fairly meagre.... I am sharing a room with Major Dubuc. The old proprietress welcomed us warmly but told us frankly that she has much to complain about with regards to the soldiers. She did not receive them with the same enthusiasm as she did earlier. Her husband has been dead since the beginning of the war but at least her daughter remains with her....

Diary entry: 16 April. Brétencourt.

The old proprietress took me to visit her little garden — a small one this year but she is very proud of it. The house has been hit by German shells in four places. One of them travelled the full length of the garden which had previously given some protection against the shells of 1914. For more than a year before the attack on Vimy, the Boche were just two kilometres away. The woman remains courageous and says she will never despair. "Ah Monsieur," she said. "The army interpreters told me at midnight to leave before dawn but how could I leave in the middle of the night? I just stayed in bed.

"The Boche did not advance so I stayed here. I watched them pass Brétencourt just as they did in 1914.... I will leave only when I see them right here in front of me, not before."

A true heroine.

6:30 p.m. We left Brétencourt for the support trenches 2000 metres east of Wailly.... Changeover was complete by 9 p.m. The night is quiet.

Diary entry: 17 April. In the trenches near Ficheux, (four miles south of Arras).

Bailleul has been taken.... to my great surprise. I remember Bailleul as being such a haven for us all in 1915 when our only distraction was an excursion to the village where we dined and caroused. Had a beautiful horseback ride, then visited all the line. There was little activity, only occasional shelling on the Arras-Amiens railway line. There is little news from the north — one could wish for more complete information.

Diary entry: 18 April. In the trenches near Ficheux.

Rose at 8:00 a.m. Weather rainy and foggy. Visited "A", "B" and "C" companies. No losses up to now. A communiqué announced (it is a little vague) that we are occupying a new line in front of Ypres.

Diary entry: 19 April. In the trenches near Ficheux.

It snowed during the night ... white patches here and there. The morning is clear and cold.... At 7 p.m., there were heavy bombardments on the left, to the north of Neuville-Vitasse. Before bed, long discussions with Lamothe & de Vienne on astronomy and the relations between the sun, the earth, the stars and the zodiac.

Diary entry: 20 April. In the trenches near Ficheux.

Very cold last night. Lamothe dreamed a lot. Clear moonlight. A sunny morning. You can feel the spring in the air....

8 p.m. We left the trenches near Ficheux and moved to the front line trenches southeast of Merlate and to the north of Bois Laux St. Marc.... We bombarded the Boche lines for two hours — the gas came floating back over our own lines and we quickly had to don our gas masks. Apart from this incident, the night was quiet. Returned to the line at 2. a.m.

Diary entry: 21 April. In the trenches (front line) south of Mercatel.

Up at 11 a.m. Weather clear and hot. Occasional shell fire around headquarters.

11 p.m.: Visited the companies by moonlight. Weather clear and fresh. Night quiet. Could make out Boislaux St. Marc quite clearly as I went as far as the Arras-Bapaume road.

Diary entry: 22 April. In the trenches (front line) south of Mercatel.

6 a.m. Extraordinary amount of activity by German planes flying low. Our own machine guns fired at them without success.

During this period, General Haig continued to hint that the Allies were in very serious trouble and that imminent defeat could be a possibility.

"Such Frightful Carnage" — March 1918

Few shared Georges' conviction about the outcome of the war when he told his mother in April 1918: "This year may see the end of the war." As we now know, however, his prediction proved to be correct.

En France
23 avril 1918

Mon cher papa,
Your present gave me a great deal of pleasure. It arrived on the 21 April, two days before my birthday! The bonbons were excellent — they reminded me of those I used to buy from the Italian grocer on the corner.

This past month has been very exciting but the crisis is over. The element of surprise which the Boche counted on no longer exists. We know their offensive fronts, their methods of attack, their reserves of forces. The Germans gambled a lot and lost. There is nothing left for us to fear.

My health is still good, and my morale too. A curious thing: the first winter I spent in France, I went frequently to Bailleul which was a welcome distraction — to dine or to make a few purchases. I got to know a grocer — an excellent man who welcomed us warmly and who invited us several times to his table. I thought this would be a very good spot to leave some souvenirs. Alas, when they fought on the Grand Place, the Boche captured the little town <u>and all my souvenirs</u>. I think therefore they will never reach Canada.

I wonder where the grocer is.... He sold the most delicious paté de foie.

Thank you again for your wishes on the occasion of <u>my thirtieth year</u>. How the time passes!

A smiling Georges Vanier, around the time of his thirtieth birthday in April 1918.

25 April, 1918

My dearest Mater,
[...] Over a month has passed since the great German offensive and the spirit of the troops is better than it ever was before. I do not think the Huns have given up the hope of ever getting through on the western front but their efforts are doomed to failure. Our reserves in guns, in men, in material are too great, too enormous to be smothered.

I think we are arriving at a decision and that this year may see the end of the war. The Germans must find a solution — favourable or unfavourable — without delay.

My good fortune has not left me and I manage to worry through without my health being affected.

At the front
28 April, 1918

My dearest Mater,
[...] The fighting up north is taking place exactly over the ground we occupied when we first came to France in 1915. Kemmel, Loker [*Locre*], Scherpenberg, Westouter-Dranouter, are all places I know much better than I know Magog. Splendid country for fighting and I am sure that the Hun is paying dearly for every foot of ground he is gaining. But he is coming to the end of his tether and fast. The more he attacks and the greater the forces he uses, the better it is for us. No one out here has any other thought than one of victory.

Since beginning this letter I have received your cablegram wishing me a happy birthday. I thank both of you — yourself and the dear Governor — for your thoughtful remembrance.

Lt. Col. Tremblay has not been very well recently and is at present in hospital. Major Dubuc is in command.

Health always good, spirit of course the best.

At the front
28 April, 1918

My dear George (Pelletier).
I meant to answer your long letter before this but recent events have kept us all very busy. The Hun is making a tremendous effort to get through but there is no chance of his doing so. His reserves are beginning to give out already.

All our eyes are turned towards America. We count on her magnificent reserves in men and material and in food. The Hun also fears the American effort and wants a decision at once.

Diary entry: 29 April. Wailly.

Tonight, we relieved the 21st Battalion on the front line facing Neuville-Vitasse.... The 21st made a raid this morning — 2 machine gunners, 2 prisoners. The Boche do not like surprises. Perhaps they will retaliate tonight. Meanwhile, I am going to confession....

7 p.m. We left Wailly following the Agny-Beaurains road. Battalion's headquarters are half way along the Beaurains-Mercatel road. During our changeover, there was one killed and ten wounded on the Beaurains–Neuville-Vitasse road.

Diary entry: 30 April. In the trenches facing Neuville-Vitasse.

At 4, I left battalion headquarters to go to Company "D" where I stayed for the rest of the tour.

[...] I ran along the fresh earth for the umpteenth time, but the earth has never done us any harm. It receives us like her own sons. When we are tired, she comforts us. When we are ill, she heals us. When we are on edge, she calms us. She is a mother to us all, and then one day we shall go back to her. This premature return must please her and take her by surprise.

In the fog, I proceeded to "Roy" and "St. Victor", the two companies on the front line.... A machine gunner opened fire on us. We crouched down and waited there a quarter of an hour....

Diary entry: 1 May. In the trenches facing Neuville-Vitasse.

9:30 p.m. Arrived at "Roy" company where I waited until there was enough light to visit the line as there is total darkness until midnight. Then I patrolled in the mud and in the water to the left and the right of our line.

[...] While passing "C" Company, I visited Dupuis and Guay and we chatted a little. Returned to camp at 1:30 a.m. Slept 5 hours when a telephone call from "C" Company brought the news that Capt. Guay had been killed! What rotten luck. He was a first class officer — one of the most intelligent in the battalion.

Diary entry: 2 May. In the trenches facing Neuville-Vitasse.

[...] Visited Dupuis whom I had seen at the same time last evening, together with poor Guay about whom we spoke. To bed at 5 a.m.

Diary entry: 3 May. In the trenches facing Neuville-Vitasse.

2:30 a.m. Intense bombardment from the Boche lines. A German brigade on the right widens the attack. The exchange lasts an hour but the results are unknown. At 4 a.m. a few of the wounded start to arrive.

Diary entry: 9 May. In the trenches near Agny-St. Beauvrains.

Changeover tonight.... Returned to Bailleulmont in trams with American drivers.
    Arrived at 1 a.m.

Diary entry: 10 May. Bailleulmont.

Rose at 11 a.m. a little tired. In the afternoon, took a horseback ride with Capt. Patenaude. Bathed in the public baths (hot shower).

Diary entry: 12 May. Bailleulval.

Mass in a little chapel in Bailleulval. A horse-back ride in the afternoon in beautiful summer weather. Captain Bourgeault left for Canada. A real veteran. There are not many left. Sad for him — sad for us.

France
12 May, 1918

My dearest Mater,
Mother's day! I cannot let it pass without retelling you my proud admiration and my undying love and my eternal devotion. You are happiest, I know, in knowing that I am contented and well, and this I can assure you from the bottom of my heart. Some of the reasons for my contentment of mind are contained in the enclosed leaflet which in very simple language sets out the great principles for which we are fighting and upon which are founded the freedom and democracy of nations.

The battalion was now in the region of Lattre-St. Quentin, where Vanier continued his diary.

Diary entry: 19 May. Lattre-St. Quentin.

The Boche flew over Lattre-St. Quentin all night. Towards midnight, there were three very powerful explosions. At 6 a.m., left on horseback to see the condition of the bridges between Avesnes le Comte and Lattre-St. Quentin. Exercises on the parade ground all morning. In the afternoon, was informed that a bomb had fallen on a cabin at Wanquetin. There are dead and wounded but I don't know how many.

Diary entry: 20 May. Lattre-St. Quentin.

6:30 a.m. Daily horseback ride through the fields to Hermaville. From 9 a.m. to 12:30 p.m., exercises on the parade ground. Visit of Canadian journalists — M.N. Chassé from l'Evenement, Quebec, M. Mayrand of La Presse, Montreal and M. Savard of Le Soleil, Quebec. They all lunched with us, then we showed them our billets, kitchens etc.

Diary entry: 21 May. Lattre-St. Quentin.

6:30 a.m. Daily horseback ride. Mass at 10:30. Sermon by Capt. Desjardins.... An inexplicable event: in spite of bright moonlight, we were not bothered for one minute last night. In the afternoon, went on horseback to Fosseux, headquarters of the brigade. Returned via Wanquetin where the bomb had fallen the night of 18/19 July — 15 dead and 20 wounded — all from the 28th Battalion. Such frightful carnage!

Diary entry: 22 May. Lattre-St Quentin.

Tactical exercises all morning. German planes flew above Lattre-St. Quentin most of the night....

At the front
30 May, 1918

My dearest Frances,
You have become a wonderful correspondent and without ever being able to reach mother's record you are creeping up and are now a very good second. You have not forgotten what I told you in a previous letter — the most prized gift at the front is a message from home.

Rumours have been going about that there is to be a French Canadian brigade but details do not seem to be decided upon. The result will be of great benefit to both races. It will be a means of drawing closer the bonds of friendship and of trust that should unite French and English in Canada.

It is not quite clear where the brigade will be formed — whether in Canada, in England or in France. We all hope fervently that some way will be found of organizing it at the front.

[...] I am glad you like your school mistress — sympathy between teacher and pupil is an essential to obtain lasting results. Learning then becomes something more than mechanical — the communion of two minds, of two personalities.

On June 8, the battalion was occupying the sector in front of Mercatel and Neuville-Vitasse when there was a sudden enemy raid involving heavy bombardment. After the barrage lifted from the front line, fifty Germans suddenly advanced. At that moment, a young Van Doos corporal, Joseph Kaeble, was in command of a section of machine gunners.

Georges Vanier recalled this incident in a speech he delivered in Montreal on May 24, 1941:

> When the Germans advanced, he [*Kaeble*] jumped on to the parapet and with the Lewis gun at his hip fired on the advancing enemy. Wounded several times by fragments of shell and hand grenades, he still went on firing and stopped the enemy. At last, mortally wounded, he fell back into the trench. There, lying on his back, he fired his last cartridge on the enemy in retreat. Before losing consciousness he called out to the wounded lying all around him: "Stand firm, boys; stop them — don't let them pass."

Three months later, on September 16, 1918, Joseph Kaeble was the first in the Van Doos to be awarded the Victoria Cross, the Commonwealth's top military decoration for bravery. Vanier called him "a through and through French-Canadian for beloved Quebec."

France
10 June, 1918

My dearest Mater,
It is evident from official newspaper reports that the French Canadian brigade will be organized within a very short time. Lieut. Col. Tremblay (who by the way has just been created C.M.G.) [*Commander of the Order of St. Michael and St. George*], has been mentioned by several newspapers as the future Brigade Commander. Any other nomination would be very distasteful to all French Canadians at the front — and I believe that consideration should and will be given to the wishes of those who <u>from the start</u> have believed in the French Canadian effort and have endeavored in every way to foster a spirit of harmony between the French-speaking and the English-speaking Canadians, both in France and at home.

    The old battalion continues to be a splendid fighting unit that reflects credit on the French Canadian race and it does one good to hear the flattering comments made by higher authorities.

    [...] I have heard some ridiculous stories about Paul Bauset, about his lying in the trenches unconscious etc. This is all pure rot. Paul was evacuated sick from the battalion with gastritis and from the hospital in France was sent to England. I liked Paul very much — his cheerfulness, his easy manner all made him popular but I am afraid he was not strong enough for prolonged trench life. Will you reassure his parents and tell them that they need have no fears about the consequences of his illness?

    The problem of what to do with Anthony is a serious one. I think it would be a mistake for him to join the R.A.F. at his age and without the mental and physical developments necessary to make rational progress in life. I would prefer him to lay a solid physical foundation at some military college where he would remain at least a year. This would fit him for hardship and strain. He is now at the age when the body will readily respond to proper and regular exercise. Only in exceptional cases can a man without this preliminary discipline of the body go through war conditions for any length of time. I am afraid we do not always attach all the importance we should to the training of the body.

Somehow, in early June, a rumour circulated that Georges Vanier had been killed in action. The family heard nothing of this until a letter reached Georges' sister, Eva, from Bernard Brady, Vanier's friend and fellow officer. It read:

4th Cdn Div. F.M. Brigade.
Wednesday 12th June, 1918

Dear Eva,
It was only the other day that I learned of poor Georges' death.... I was so anxious to let you know that I sympathized with you in this loss of so excellent a brother. As a civilian, I always admired him so much as a gentlemanly, scholarly young man, and who could help admiring his splendid spirit in putting his career (for the present) in the background and in spite of poor health, offering his services to do what he could to beat off the common enemy.

You have no idea how much he was thought of in his battalion. Always kind, just and fair to his men....

Do convey these few expressions to the family and let me say what a pity it is that we are losing our best and bravest....

With kindest regards to Mr. Trudeau and the baby, I am, sincerely yours

Bernard W. Brady

The minute the letter reached Eva, her brother John immediately contacted the Secretary of State in Ottawa for confirmation of the news. Ten days later, on July 16, a reply from the Department of Militia and Defence informed them that there was "No record of casualty Captain (Acting-Major) George Philias Vanier."

The following day, the Secretary of State also wrote: "It is very evident that the reported death of your brother was due to a misapprehension, for were an officer of his seniority a casualty, it would unquestionably be reported."

Meanwhile, to his family's enormous relief, Georges' letters home continued to arrive.

France
20 June, 1918

My dearest Mater,
I have had a perfect avalanche of presents since I wrote my last letter and I have given very great pleasure to everyone in the mess. The maple syrup (delicious by the way) and the maple sugar were particularly sought after — they brought back such vivid memories of home. Maple syrup and maple sugar are unheard of articles in Europe — curiously enough all Europeans who have tasted them become ardent converts.

One of the boxes contained a piece of blessed palm [*a palm leaf blessed on Palm Sunday*] sent by papa. Will you thank him for me?

Miss Martin's [*Camille Martin's daughter, Thérèse*] letter contained in one of yours reached me and brought back the happy times spent with dear Mr. Martin, one of the finest of scholars and of gentlemen. I look forward to the day when I will be able to resume our little chats.

I spoke to you in a former letter of the French-Canadian brigade. It would appear from an authoritative statement published since I wrote that the intention is not to organize at once a French Canadian brigade but to form gradually several French Canadian battalions in the four Canadian divisions. I still believe however that sooner or later we will have our own French Canadian brigade.

On July 1, the Battalion went into rest billets at Lingnerevil and Lattre-St. Quentin. The past three months had taken a huge toll with some four hundred of their men killed or wounded, and Major Chassé taken prisoner. Nonetheless, spirits remained high.

At the front, France
4 July, 1918

My dear George (Pelletier),
[...] Independence Day is being celebrated with enthusiasm

throughout France and even in villages near the front. American flags are seen flying everywhere.

There is a deep-rooted sentiment that the new and virile forces of America will deal the decisive blow for victory in the world war.

France
9 July, 1918

My dearest Frances,
[...] A feeling of added confidence is growing since the advent of the Americans in such great numbers. We cannot see the end of the war yet — possibly it will come next year if the allied forces are strong enough for an offensive on a tremendous scale. Time is a factor which helps us and which is beating the Germans but whether victory comes next year or the year after is not of paramount importance to us.

France
18 July, 1918

My dearest Mater,
[...] We are all very much elated over the defeat of the Germans in their latest offensive: it is unquestionably a most serious blow to them and may possibly mark the culmination of their operations this year. The American troops that I have seen are magnificent. I do not say this in empty praise but quite literally. They have a splendid physique, quick to learn and courageous — what more does one want?

Gradually, the German offensive spent itself and by July 22, the enemy was in retreat from its bridgehead south of the Marne. The Van Doos were moving too, south from Arras to the area around Amiens. The hour of reckoning, so long awaited, had come at last.

11

CASUALTY OF WAR
AUGUST 1918

"I have been protected in a special manner the last three days. I have seen some of my comrades fall beside me and I have had so many narrow escapes myself that I am beginning to think that one should not worry much about possible eventualities."
Georges Vanier to his mother
11 August, 1918

"Providence — thanks to the prayers of all the dear ones at home — has protected me in a special manner and I have come through without a scratch."
Georges Vanier to Frances
17 August, 1918

On August 8, the Canadians joined the Australians in the final British offensives and managed to pull off a highly successful attack on Wancourt. In a speech marking the fiftieth anniversary of the Van Doos 22nd on September 26, 1964, Vanier recalled that day:

> On August 8, we knew that the enemy was beaten. The 22nd attacked and in two days they advanced

eighteen kilometres from Marcelcave to Méharicourt. Ludendorff [*the German General*] described August 8 as "the black day of the German army."[1]

At 9:05 a.m. on August 9, the battalion received orders to attack in the direction of Méharicourt.

Diary entry: 9 August

Colonel Tremblay sent me to reconnoitre in front of Caix to clarify the situation. He gave me a rendezvous point at the last house in Caix on the road to Harbonnières.

Vanier left on horseback by way of Guillaucourt, leaving the rest of the mounted troops in the valley. At 10:00 a.m., he dismounted to the east of Caix and met Tremblay as arranged. The battalion followed on the right flank through Caix and Vrély against strong opposition and with heavy losses.

The 22nd Battalion was ordered to attack again. They had three objectives: the first was Vrély, ten miles southeast of Villers-Bretonneux. The second was Méharicourt and finally, the village of Chilly. By 2:45 p.m., they had captured the village of Vrély. They planned their second attack that night.

Vanier continues his diary:

3:30: A messenger arrived and announced that the General [*Brigadier-General J. M. Ross*] had been wounded. Colonel Tremblay has been asked to command the Brigade so he put me in command of the battalion.

We struck out at once towards Méharicourt. There was very strong resistance along the road between Vrély and Méharicourt and Company "A" suffered many losses but we managed to dislodge several snipers and machine-gunners. All in all, we captured fifteen machine-gunners and a total of two hundred men.

CASUALTY OF WAR — AUGUST 1918

They continued on to Chilly and, still under constant machine-gun fire, eventually took Monchy-le-Preux and Wancourt. By the end of the night, they had reached all their objectives. As Vanier wrote later to his sister Frances:

The advance was unprecedented — 22,000 yards in a little over two days. The Huns were no match for our men who charged M.G.'s [*machine guns*] with perfect coolness as if they were on the parade ground. Their indifference before death was little short of sublime.

Vanier later spoke of the event in a CBC broadcast taped on January 14, 1965:

> The effect on the troops of that successful breakthrough was extraordinary. It was the first time that we were attacking and advancing in terms of miles instead of yards. We felt somehow that the Germans were beaten and after years of crawling, of dugouts and shell holes and mud, hope stirred our hearts.

Over the Top: This painting by Belgian artist Alfred Bastien was made in July/August, 1918 when he was attached as a war artist to the 22nd Battalion. It depicts the Van Doos during an attack near Neuville-Vitasse in August, 1918. Interestingly, some speculate that the tall soldier in the foreground with a pistol in his right hand is Georges Vanier.

This victory turned out to be a critical turning point in the war and earned a congratulatory telegram from General Currie: "From the depths of a very full heart I wish to congratulate you all on the wonderful success achieved." Thus began what became known as "The Last One Hundred Days."

Vanier's actions in the Battle of Amiens did not go unnoticed: soon after the event, Lieutenant-Colonel Tremblay recommended him for a D.S.O. in the following statement dated August 16, 1918:

> Captain (Acting Major) George Philias Vanier was my second-in-command during the operations of the 8th and 9th of August 1918. He was placed in command of the front line companies, and the skill and fearlessness he showed during these two days were of the highest order. On the 9th August especially, at the capture of Vrély and Méharicourt, the leading companies found themselves confronted with very serious opposition, and it was largely due to his leadership and magnificent courage that the enemy was overcome and the objective reached.
>
> After the capture of Vrély, when I was called to command the Brigade, this necessitated Major Vanier taking the command of the Battalion which he led with marked ability.

Lieutenant E.A. Blais, assistant adjutant, added his own comments to the nomination, stating that Captain Vanier, acting as second-in-command, led two of the companies "with the greatest fearlessness and determination. During the whole attack he showed qualities of great bravery ... giving splendid example to all."

It was during the same attack that Jean Brillant, a young lieutenant with the Van Doos was mortally wounded. Vanier recalled the incident later in a speech at ceremony in Montreal on May 24, 1941:

For two days he [*Brillant*] fought like a lion, and then — when he had been wounded three times — he fell. I can still see my friend on his improvised stretcher, the colour of his cheeks already livid, but he was smiling and the expression in his eyes was serene.

For his bravery, Brillant became the second member of the Van Doos to win the Victoria Cross, which was awarded posthumously on September 27, 1918.

The success of the Amiens offensive convinced General Haig that the time had come for an all-out assault against the enemy. As preparations began, orders changed constantly and troops moved most nights in preparation for the attack. Thanks to a brief lull while the 22nd Battalion waited for their orders in the Bois de Blangy, ten kilometres east of Amiens, Vanier seized the chance to write home.

In the field
11 August, 1918

My dearest Mater,
You will pardon the brevity and the looseness of this letter when you know under what conditions it has been written. What you wish to know above all I can tell you at once. I am well — in fact I do not think I have ever been quite so well in body and in spirit. I have been protected in a special manner during the last three days. I have seen some of my comrades fall beside me and I have had so many narrow escapes myself that I am beginning to think that one should not worry much about possible eventualities.

Basil Hingston [*an old friend*] was killed on the 8th August at midday. Before dying he received the services of the doctor and of the priest. He was anointed by Major Fortier of Ottawa College. The day before his death I had quite a long talk with him in a front line trench. He was always the same quiet, gracious, courteous gentleman. I was not with him when he died although unknowingly I happened to be only two or three hundred yards from him. Lieut. Blais, our assistant adjutant, remained with him until his death and gave me the above sad information. Major Fortier saw to the removal of the body. Basil was mortally wounded in the chest and in the right arm.

I hear Father Hampton is rector of Loyola College. Will you give him what first-hand news I have been able to obtain?

Diary entry: 13 August

Front relatively quiet. Intermittent bombing of Méharicourt. Orders for the attack constantly changed. Instead of joining the attack, tonight we will relieve the 102nd Battalion on the line north of Chilly.

9:30 p.m. Left Méharicourt for the first line. Just as we left, Boche planes dropped a shower of bombs which we could see in the moonlight. Changeover completed by 2 a.m.

Diary entry: 15 August. Trenches north of Chilli.

A quiet night. In the morning I continued working on recommendations for decorations. In the afternoon, I visited the front line.... The Boche are quiet. Not much artillery fire.

At the front
15 August 1918

My dearest Mater,
[...] I received the snapshots sent by Frances. You and the Governor do not seem to have changed in the least — you both look as young as when I left you — so long ago it seems. Frances of course has grown tremendously but seems to have preserved her babyish face and expression. The longer she can keep both, the more charming she will be. Her letters are always whimsical and loving and give me the greatest pleasure.

Of course you know — it is a secret for no one — that we have been through some severe but very consoling fighting and our heart's desire is to be given another chance at the retreating Hun.

We have now the military initiative — in two months it has completely passed from the Germans, thanks to the genius of Foch, and we mean to keep this initiative.

At the front
17 August, 1918

My dear Frances,
[...] You have read in the papers of the advance of the Canadians: as the matter is common property I can mention it without giving any details that would be of value to the enemy. The achievement of the battalion on the 8th and 9th August were as memorable as anything it has done since its arrival in France with the possible exception of Courcelette. The men upheld the highest traditions of their predecessors. The battalion showed that it had lost none of its fighting and aggressive qualities and it earned the praise of higher authorities.

The advance, of course, was unprecedented — 22,000 yards in a little over two days. The Huns were no match for our men who charged machine guns with perfect coolness as if they were on the parade ground. Their indifference before death was little short of sublime. We all felt more than ever that we are going to gain a complete victory — one which will leave no room for doubt and which will eliminate once and for all the spirit of Prussianism.

Providence — thanks to the prayers of all the dear ones at home — has protected me in a special manner and I have come through without a scratch.

Some time ago I received a package of comforts from you together with a small leather case containing a pair of beads, a cross and a medal of our Lady of Mount Carmel. I carry the case with me at all times.

Diary entry: 17 August

Relieved tonight by the 87th Canadian Battalion. Night is relatively calm. Lieut. Col. Tremblay, Commander of the Brigade, came to see us. Heard that the French have taken Roye and

Sassigny. If it is true it will be difficult for the Boche to hold the corner of the land from here to the Somme. Changeover completed at midnight. All followed the railway line from Chaulnes-Amiens, passing by the Gare Rosières-en-Santerre (a few shells fell on the station) as far as the Harbonnières-Villancourt road. We are billeted in the woods at Wild Bois between Caix and Harbonnières.

Diary entry: 18 August

Billeted in Vallon which was all overgrown with trees. Counting on a few days of rest in the same billets. Some planes visited us the other night, dropping a few bombs 500 metres away. No damage. Lieut. Col. Tremblay visited us. The attack as far as the Somme will probably take place on the morning of the 22nd. (Nothing certain. Orders change continually in order to put off enemy agents.) All our movements are made at night.

Diary entry: 19 August. Bois between Caix and Harbonnières.

We have received orders that we will move tonight — to an unknown destination.
    9:30 a.m. Left for Bois de Blangy, east of Amiens (10 kilometres) and followed the road from Guillaucourt, Wiencourt, l'Equipée, Marcelcave (the ground reconquered and travelled through on the 8 and 9 of August) going north of Villers Wrentonneux. Surrounded by the smell of horses and of dead men. This was the site of the great success of the Australians. Arrived at Bois de Blangy at 3:30 in the morning, the men exhausted.

Diary entry: 20 August. Bois de Blangy.

Stretched out on a plot of grass in the underbrush and slept for an hour. Spent another night under the stars (if there are any). Our cars, portable kitchens etc. leave tonight by train for Frevent. Visit from Lieut. Col. Tremblay who dined with us. In the afternoon, walked to highest point of the Côte 116 south of Bois de Blangy.

There was a sunset of deep crimson and gold and I could see the towers of Amiens Cathedral silhouetted against the sun. It was one of the most beautiful moments of my life. What an honour to have contributed, even in a small measure, to the deliverance of Amiens and its celestial cathedral. In the west, the sun is setting and a full moon is coming up.

Diary entry: 21 August. Côte 116 (south of Bois de Blangy).

Rose at 7:30 a.m. Thick fog, reminiscent of the morning of the August 8 attack. Little by little, the sun dissolved the mist and uncovered first the Bois de Blangy, then the north side of the Ancre, and finally the steeple of Amiens Cathedral. We leave tonight for Ternas, the sector between Frevent and St. Pol.

7:30: leave by bus. Informed that we will go to Ternas.

The final assault along the Somme was fixed for August 22, but orders changed frequently. The exhausted men of the 22nd were still in the Bois de Blangy waiting for their instructions.

The entire Canadian Corps, including the Van Doos, was now moving back north from the region of Amiens to the area around Arras.

Diary entry: 22 August. Ternas.

The heat is oppressive, a bit like the heat of Canada. It is impossible to do any exercises. I stretched out on the grass. It seems we will move again tomorrow. There is a bright moonlight and all through the night, the continuous ron-ron-ron of the airplane motors and the sound of distant explosions.

Diary entry: 23 August. Ternas.

We leave at 12:30 p.m. for Pt. Houvin. Hot sun at noon. Several men collapsed from the terrible heat. At Pt. Houvin, we boarded animal cars for the journey by train to Aubigny. Extraordinary activity in the station at St. Pol.... Arrived in Aubigny and marched to Wanquetin at 9 p.m. in the driving rain. Very badly installed for the night. *C'est la guerre.*

Diary entry: 24 August. Camp near Wanquetin.

Another move tonight. Have just learned about the death of my friend Trevor Penny who was a very genial companion. We were enthusiastic supporters of the O.T.C. [*Officers Training Corps*] at McGill after the declaration of war. In the afternoon, a visit from two Canadian journalists (M. Livesay and another whose name I forget).

    7 p.m. We left for Berneville. Slept very well in a small cabin on bundles of straw. The constant ron-ron-ron of German planes and search lights and bombing continues all night long.

At last, the final assault along the Somme was about to begin. By August 24, the men of the 22nd had reached the village of Wanquetin, then moved on to a camp near Berneville.

Diary entry: Sunday, 25 August. Camp near Berneville (two miles west of Arras).

After a night of searchlights, German planes and bombs, we rose at 9 a.m. Attended Mass in the parish church at Parvins....

    2 p.m. Received news that we will move tonight, and probably attack tomorrow morning.

    5:30 p.m. Major Dubuc sent me to reconnoitre the "Assembly area" — torrential rain and lightning which illuminated the sky as in daylight. Then moonlight. Waited for the other companies until 11 p.m. on the Beaurains-Ronville road.

Casualty of War — August 1918

Diary entry: 26 August. Beaurains-St. Sauveur etc.

The day of the attack.

Left at 1 a.m. with Major Dubuc for the Brigade. Colonel Tremblay sent me to the quarters of the 3rd Division and the 7th Brigade. I will be liaison officer. He gave me all the information on a map. I am to return to Beaubourg St. Sauveur and find a large cave. Cross Rouille and proceed to Faubourg St. Sauveur.

I had left the camp the night before not knowing that I would be liaison officer so I didn't take any toiletries with me or anything to eat. I really learned the agony of hunger the morning of the 26th. Luckily, I found two boxes of "Bully Beef" left behind in the trenches and they saved my life.

Col. Tremblay informed us that the Brigade will attack on the 27th. Our final objective will be Cagnicourt.

On August 26, Major Dubuc was in command, with Georges Vanier acting in liaison with the 4th Brigade as they prepared to launch an attack on the village of Cagnicourt — an assault that would take them through the village of Chérisy,[2] four miles southeast of Arras. As they crossed to capture the ridge beyond the Sensée ravine, a bullet struck Dubuc in the head. It cost him his eye but not his life. He was taken from the field and the command passed to Archambault. Later the same day, he too was wounded. Tremblay, now Brigadier-General and in charge of the whole operation, made an instant decision: he put Georges Vanier in command.

Vanier rejoined the unit as commander at dusk on August 26. The men were exhausted and crouched in shell holes or what was left of the trenches. At 9 a.m. the following morning, they received orders to renew the attack before noon. Vanier was one of the few officers left so he advanced at the centre of the battalion under cover of a light artillery barrage. They did not get very far: in the first few minutes of their attack, the battalion met a hail of machine-gun fire. Suddenly, a bullet hit Vanier and pierced his stomach. A stretcher-bearer rushed over to dress his wounds. That same moment, another shell exploded beside the two killing the stretcher-bearer instantly. The second shell also caused serious damage to Vanier's left leg and shattered his right leg at the knee. As he was being carried on a stretcher to the dressing station, he met Major Fortier, the padre, who asked him if there was anything he wanted. As Vanier recounted in a CBC broadcast taped in 1965:

> I asked him for three things: absolution for my sins, which he gave me; a cigarette, which he gave me (it was the first one I had smoked during the whole of the war); and rum, which he did not give me for the very comforting reason that I might have internal injuries as well.

He recounted details of his injury in a letter to his mother dated September 6:

On the 28th of August the battalion attacked. As Major Dubuc had been wounded the previous day (I cannot say yet exactly how seriously), I happened to be in command. Very shortly after zero hour, I was shot (machine-gun or rifle bullet) through the right side splitting a couple of ribs. The wound however was a very clean one (most bullet wounds are) and I should have been very fortunate indeed to come off with it only. But this was to be one of my bad days: as I was being dressed by the bearer a shell exploded at my side causing rather unpleasant shrapnel wounds to my right and left legs. I was evacuated in good time from the battlefield and taken to the Casualty Clearing Station at Ligny St. Flochel which I reached at about 9 p.m. and where I received every possible medical and surgical treatment. They were splendid to me.

The right knee was shattered and the Medical Officer then said even if the leg were saved I would never be able to use the knee. I asked him if he might wait until the following day for a reply. He agreed and the leg was amputated next day. A short time after my return to bed following the operation, I suffered a severe haemorrhage and was hurried back to where the operation took place. There a transfusion was done in direct contact with the donor. The immediate effect was a feeling of active physical resuscitation. I have no doubt whatever that the transfusion saved my life.³ When it was over, somebody suggested — perhaps I did — that a glass of port might do me good. Everybody agreed, and another voice was heard (it was the man next to me who had given his blood) saying: "I'd like one too."

Soon after the amputation, Major-General Burstall, the general commanding the 2nd Division, visited Vanier at the Clearing Station. As he later recalled in his CBC talk:

> [*General Burstall*] assured me that the High Command had been much impressed by the terrible losses of the 22nd but that these were not in vain. On the contrary, they had facilitated the advance of the troops who came after them and thus they had contributed to the victory.

The next morning, Vanier was moved from the Casualty Clearing Station to the Red Cross Hospital in Boulogne. He left the C.C.S. with a heavy heart, noting in his diary on September 3:

As I left today, I took a last look at the old farms, the old roads of France that I have come to know so well. My heart is heavy indeed.... They put me on a hospital train which was waiting at the Ligny station. It was an enormous carriage containing about thirty officers lined up in ten rows of three with a corridor down the centre. The heat was intolerable, the blinds closed. Because of my wounds, they placed me on a platform. The train left only at 9 p.m. I had a light meal of tongue and soup.

After what he admitted was "a long night of suffering," relieved only by constant injections of morphine, Vanier reached Boulogne at 7:30 a.m. An ambulance met him there and took him to the No. 8 British Red Cross Hospital.
  Two telegrams carried the news to his parents.

TELEGRAM 6 September 1918
GEORGE WOUNDED LEGS HOSPITAL DOING WELL.
TREMBLAY

TELEGRAM 9 September 1918
SINCERELY REGRET INFORM YOU CAPTAIN ACTING MAJOR GEORGE PHILIAS VANIER M C INFANTRY OFFICIALLY REPORTED SERIOUSLY ILL BRITISH RED CROSS HOSPITAL LE TOUQUET SEPT 5TH GUNSHOT WOUND AMPUTATION RIGHT LEG.
    DIRECTOR OF RECORDS

The next day, Georges himself sent his family the following telegram:

IN 8 BRITISH RED CROSS HOSPITAL FRANCE NO CAUSE WORRY
GEORGES VANIER

No. 8 British Red Cross Hospital, Boulogne
6 September, 1918

My dearest Mater,
By this time you will have received reassuring cablegrams and field postcards and possibly letters from friends of mine.
    First, to be quite frank, I will admit that I have not been in fit condition to write a coherent letter before without running the risk of endangering my general health.
    [...] On the 3rd September, I was shipped by hospital train to this base hospital. This quick movement will give you an idea of my stamina and the high opinion they had of my resistance. My present state is more than satisfactory — temperature and pulse normal, sleep coming back to me etc. And I wish to impress on you the necessity for not worrying. I do not expect to be at the base hospital very long but count on reaching England within a week. I have

already written to Mr. Bull who, I think, will try to have me as near him as possible.

From today on, I shall write you a daily letter (even if very short) to show you that I am really making rapid strides to complete recovery. Remember there is NO CAUSE FOR WORRY.

Diary entry: 6 September. British Red Cross Hospital, Boulogne.

Couldn't sleep last night, in spite of the morphine. Woke early scarcely rested. The weather is still very heavy.

12:00 noon: Right leg was dressed without pain.

At 6:30 p.m., I felt a sharp pain in the muscles of the calf of my left leg — exasperating. The heat is intolerable. The papers have announced that the whole Allied line from Ypres to Rheims is on the move.

Diary entry: 7 September

No morphine last night. However, it was a good enough night if only my sleep would return. Torrential rain off and on hasn't yet taken away the humidity. Less pain in the side. Major Dubuc appeared on the list of the wounded (Times 7/9/18). A night of thunderstorms and rain. Slept very badly without the morphine. Intermittent pain in my left leg and in my right side. Suffering a great deal. Scarcely any sleep.

No. 8 British Red Cross Hospital, France
7th September, 1918

My dearest Mater,
My case could not possibly be progressing more favourably than it is. The doctors here seem to think that I will reach England within four or five days and then of course a relatively long period of convalescence will follow — possibly one month and a half. I suffer very little during the dressing of my wounds: this is due in large

measure to the particular attention paid even to the minutest details of all operations and dressings. Major Roy and Lieuts. Aitkens and Bourgault all of the 22nd are in the same hospital and doing well. Lieut. R. McMurtry, lawyer of Brown and Co. Montreal, is here also with a fractured leg.

Very few of the old 22nd officers now remain with the battalion. Majors Dubuc, Archambault, Roy Routier and myself were all wounded — besides almost a score of others killed and wounded. I believe Lt. Col. DesRosiers will come across to command the battalion with Major Henri Chassé as second-in-command.

My being wounded at this particular time was unfortunate in another sense. I have been since October 1916 an acting Major which means that I had the apparent rank and pay of a Major but the substantive rank of a Captain. Now that I cease to belong to the 22nd Battalion, I revert for pay to the rank of Captain although I retain the honorary rank of Major. However, when I reach London I will endeavour to have my case settled in such a way as to retain Major's pay. In the ordinary course of events, my promotion would have come through in a few weeks as Major Dubuc was to have been promoted Lieut. Col. in the stead of Colonel Tremblay who should get a brigade very shortly.

Rather hard bit of luck, don't you think? For poor Major Dubuc also?

Diary entry: Sunday, 8 September. Boulogne.

Woke very early. Washed and dressed by 6:30 a.m. At 7:10, took communion.

At first, the weather was overcast but later it cleared up. There was a raging wind all day. In the afternoon, I had a surprise visit from Lt. Col. DesRosiers of the 10th Reserve who now has taken over as commander of the 22nd. Chassé will be his second-in-command. He stayed two hours with me. We talked about everything — the battalion, the brigade, the future of French Canada. His visit really boosted my morale. He is a sterling man who will make an excellent commander of the battalion. A disappointment for Chassé, no doubt.

No. 8 B.R.C.H. Boulogne
8 September, 1918

My dearest Mater,
This morning early — Sunday — I received Holy Communion from the hands of a priest who has been very kind to me since I reached this hospital.

This afternoon, I had the surprise of my life when Lieut. Col. DesRosiers dropped in to see me. He was on his way to the battalion to take command — as foreshadowed in one of my former letters to you. He had the afternoon off in Boulogne and had the happy idea of looking up some of the larger hospitals for recently-wounded and thus ran into me almost immediately.... All our senior officers have been hit with the exception of Major Dupuis who seems to stick on through everything. The old battalion will no longer be recognizable. If Major Dubuc's wound is not too serious — which God grant — I should not be surprised to see him become Lieut. Col. in command of 10th Reserve Battalion instead of Lieut. Col. DesRosiers. He richly deserves his promotion. It would give him a well-earned rest. I am told however that his face wound is quite serious.

This hospital is only a few hundred yards from the sea and the strong fresh breezes keep the room aired and cool. The attention and the meals leave nothing to be desired. My general health is exceptionally good; I do wish I could make you realize there is no cause whatever for worry. If I were certain you were reassured and content I should be much happier myself.

Do you remember Romeo Dupuy who was platoon commander with me in "D" Company under Major Dubuc? He has died of wounds poor chap. So has Lieut. [*Roddy*] Lemieux, son of Sir Rodolphe. The same ambulance conveyed us from the advanced dressing station. He looked very low at that moment. I lost track of him then, until I read of his death in the official lists.

Though Vanier put up a brave front to his mother, he was in fact suffering a great deal as we see in this diary entry:

Diary entry: 9 September

A long night of insomnia. God! How the nights are long! Every half hour I hear the distant echo of the sea, and the sea winds; the weather is cool. The French continue their advance towards St. Quentin and La Fosse. Still no letters; agonizing pains in the right leg.... Sudden attack of faintness. Must have been reading too much — a hundred pages of Nemesis by Bourget,[4] a book given to me by Lieut. Col. DesRosiers.

The Times (9/9/18) has announced that Lieut. Dupuy, Lieut. Lemieux (who died of wounds), Lieuts. Chenier, Lamothe, Blais, Laverdure, Maranda and Major Routier — have all been wounded.

No. 8 British Red Cross Hosp.
Boulogne
9 September, 1918

My dearest Mater,
A terrific gale has been blowing all night: in fact the hospital ships which were to cross the Channel today were prevented from doing so.

The wind and the rain have brought the cool weather in their wake which makes sleeping easier. My normal sleep is returning very quickly. The return of the sleep, I consider to be as important as the healing of the wounds.

The doctor prefers to keep me here some time yet to make sure of the state of my general health and of my strength to undergo the channel trip. I am anxious to receive word from you that you are reassured as to my condition and that you are not worrying. It is only a question of time before I am quite as fit as I ever was.

Diary entry: 11 September

A good night with more sleep, more calm, no morphine. Torrential rain. Long list of losses reported in the Times (11/9/18) — Lieut. Aitkens, Capt. Archambault, Lieut. Bourgault, Lieut. deVienne,

Capt. R. McMurtry (of Brown & Co., Montreal) ... and myself — all wounded.

Diary entry: 12 September

Progress every day. General health is much better. Tomorrow, we must dress all the wounds. A cheerful prospect.

No. 8 British Red Cross Hospital, Boulogne
12 September, 1918

My dearest Mater,
Each day brings further progress in my general health. I eat quite as well as I did before I received my wounds and in every way I feel quite as fit. So please do not worry. I will keep you informed at all times by cable and by letter.

Diary entry: 13 September

All wounds dressed. Very sick. Sharp pain especially in my right leg. Restless night.

Diary entry: 14 September

Suffered a great deal today, always in the right leg. There were moments when the pain was almost unbearable. The weather is grey and depressing.

Marvellous news about the American advance at St. Mitirel. Bad night. Morphine.

Diary entry: 15 September. Boulogne.

The sun is dazzling. In the afternoon, a procession of strollers passed beneath the window (I could hear them without seeing them). At night, clear moonlight and the sound of young people singing. My right leg is still very painful.

11:10 p.m. An alarm sounded. Cannon shots. At midnight, the "all-clear".

Diary entry: 16 September

Slept little last night. Right leg a little less painful.

Diary entry: 17 September

A more restful night. Moonlight. Two alerts but no sound of bombing. The streets emptied in two or three minutes. Very nervous.

News of the V.C. [*Victoria Cross*][5] given to Kaeble [*Joseph*] appeared in all the papers. The first for the 22nd.

No. 8 British Red Cross Hospital, Boulogne
17 September, 1918

My dearest Mater,
I had the surprise of my life this afternoon when Monseigneur Georges Gauthier [*the Bishop of Montreal and family friend*] came to the hospital to see me! I thought him thousands of miles away! I was so dumbfounded at his appearance that I quite forgot to question him about his mission in France. He was very kind to me, said all kinds of comforting things and promised to write to you and the Governor. He asked me particularly to remember him to you when I wrote. He has changed little since I saw him over three years ago.

You have no idea what a comfort and relief Bishop Gauthier is! Or it was to me! His was the first face from Canada I had seen for such a long time!

Vanier continued to be in considerable pain, noting in his diary on September 14 that "I am in so much pain today, always in the right leg," though two days later he wrote "I slept a little last night and my right leg was a little less painful." But again, on September 18, his exasperation surfaced when he noted: "The same routine over and over again. My, how the hours are sometimes long!"

No. 8 British Red Cross Hospital, Boulogne
24 September, 1918

My dearest Mater,

The doctor tells me that he is going to send me across to England to-morrow: I feel almost sorry to leave this hospital because of the exceptionally kind and efficient treatment I have received. All the sisters and nurses are most gracious and look upon you less as patients than as friends in distress.

Each day marks fresh progress in my condition. This may seem astonishing to you but I am told that in three weeks I may be getting about, with difficulty, of course, but still getting about.

I received a letter from Major Dubuc in London confirming what I told you in a previous letter. He has lost his right eye but apart from that his general health is not affected.

Colonel Tremblay has been promoted Brigadier General in command of the 5th Canadian Brigade — a well deserved honour.

On September 25, under sunny skies, Vanier crossed the channel by boat to England and moved into the Third London General Hospital at Wandsworth, London to continue his convalescence. Though he had expected to be getting about in three weeks "with difficulty, of course, but still getting about," his next letter home was not quite so optimistic.

3rd London General Hospital
Wandsworth (London)
26 September, 1918

My dearest Mater,

I reached this hospital at one o'clock this morning after a most pleasant crossing from Boulogne and a quiet and easy journey in the train from the coast to London. The trip has tired me very little and I feel as fit as when I left No. 8 British Red Cross Hospital in Boulogne.

By this time of course you know what my injuries are, so that I can discuss them without giving you cause for worry. I know you wish to know the details of what happened. On the 28th August shortly after the beginning of one of our attacks I was hit in the right side by a bullet which made a through and through wound fracturing two ribs in its course. As I was being dressed by a stretcher-bearer a shell exploded at our side killing the poor stretcher-bearer instantly and causing severe wounds to my right and left legs but particularly to the right. Fortunately no bones were broken in the left leg and I expect to have back the complete use of it very soon. But the right was badly shattered more especially about the knee and it was found necessary to amputate just above the knee.

Do not think that I have suffered because with the modern surgical methods pain and discomfort are reduced to a minimum. By this time, of course, the stump is almost healed and I shall probably be about without a bandage in a few weeks.

On reaching London, I telephoned to the Bulls who are coming to see me. Major Roy of our battalion is two beds away from me: he is recovering from an abdominal wound.

There is absolutely no cause for the slightest worry on your part. The loss of the leg does not affect me in the least.

On September 27, another member of the Van Doos, Lieutenant Jean Brillant, was awarded the Victoria Cross for gallantry. Brillant had been mortally wounded on August 10 in the front line of the attack.

Diary entry: 30 September

Began and finished "With the Turks in Palestine" by Alexander Aronsohn (Constable London). A pitiful picture of the condition of the Jews in Palestine under the Turks and a review of the politics of the Allies.

Finally the weather is clearing. Began "J'Accuse"[6] [*an open letter written in 1898 by Emile Zola in response to the Dreyfus Affair*] — a remarkable book that I have often wanted to read.

It was General Tremblay himself who conveyed some news that greatly cheered Vanier. In a letter dated October 8, Tremblay informed him that he had been awarded the Bar to his Military Cross and also the Distinguished Service Order (D.S.O.) The citation for his Bar read as follows:

> For conspicuous gallantry and devotion to duty. The battalion commander having become a casualty, this officer organised the remnants of the battalion which had suffered heavily the previous day, and led the men in the second attack with great dash. He was first seriously wounded in the side but carried on until severely wounded in both legs.

The citation for his D.S.O. read:

> For conspicuous gallantry and devotion to duty. As second-in-command he led a portion of the battalion in the attack and capture of a village. The O.C. of the battalion being then called in the command of the brigade, this officer took charge of the battalion and led it with great skill to the attack and capture of a large village. His courage, example and will to conquer imbued all under him with the finest fighting spirit.

Congratulations followed from General Gaudet. "My greatest admiration for your courage and for your enormous dedication and self-sacrifice."

3rd London General Hospital
9 October, 1918

My dearest Frances,
Your cablegram cheered me up, as do all good wishes from home. Your prayers are evidently listened to because I am recovering rapidly and my wounds are healing quickly.

[...] Most of my day is spent reading. Today however I have indulged in another pastime — watching spiders spin webs. They have put me in a sort of summer-house outside the regular ward and when I woke this morning I found four spiders industriously spinning beautiful, regular webs outside of my four windows — trying to seal me in as they did the King in English history whose name I forget. [*Possibly Robert the Bruce, King of Scotland, who watched a spider while in hiding on Rathin Island and drew inspiration from its perseverance.*]

3rd London General Hospital
Wandsworth (London)
9 October, 1918

Mon bien cher papa,
It is already a long time since I have wanted to write to thank you for your numerous cablegrams. ("Love and best cheer from all." "Delighted to hear you doing well. If in need of anything cable. Love and good cheer from all at home. Philias Vanier." and, this morning "Happy to know you are so well. Not worrying. Love from all.") Rest assured that such signs of affection are a great consolation for me.

Maman will have read you my letter with all the details of the 28th. Already the wounds in my side and one of the wounds on my left leg are healing. The other wound on that leg will take another two weeks and I look forward to the moment when I can lift myself up with the help only of the side bars on the bed. This will encourage me, after the relative inactivity to which I have been consigned, though I was in no pain or discomfort during that period.

I sleep well at night and in no way suffer from my wounds. I would be very happy to be reassured that neither you nor mother are suffering in any way from my accident. After all, equally serious accidents are commonplace.

Diary entry: 13 October

Reading "A Royal Tragedy", [*by Chadelle Misatovitch*] the history of the assassination of King Alexander and Queen Draja of Serbia.

3rd London General Hospital
Wandsworth, London
16 October, 1918

My dearest Mater,
Since my last letter to you, my condition has steadily improved and there have been no setbacks. I would very probably be up on crutches by this time if it were not for the injuries to my left leg, which are healed but which have left the leg weak. Besides I must be careful because there is always the possibility of the wound re-opening if I attempt to do too much.

The Bulls have been very kind to me and are anxious for me to go to their home now, but I think it unwise as I am still too helpless: later on I will feel more able to look after myself.

Diary entry: 17 October

Finished "A Royal Tragedy". What struck me most was the hypocritical and criminal politics of the Russian factions and of the horrible cruelty the Balkan officers were capable of. The story of the assassination [*of the King and Queen of Serbia*] is terrifying.

Diary entry: 19 October

Read "Literary Lapses" by Leacock.[7] Very amusing, a little ludicrous in some places.

In mid-October, Vanier received a visit from Lieutenant-Colonel Hugues de Harding who sent his parents a report, in French, on their son's condition.

10th Canadian Reserve Battalion,
Bramshott, Hants.
18 octobre 1918

Madame,
During my visit to London a little while ago, I dropped by the Clapham Junction Hospital to see your son, George. I found him happy as a schoolboy, surrounded by friends and in excellent spirits. He instantly won, and certainly not for the first time, my warm admiration.

The wound in his side is already closed and scarred over. His leg gives him no pain. In short he is well along the way to being completely healed. I was told that he will soon be leaving to stay with Mr. Perkins Bull and his family to finish his convalescence....

It is really something for him, at his age, to have survived. The thought that he will soon see his loved ones again is the best tonic for him. He has completely regained his famous appetite.

Wounded in glory, covered with honours, surrounded with respect and affection, life seems to him to be sweet and beautiful. I congratulate you, Madame, for having such a son.

We were already friends before the war, but these two years that I have spent with him at the front have made him seem almost a brother to me. I can thus share both your joy and your fully justified pride.

    Hugues de Harding
    Lieutenant Colonel.

3rd L.G.H., Wandsworth
1 November, 1918

My dearest Mater,

You will be pleased to hear that my recovery has had no setbacks: my left leg is getting stronger each day. The bone does not seem to have been affected: the wound is quite healed and I get about (for a very short time each day) on crutches. I no longer stay in bed but sit up in a chair or couch and altogether my general health has improved wonderfully. The Canadian Red Cross people have been very kind to me and have taken me out for motor drives through the parks and to the city to make small purchases.

General Tremblay has been especially thoughtful and during his short stay in London, came to see me twice besides sending gifts of flowers, fruit and chocolates.

My deepest regret is that I cannot carry on with him in France until the victorious end.

12

CONTINUED CONVALESCENCE, AND ARMISTICE
NOVEMBER 1918

"My greatest, my supreme consolation is to have led the noble battalion in the assault. How I would have hated to have received my own wounds from somewhere behind."
Georges Vanier to his father,
5 December, 1918

"I am happy at the thought that I had the courage to return to my boys in 1916 and that God gave me the strength of body and of mind to do my duty under fire. It is a tremendous consolation that will comfort me until my dying day."
Georges Vanier to his mother,
13 May, 1919

Vanier moved on November 4 to the I.O.D.E. (Imperial Order of the Daughters of the Empire) Hospital, a Canadian hospital on Hyde Park Place in the heart of London. There he was under the care of Dr. Donald Armour, a Harley Street surgeon who later became a close friend of the family. After Armour's death in the 1930s, Georges spoke at a memorial service in London, recalling him as "one of the best":

> [...] I well remember him in November 1918 at the I.O.D.E. hospital in London where nurses and patients loved him equally. He had a way of making you hopeful and wishful of life even when you didn't care very much what happened, and I feel sure that many of his wounded came through because he told them to.... I can see him coming into the ward with his quick determined step, his splendid head thrown back, and I can still hear his deep, resonant, laughing voice that literally made those of us who could, sit up: to everyone in the hospital he embodied the spirit of strength and kindness.

Diary entry: 4 November

Colonel Armour examined my right leg and decided a second amputation is necessary. It will be done in a few days. Very comfortable here at the I.O.D.E.

From outside the hospital walls, important news began to filter in.

Diary entry: 9 November

There is news that the Kaiser [*of Germany*] and his son have abdicated. The Boche have until Monday at 11 a.m. to accept the conditions of Armistice.

In the afternoon, I attended the Adelphi Theatre to see "The Boy". I was carried into the lobby by a small motor cart — what an object of curiosity!

Continued Convalescence, and Armistice — November 1918

On November 10, the Kaiser crossed the border into Holland, never to return. Meanwhile, German and Allied leaders met in a railway carriage in the Forest of Compiègne, north of Paris, to sign an agreement that included several conditions: the Germans were to hand over vast stocks of war material and most of their fleet; they were to withdraw from all invaded territory in the west and from Alsace-Lorraine; and the Allied armies were to occupy all German territory on the left bank of the Rhine and the bridgeheads for fifty miles beyond it. Fighting was to cease at 11 a.m. on November 11, 1918.

Back at the I.O.D.E. Hospital, Georges Vanier was bracing himself for another operation scheduled for 8:30 a.m. the next day.

Diary entry: 11 November

7:45 a.m. Injection of morphine.... 8:30 a.m. Operation. Lieut. Col. Armour did the operation. I woke up from the anaesthetic to the sounds of cannons — cannons of joy — announcing the Armistice at 11:00 a.m.

I.O.D.E. Hospital
12 November, 1918

My dearest Mater,
On the news of the Armistice, London went wild with joy! Hundreds of thousands of people thronged the streets shouting, singing and dancing: the King and Queen were given a tremendous ovation in front of Buckingham Palace. Still I should have preferred very much to have been with the battalion in France: I can imagine what wild scenes took place along the battle front. [*There were very few, in fact.*] There is only one original officer with the 22nd now — Major Chassé: some of the others are almost fit enough to go back. All Canadians in England are being sent to Canada as soon as possible. I think that many thousands will arrive before the New Year. I do not know yet when I will be leaving but it cannot be for some time — certainly there is no chance of spending Christmas together.

On the news of the Armistice, London went wild with joy. Here, thousands jam Trafalgar Square during a victory parade.

My health is steadily improving and there have been no unpleasant complications from any of my wounds. The left leg keeps getting stronger and bears my weight for a short time each day.

I.O.D.E. Hospital
16 November, 1918

My dearest Mater,
[...] The London celebrations have by no means subsided yet. The people in their frenzy have gone to such lengths as tearing down boardings and signs and making bonfires with them in the public squares. Nelson's monument in Trafalgar Square was damaged by the celebrants. The Canadian troops in France will be marching towards the Rhine in a few days — one of the greatest disappointments of my life will be my inability to take part in this march. What a tremendous reward and consolation to see the goal of all our ambitions — to

CONTINUED CONVALESCENCE, AND ARMISTICE — NOVEMBER 1918

actually tread on German soil and to feel that the efforts and the sacrifices of years have not been in vain.

To while away the hours, I read almost continuously: this prolonged rest will have brought me back to my old friends — the books — which I had more or less deserted during the busy days in France.

I.O.D.E. Hospital
28 November, 1918

My dearest Mater,
Lieut. Col. Dubuc, who is sailing for Canada in a few days, has kindly offered to give you this letter when he calls on you. He will tell you — and in this way confirm what I have said in my letters — that I look very well and that my complete recovery is only a question of time. I have thought very seriously of the advisability of being fitted for my leg in England or of waiting until I return to Canada. For many reasons I consider it much wiser to have everything done here. The surgeons over here have had a much wider experience in amputations and in the treatments preliminary to the final fitting: moreover it will give me great personal satisfaction to be quite crutchless before I reach Montreal. All this will mean a slightly longer separation — which I regret as much as all of you — but the advantages outweigh the additional sacrifices.

I know this letter will reach you before Christmas — when I should so like to be with you — and I wish you to accept for yourself, for the dear Governor and for the whole family — my heartfelt wish for a happy and merry Christmastide. To the kind friends who ask after me, please give my best regards. This will be the last, the very last Christmas which will see us separated.

As Georges continued his recuperation in London, the Van Doos became part of the Allied occupation force in Germany. His old comrade Major Henri Chassé wrote from the German frontier on December 3:

My dear Georges,
Lieut. Col. DesRosiers is on holiday in London so it is I who will have the very great honour to enter Germany tomorrow with the battalion. We will go to the other side of the Rhine (1st and 2nd Divisions) as occupying forces for a few weeks. I am anxious to see the reception we receive in Germany. Our journey through Belgium has been a series of receptions and triumphs. We have been received with open arms.

We march for 25 kilometres a day. It is a superb journey. Yesterday, we reached the highest point of Belgium, in the Ardennes — an altitude of 667 metres. We almost reached the clouds and it was very cool....

Your friend, Henri Chassé

Le 5e decembre 1918

Mon bien cher Papa,
I apologize for having so seriously neglected my correspondence; you can be sure it is not out of any ill will on my part. Your letters have been a real blessing to me, and your generous offer to send me anything I need has touched me deeply.

I have before me this minute your postcard from Notre Dame du Portage, and your letters from Trois Pistoles de Cacouna and from the Saguenay: they arrived at the very moment when the battalion was paying very dearly for its claims to fame. The month of August will be a memorable one in the history of the 22nd.

Curiously enough, it had originally been decided that I should not take part in the attack of August 28th, since I had participated in the assaults of the 9th and 10th of August. The wounding of Colonel Dubuc, however, meant that I had to take command of the battalion on the afternoon of August 27th. The next day, the 28th, at noon, half of the entire brigade attacked and the 22nd suffered heavy losses. My greatest, my supreme consolation is to have led the noble battalion in the assault. How I would have hated to have received my own wounds from somewhere behind!

In the various hospitals I have stayed in, everyone spoilt me shamelessly — all care and treatment was given with kindness and affection. Before August 27th, I had no idea of the immensity and generosity of the work performed by the women nurses in war.

All my wounds have now scarred over: my blood must be in good shape, according to the doctor, because the scars have formed so quickly. For the moment I have need of nothing, and lack little. New Year's Day, my thoughts will fly to you, and I would ask you your blessing in advance.

I.O.D.E. Hospital
7 December, 1918

My dearest Mater,
I am now getting about on crutches — not as yet about the streets because I do not believe in taking unnecessary risks. I get up and down stairs quite easily. The left leg has done much better than I expected — the nerves and muscles do not seem to be affected in any way. This of course is a great consolation.

I continue to make friends in hospital — not a day passes without my having two or three visitors in to see me.

I have received two invitations for Christmas dinners — one for 2 in the afternoon at the Perkins Bull Hospital and one for 8 at night with some charming English friends of Mrs. Armours (of Vancouver) who has been very kind to me. I expect to be able to accept both.

The I.O.D.E. Hospital is moving to the Petrograd Hotel where 170 patients will be accommodated: I am afraid I shall not like life there quite as well as at Hyde Park Place where we are all "en famille".

In early December, the I.O.D.E. closed its doors and transferred its patients, including Vanier, to the Canadian Red Cross Officers' Hospital, also in central London.

Cdn Red Cross Officers' Hospital,
North Audley Street, London W.1.
15 December, 1918

My dearest Mater,

The IODE hospital has ceased to exist and all patients have been transferred here which will gather in all Canadian officers distributed throughout England.

A few days ago I was measured for a peg leg. A peg leg is a sort of preliminary leg which must be worn for a month or so before any work can be done on the artificial leg proper. This enables the stump to harden and prepares it for the harder work it will have to do later on.

The Hon. Philippe Roy, Canadian Commissioner in Paris, has made me an offer to accept the secretaryship of the Commission. The salary would be approximately $4000 a year. There are certain advantages connected with the position. I would get in touch with the leading men of affairs and of politics in Canada and the position might lead to some other position of importance. The proposition made by M. Roy is the following: I would go to him as soon as possible, perhaps about the 15th February, remain with him for three or four months when he would sail for Canada and I would remain in charge of the commission. Then (sometime in the summer) I would be given the opportunity of going to Canada myself.

Of course if I accepted the position it would be for a short time: the year 1919 in Paris will be full of momentous events really unprecedented in the history of the world and I would get in touch with men of mark and of ability.

Will you tell me frankly what you and the Governor think of this (by cable if you think it wise). Please think of the matter solely from the viewpoint of my future and of my good. When considering the matter remember that I have no intention of definitely settling down in Europe.

The left leg is in splendid shape and I hobble about in wonderful fashion.

Vanier spent Christmas at the Perkins Bull Hospital, dining on mushroom soup, scalloped oysters, roast turkey and plum pudding.

Mr. Perkins Bull wrote about the occasion to Mrs. Vanier.

Georges was with us for Christmas dinner yesterday. He is doing well but was tired at the end of the day — he has quite a long way to go yet to be himself but he is well on the way. He is happy but is still rather bloodless and weak.... I see his doctors regularly and know he is doing well. He had some setbacks, not dangerous but causing delay.... He had lost so much blood.

Canadian Red Cross Officers' Hospital
North Audley Street, London W.1
1 January, 1919

My dearest Mater,
On the first of the year, I wish to reach out and hold you all in spirit. My greatest desire would be to rejoin the family circle. Will you give my most affectionate New Year's wishes to all the dear ones?
    I received your Christmas box in perfect condition: the contents were delicious. I am writing to Mr. Martin to thank him for his beautiful rose.

Canadian Red Cross Officers' Hospital
6 January, 1919

My dearest Mater,
[...] I am getting stronger each day and better in every way. I have now my preliminary peg and I make use of it each day for a short time. In a month or two the question of my regular artificial leg will be raised (not the leg, the question).

Granville Special Hospital, Buxton, Derbyshire
18 January, 1919

My dearest Mater,
A few days ago I was moved from London to this hospital where I

am to receive special treatment for my stump and to undergo preliminary training in the use of my peg leg which I have been given and upon which I hobble fairly well.

[...] Your cablegram in answer to my inquiry regarding the secretaryship in Paris is another proof of how broad and unselfish an outlook you take on all matters concerned with my future. I have written to Mr. Roy accepting the position but under conditions which I hardly believe he can accept. Firstly, I am to remain in uniform and not be demobilized until my condition becomes permanently settled, i.e. until I am sure whether my side and left leg will give me further trouble. Secondly, I am to go to him between the 15th Feb and the 1st March. Thirdly my stay with him is to be limited. Fourthly, the salary is to be $5000 a year. If he accepts these terms I will advise you by cable. Frankly I am not very sanguine — particularly because of the rather high salary but I could not ask for less at my age and with my training, to speak quite frankly with you.

But really it was rather splendid of you and of the Governor to be so unselfish, and I appreciate your attitude more than I can say. It has made my conditional acceptance much easier.

[...] When my leg was amputated in France, the work had to be done hurriedly and more attention was paid to the saving of my life than to the details of making a clean comfortable stump (if I may put it thus) with necessary flap of flesh over the end. As a consequence, when the stump healed a rather broad scar remained with the bone hardly covered by the scar tissue. This condition would have always given me trouble so that Colonel Armour, one of the best Harley St. surgeons, suggested that I have the scar tissue removed and a piece of the bone cut off. I agreed at once and the operation was completely successful and in less than three weeks the stump was again healed. Now I have a clean scar about 1/8 of an inch wide: I suffer no pain whatever and there is no question of any other operation even at some remote period. My left leg gives no trouble whatever and my right side is in no way painful. The lung was not pierced but I escaped almost miraculously. The surgeons here have given me a complete re-examination and look upon me as a curiosity without any claim to existence!

Did I ever tell you that when I received the bullet wound in the right side, my revolver at the same time was smashed by another bullet which would otherwise have lodged in my abdomen? The result was only a bruised patch just about where the appendix lies.

Granville Special Hospital, Buxton
30 January, 1919

My dearest Frances,
[...] We have had Canadian winter weather during the last two days: the ground is covered with snow and all the able bodied citizens seem to be sliding and sleighing. Personally I get about for the most part in a sea-going cab which insists on skidding downhill and which has to be pushed uphill because the horse at times gets stubborn and refuses to budge. The cabby is so kind-hearted that he cannot be persuaded to use force or violence. But if the hills are steep and numerous the distances are short and I rather enjoy the amusing contretemps.

I get about quite well on my stump and in a month or six weeks I should be ready for measurement for my artificial leg proper. I am very sanguine about my future ability to get about and even to ride and possibly to play tennis.

Granville Special Hospital, Buxton
1st February, 1919

My dearest Mater,
Lieut. P. Gélineau of our battalion, one of our bravest and best officers and a great friend of mine, will hand you this letter and will give you news of me. I would be very grateful if John and Eva would do all they can to make his stay in Montreal pleasant.

I am sending you an etching which I wish you would keep for me. As you will see from the signature Clarence Gagnon[1] is the artist: I chose the etching at the same time that I ordered the painting of the village winter scene for the Governor. I wish you would not have the canvas or the etching framed until I obtain information about the kind of frames Gagnon wants.

Granville Special Hospital, Buxton
1 February, 1919

My dearest Mater,
[...] Two of my friends Capt. White and Lieut. Gélineau of the 22nd Battalion sailed this morning for Canada.... Gélineau is taking with him a small canvas by Clarence Gagnon which I mean to offer to the Governor: I chose the subject myself and I am very well pleased with the execution of it.

My stay in Buxton is most beneficial. Each morning I receive one hour's massage — stump, left leg and scar in the side — all wounds are quite healed and the massage is loosening the scars and strengthening the muscles and stimulating the nerves.

Each afternoon I spend three quarters of an hour at the gym rowing and punching the bag in an attempt to develop my arms, chest and shoulders.

In my enumeration, I forgot to mention that at eleven o'clock each morning there is a walking class for "peg" cases where I am put through such antics as walking on a narrow strip of wood, walking backwards and sideways upstairs, downstairs and in every other imaginable fashion. I am making rapid strides and I can now walk on my peg without crutches or sticks <u>for a short distance.</u>

I believe I will remain another month in Buxton and then be transferred to Roehampton, London (near Putney)[*Queen Mary's Hospital, well known for the provision of artificial limbs*] for the fitting of my artificial leg proper.

[...] I am glad Colonel Dubuc should have sent you a picture of the battalion but I am afraid I look rather a sorry sight in the picture: it was taken after the March offensive when I was a bit overworked.

Granville Special Hospital, Buxton
1 February, 1919

My dearest Frances,
[...] Your reference once again to your little friend who thinks that the English are barbarians compels me to say that she has fallen into the rather common error among some classes of believing that

Continued Convalescence, and Armistice — November 1918

Georges Vanier (second from left) with fellow amputees in spring 1919, probably in Roehampton where artificial limbs were fitted.

this war was really engineered and instigated by British commercial circles and that Canadians who came to fight were offering themselves a sacrifice on England's altar. She is quite wrong.

The most inspiring motive to sacrifice all — even life if necessary — sprang from the Hun brutality and the Hun atrocities in Belgium. During the last months of 1914, I could not read the harrowing account of Belgian sufferings without feeling a deep compassion and an active desire to right, so far as it was in my power, the heinous wrong done. I wish your little friend could have seen, as I saw in March 1918, the poor peasants of France fleeing with some small belongings — weary and half clothed — before the new barbarian onslaught.

To cite only one incident. While the battalion was marching during the night to take up a forward position to stop the German onrush, we met a girl of about fifteen leading an old horse harnessed to a still older cart which recalled the old hay carts of the province of Quebec. In the cart were a child of three or four, a few bundles of hay, a loaf of bread and some other eatables. I asked the girl where she was going and she answered "I do not know, Monsieur. This morning my father was killed by a shell. I was alone. I did not know that the Boche were advancing so I fled without knowing where I am going."

That was one of the moments when I did not care whether the English were barbarians or not but when I did care whether we could save the poor people of France from the horrors of every imaginable crime.

You may tell your little friend that the "English barbarians" for four long years have been sacrificing their finest manhood in the service of humanity in order to make the world inhabitable for her and her children and her children's children. Strange barbarians these!

Granville Special Hospital, Buxton
5 February, 1919

My dearest Mater,
[...] You need have no scruples about your advice to accept Mr. Roy's proposition. I have written to him setting the rather drastic conditions mentioned in one of my former letters and I do not believe he will accept these conditions. In any case, I am not <u>particularly</u> anxious to obtain the position because in spite of certain apparent advantages it has also certain marked disadvantages.

During the last month, I have gained weight appreciably and I hope to surprise you when I return.

[...] I hope the Governor will be pleased with my little present and I should be happy to hear from you exactly what impression my choice makes on him.

Granville Special Hospital, Buxton, Derbyshire
8 February, 1919

My dearest Frances,
Your delightful little letter dated 22nd January reached me last night. I observe that you sign "Frankie". Is this a nickname that you have been burdened with? Personally I prefer "itty Goo".

Continued Convalescence, and Armistice — November 1918

There is only one "terribils awfits" thing about Buxton — the cold. We have not central heating but instead fireplaces in each room which blaze as long as coal can be procured.

Recently a new orderly came on duty and Captain Cathcart (my room-mate) and myself decided that we must have a confidential talk with this important personage. We called him in and informed him that his two most important duties in the hospital were firstly to see that a fire was at all times blazing in Room 23 (ours) and secondly that the coal box in Room 23 must at all times be filled to overflowing. He was allowed to leave our August presence only after we had thoroughly impressed him with the dire calamity that would overtake him should he neglect these his most important duties.

The result has been miraculous. The rest of the hospital patients are allowed to freeze (more or less) but Room 23 sometimes presents the aspect of a Turkish bath.

So far so good. But the horror of the thing does not end here. Our room communicates with a second room in which two other officers whose eyes bulge when they see the coal being brought into Room 23 and whose hearts grow black with rage. We fear some awful tragedy of revenge: whenever I stoke the fire, Cathcart — to drown the noise — either attempts to sing or throws the furniture about and the sound of the shovelled coal does not reach the ears of the infuriated patients in Room 22.

The other night we heard a strange song from Room 22 and Cathcart swore it was the Scottish death-song (the patients in 22 are Scots). We waited in fear and trembling for the onslaught: finally I ventured forth and attempted to placate them with offerings of candied ginger and of "Cresca" figs. But the suspense is terrible: Cathcart and myself spend — alternately — sleepless nights watching the fire and the precious box of coal. Needless to say we keep a vigilant eye on the frenzied inhabitants of 22.

9 February, 1919

My dear George [*Pelletier*],
Your letter pleased me very much. I quite agree with you that

Roosevelt[2] [*former U.S. President Theodore Roosevelt*] was an outstanding figure not only in America but in the world. His imagination and earnestness will place him among the foremost few of this generation with a claim to at least relative immortality.

Granville Special Hospital, Buxton
21 February, 1919

My dearest Mater,
[...] I am very glad that you agree with me about my discharge: it would be unwise to accept it until I know definitely the extent of my final disability.

[...] You ask if the wound in my side is healed. Yes, ages ago. It was quite closed two weeks after I was wounded. At no time did the doctors think that the lung was affected but of course for the first week certainty in this matter was impossible.

My stay in Buxton has worked a great change in me and has put me on my feet again (unfortunate metaphor!). The authorities here are making me a new peg-leg with knee-joint as a convenience when I sit down. In this way I shall be able to sit at a dinner table without knocking the shins of the people sitting opposite.

Buxton is still enjoying winter weather — snow and ice with the accompanying sports. It makes one think of Canada. Every week or so we have a thaw when the streets become almost impassable.

I was sorry to hear of Sir Wilfrid Laurier's death: he had some very good press notices in England but most of the newspapers cannot forgive him for his attitude during the war. Without a doubt he will rank among the ten or twelve greatest Canadians. His loss to the country is a great one — we have too few public men with as high a regard for probity — private or public.

Granville Special Hospital, Buxton
23 February, 1919

My dearest Mater,
[...] It is likely that, by the middle of March, I shall be back in

London for my leg fitting at Roehampton. To while the time away, I intend to take up Italian.

The Canadian Officers' Club,
8 Chesterfield Gardens, W.I.
28 February, 1919

My dearest Mater,
I have come up to London for a few days. You will observe, by the heading, that I have had the good fortune to obtain — I shall not say a room, but a bed at this most comfortable of clubs in the heart of London. The club was formerly the residence of Lord Chesterfield who has consented to lend or let it for the use of Canadian officers.
[...] I am looking forward to spending the summer on Lake Memphramagog. I am sure that a few months there will make more difference in my convalescence than six months in England.

Granville Special Hospital, Buxton
11 March, 1919

My dearest Mater,
Yesterday your letter dated 22nd February reached me. I cannot understand how Dubuc found out in Ottawa that I had been offered a secretaryship unless Mr. Roy wrote to friends in Ottawa that I meant to accept. In any case, the matter is closed once and for all.
I told you, I believe, in my last letter that a new ruling has been passed with reference to those who require artificial limbs. The authorities wish to send us all back to Toronto for fitting but I, for one, do not wish to go. I am told that there is a waiting list at Toronto and that I would be kept in a queue for two or three months. In order to obtain my leg over here, I may be forced to say that I wish to be demobilized over here. When I have the leg, I can always say that I have changed my mind and that I prefer to return to Canada for discharge. So do not be surprised if you hear that I have asked for my discharge over here — you will know exactly what it means. I prefer

to warn you beforehand because rumours — usually absurd — spread quickly and from heaven knows what sources.

I expect to be in Buxton for quite three weeks yet then to go to The Perkins Bull Hospital for the fitting of my leg at Roehampton (ten minutes walk from Putney) and then — home.

Granville Special Hospital, Buxton
18 mars, 1919

Mon bien cher Papa,
I hope that Lieutenant Gélineau gave you the painting by Gagnon that I bought for you. I feel very guilty not to have replied sooner to your kind letters which brought me much comfort during a very difficult period.

I am specially grateful to you for having given me your blessing on New Year's Day. Even if I am so far away from my dear friends, I feel united with them in spirit.

I very much look forward to seeing you again and giving you a hug.

Maman has written that you are still bursting with energy: I fear that you will appear more young than I!

[...] The death of Sir Wilfrid [*Laurier*] has caused me great pain: he was a remarkable and very impressive figure. I don't believe we will ever have another French- Canadian Prime Minister. The British newspapers were rather reserved about it. They reproach him for his attitude towards conscription in Canada and for his opposition to certain war measures. They all agree on one thing however: that he was above all a great <u>Canadian</u>. They are quite right.

[...] I have acquired such an astonishingly good balance on one leg that I could perhaps become a professional acrobat!

In mid-March, Georges received the sad news that his old friend and mentor, Camille Martin, had died. But he was comforted by the words that Martin's daughter had written to his mother: "Tell Georges that his good old friend carried into his tomb the little seed of wheat and the roses he had sent him from France. I wanted him to keep them forever."

Granville Special Hospital, Buxton
28 March, 1919

My dearest Mater,
[...] The news of Mr. Martin's death depressed me more than I can say. He was one of those I looked forward to seeing with particular pleasure. I had the very deepest affection for him and great admiration for his remarkable power of intellect and of heart.

He was above all a large-hearted man. His love for France was almost a religion and it is to him I owe — to a large extent — my own love for and my pride in this most wonderful of nations. I wish from the bottom of my heart that he had lived for a few years yet: I should so like to have talked over all the adventures and experiences I have been fortunate enough to go through. We would have had so much matter for common thought. But the Almighty's designs are sometimes obscure and who dare say that they are not for the best? I feel keenly for dear Miss Martin who has been an angel of consolation and of devotion. I am cabling and writing my sympathy to her.

[...] To be quite frank my new peg leg with knee has not been a success. They do not seem to get it comfortable. At present it is in the workshops of the "arts and crafts": when it comes back it may possibly be induced to be a little more considerate.

I do not think that I would care for the blue room. You know how much I like a large airy room. I am quite satisfied with my old room filled with books and it will seem like returning to old friends when I see them all smiling down on me.

Granville Special Hospital, Buxton
9 April, 1919

My dearest Mater,
Trudeau [*Joseph, sister Eva's husband*] has been to see me and gave me the very much appreciated gift from you and from the Governor. You knew my taste in these matters and I shall be able to wear the cuff links even in uniform. Thank you very much indeed.

Not long ago I received a parcel — evidently long delayed in transit — of maple syrup and almonds which arrived in perfect condition. This parcel also contained cards from you and from the Governor which were very touching in their thoughtful remembrance of past days when we received the New Year's blessing around the paternal bed. I was moved more than I can say.

I have rather good news for you respecting my promotion and my leg. Things were not shaping satisfactorily and I saw visions of further delay and possible failure in putting through my majority and in obtaining my leg in England. I went direct to General Turner in London and I was most cordially received. In the matter of the promotion (where he has jurisdiction) he gave orders that my substantive majority be recognized at once. I expect to see the official announcement in a few days. In the matter of the artificial leg he took me in his car to see Sir Edward Kemp,[3] the overseas minister of militia and I was very well received and obtained permission to be fitted with a leg in England instead of going to Toronto and wasting several months there — possibly during the summer.

The 22nd Battalion is already in England and I received a letter from General Tremblay yesterday. The battalion reached England long before expected and it will be quite impossible for me to return with it. In a way, it is perhaps as well: the attendant excitement and exertion might not have an exactly soothing influence.

Perkins Bull Hospital
Putney Heath, London S.W. 15
16 April, 1919

My dearest Mater,
I am once again in my old English home. Here I received as warm a welcome as in June, 1916. Of course few of the patients and V.A.D.'s are the same but the same spirit of cordiality and of hospitality reigns.

At last I am well on to obtaining my real artificial leg — and I can assure you I am not worried. I ran into General Tremblay the other day and we revived past and pleasant memories. When he goes to Montreal he will visit — and I know that you will not forget that he has always been most kind to me and that he and I will ever remain the staunchest of friends.

I am enclosing a letter for my "album de guerre" [*war album*]. Its interest lies in the fact that I received it a few hours before the attack of the 28th August when the amiable Hun decided to send me on indefinite leave. You may read it if you like — the contents are quite innocuous.

Canadian Red Cross Hospital, London
24 April, 1919

My dearest Mater,
[...] On the 22nd April I was moved from Buxton to this hospital en route to the Perkins Bull Hospital where I will receive my artificial leg. I have told you I think that Roehampton is only a few minutes walk from Putney.

I appreciate your kind wishes for a happy birthday. I spent it in a quiet manner with Major Hudon, whom I met in London. As a matter of fact he is staying with me in this hospital.

It is quite out of the question for me to go back with the 22nd Battalion. I don't think I could stand incidental excitement and responsibilities — even were I fitted with a leg. Without a leg the matter is quite unthinkable.

Major Hudon revived old memories when he explained what trouble you had gone to in 1916 to have me recalled to Canada on leave. I may have appeared ungrateful at the time but subsequent events have justified — so I believe at least — my decision. I regret nothing that has taken place since then and my proudest boast will always be that I was able to give something of myself to France as a testimonial of my great love for her. The thoughts give one a satisfaction quite superior to all material gratifications.

My health is splendid — I am gaining weight and with the air and exercise of Magog I will be my old self again. You know how I long to get back to you all.

Perkins Bull Hospital, London
19 April, 1919

My dearest Mater,
I have splendid news for you today. In this morning's Times appeared my promotion to the rank of Major to date from the 10 August 1918. I shall forward the clipping to you in a few days.

Canadian Red Cross Hospital à Londres,
24 avril 1919

Mon bien cher papa,
Your letter of 8 April, which I received this morning, gave me much pleasure. Thank you for your kind thoughts and your good wishes on my birthday.

I share completely your pessimistic views regarding Europe and even the whole world. Wars are not over: they are only beginning. I do not foresee another war like the one we have just lived through but I do predict several social and revolutionary wars. There is no doubt that England right now is going through a domestic crisis which will have serious consequences.

I do not defend Russian Bolshevism — far from it. However I do realize it is the sort of violent reaction that inevitably follows an autocratic regime when the people are oppressed and <u>kept</u> in ignorance of their rights and responsibilities. The situation in Russia before the revolution was dreadful. The aristocracy gradually became more and more decadent. You only have to read "The Last of the Romanoffs" by Charles Rivet to appreciate the desperate situation of the Tzarist regime. Reading this historic book written by the Times correspondent in Petrograd instills in you such a strong repulsion that you remain deeply marked by it.

The Times this morning speaks of a "manifesto" from the French socialist group. The constitution and the laws of France could suffer considerable modifications. Even Canada will have its own internal crises — I already see elements of separatism between west and east. The next election will be a contest between those who support and those who oppose the tariff.

The creation of an independent party in Canada is absolutely necessary. As long as the politicians will be forced to blindly follow a party, people will be led by jokers and scoundrels. It takes considerable courage to be independent: it is much easier to accept the status quo.

I was deeply touched by your transcription of a passage from the newspaper containing the ideas of Sir Wilfrid [*Laurier*] on death and life after death.

Perkins Bull Hospital
2 May, 1919

My dearest Mater,
[...] I am very sorry that my departure for Canada has been so long delayed but I do believe that it is better to obtain my artificial leg in England. In the army everything — except in an attack — moves slowly. You see how long I had to wait before my temporary majority came through — and then only after seeing General Turner.

P.S. Tomorrow — monster parade of overseas troops in London. I mean to attend. The 22nd will take a prominent part.

Perkins Bull Hospital
11 mai 1919

Mon bien cher papa,
I received only this morning your cablegram on the occasion of my birthday. I am very touched by your thoughtfulness and am infinitely grateful.

The 22nd left yesterday, <u>I believe</u>. I would have liked to accompany them but that is one of the hazards of war that we must accept.

I met General Watson of Quebec who insists that I return to Canada with him. He leaves the 11 June but it will be impossible to arrange my departure for this date.

The military authorities are very slow in giving me my leg so I have ordered a leg outside of the army and I have been promised its delivery in about a week. That will allow me a few weeks to use it before my departure.

You know how anxious I am to see you all again. A few days after my arrival I would like to leave Montreal for Magog. What do you think?

Perkins Bull Hospital, London
13 May, 1919

My dearest Mater,
[...] The 22nd sailed for Canada a few days ago and I entrusted an enormous trunk to Major Archambault. It is filled with all sorts of things — souvenirs, old clothes, boots etc. I wish you would keep everything together until my return. Of course open the trunk if you wish; some of the contents may prove interesting. The torn, bloodstained tunic is the one I wore on the 28th August.

The boots (ankle) covered with mud you will recognize as the Dangerfield's. I was wounded in them: you will notice a great quantity of dirt adhering to them. Please do not clean the boots: I wish to keep the soil of France which clings to them and to sprinkle some of it over the grave of our dear Mr. Martin.

I feel sure of sailing with General Watson on the 11th June but I do not intend to remain more than a few days in Montreal after which I mean to go to Magog to recuperate. I need not tell you that after the shock of losing a leg and the consequent inaction I am not in good condition. I am organically as well as I ever was but I do not look well and I prefer not to give you a wrong impression which would prove disappointing when you saw me. When I left Canada, I weighed 170 lbs. In France during March 1918 I weighed 200 lbs but the German offensive kept us so busy and so worried that when I was hit, I only weighed about 175 or 180 lbs. Now I weigh 150 lbs which added to the weight of the lost leg (22 lbs) makes 172. So that I am no stouter than in 1914. However weight will come back with exercise.

Remember one thing: if I am not fat, I am happy at the thought that I had the courage to return to my boys in 1916 and that God gave me the strength of body and of mind to do my duty under fire. It is a tremendous consolation that will comfort me until my dying day.

Continued Convalescence, and Armistice — November 1918

Perkins Bull Hospital,
22 May, 1919

My dearest Mater,
[...] I am delighted that Dad should have met Colonel Clark Kennedy. He is a prince and a gentleman — quite one of the bravest men I have ever met. The night before the attack of the 28th August we spent the night together in a dirty abandoned German dugout. Clark Kennedy has always been an inspiration to all under him. He was our brigade Major for over a year and I do not believe a more efficient one was to be found in France.

I am glad Trudeau gave you good news of me: he probably told you I looked better than I really do. I repeat what I said in a former letter — I <u>do not</u> look well so expect to be disappointed in my appearance. However time will improve all that.

I am delighted that the oil painting and etching met with entire approval.

Perkins Bull Hospital
5 June, 1919

My dearest Mater,
This morning's mail brought me your two long and delightful letters. I am glad that General Tremblay, Captain Blais and Mr. Lafontaine called on you. I knew you would like them all. Tremblay is a prince, and he has been wonderful to me at all times. Very often he has been anxious to spare me fatigue and danger and on two or three occasions wanted to leave me out of shows in which he was taking part. I felt that as long as I followed him, no harm would come to me. I have been in tighter corners than the one in which I was hit but always I felt certain that his star would bring us through.

I am looking forward to my return to Canada with General Watson on the 11th June.

Vanier's return to Canada was postponed once again. This was perhaps fortuitous since, on July 14, he was able to attend a ceremony at Buckingham Palace to be invested by King George V with the Bar to his Military Cross and his Distinguished Service Order. The same day, he wrote to his mother about the occasion.

Today I had the honour of receiving from the hands of the King the Cross of the Distinguished Service Order and the Bar to the Military Cross. The King was very considerate to me, wishing me not to stand when speaking to him and questioning me at length about the condition of my stump and the comfort of my artificial leg. He looked extremely well and I should say that, with age, his appearance improves. He has a quiet, direct manner which pleases by its manliness. He reminds one of the soldier or sailor rather than of the courtier.

Four days later, on July 18, Major Georges Vanier, DSO, MC, boarded the S.S. Minerva *for his journey home to Canada.*

EPILOGUE

"Today ... we think of those who chose the road of combat, of danger and suffering and, in too many cases, of death — the road which leads a nation to greatness. We think of those who died on the field of honour and the words of Lacordaire spring to mind: 'Oh Lord, will you not bestow a special grace upon those brave souls who arrive before You in the folds of their country's flag.'"
> Georges Vanier speaking at the 50th anniversary of the Royal 22nd Regiment, 26 September, 1964.

Following the Armistice of November 1918, representatives of the victorious Allied and Associated powers (the United States, France, Britain and Italy) met outside Paris in January 1919 to hammer out what was to become known as the Treaty of Versailles. Under its terms, the treaty was instrumental in the creation of the League of Nations, an international body designed to promote peace. In addition, it obliged Germany to return Alsace-Lorraine to France and to cede much of its eastern provinces, including West Prussia to Poland; it placed strict limits upon the size of the German armed forces and, most contentiously, it obliged Germany to accept the burden of reparations for war damage. It took barely twenty years for Adolf Hitler to come to power and nullify those parts of the treaty that penalized Germany, thus paving the way for another bloody conflict that would engulf the world.

Georges Vanier returned to Canada in July 1919. He had decided against the job with the Canadian commission in Paris and contemplated returning to his old Montreal law firm. But the more he deliberated, the clearer it became to him that his heart still lay with the Regiment. He travelled to Ottawa to consult Sir Arthur Currie, Commanding Officer of the Canadian Corps during the last year of the war and now Inspector-General of the Armed Forces. When Vanier asked about his prospects for re-joining the army, Currie laughed uproariously at his request. "But Vanier, you've only got one leg," he said. "I know," Georges replied. "But don't you want officers with *brains* as well as legs?"

Vanier was not discouraged by Currie's misgivings. Despite his disability, he returned to the Van Doos in 1920 as second-in-command to his old friend, Henri Chassé. Such was the reputation of the 22nd that an Order-in-Council of 1920 made the Regiment part of the regular Canadian army. Soon after, they moved into new quarters in Quebec City's historic Citadel. "A French-Canadian regiment in the garrison of the Citadel of Quebec!" exclaimed an editorial in a local English-language paper. "...The ghosts of Champlain, Frontenac, Montcalm and de Salaberry ought to shake with joy in their graves when they see their descendants taking possession of the Citadel."

RETURN TO REGIMENT

Georges Vanier remained with the regiment until 1922 when he was asked to serve as aide-de-camp to Governor-General Lord Byng of Vimy who, as Sir Julian Byng, had led the Canadian troops to victory at Vimy Ridge in April 1917. This marked the beginning of a deep friendship that was to continue until Byng's death in 1935. Three years later, Vanier returned to the regiment to take command of what had become, by decree of King George V, the Royal 22nd "in recognition of services rendered during 1914–18." In 1951, he was to become Colonel-in-Chief, succeeding his old friend "Tommy" Tremblay. Tremblay spoke of the new Colonel-in-Chief in glowing terms, calling him a "gentleman soldier" and noting that "in the regiment, he was the best possible comrade, always ready to help others, even under the most difficult circumstances."

Vanier was back in Montreal in 1919 when his friend Tremblay introduced him to a beautiful young woman. She was Pauline Archer, the daughter of a Montreal judge, and she was smitten immediately with the dashing war hero. Soon after their meeting, Pauline told Georges she was planning a visit to Europe. He was delighted with the news and immediately thrust in her arms a bundle of his carefully annotated World War I maps so she could visit the battlefields he had fought on and even retrace his footsteps. After an eight-month courtship, he asked for her hand in marriage. She was expecting a ring but instead, he offered her a small silver-topped bottle containing a lump of earth he had saved from the boot of his wounded leg. She kept it all of her life.

The wedding of Georges Vanier to Pauline Archer on September 19, 1921. The couple left the Montreal Basilica under an archway of swords held by Vanier's fellow officers.

The couple were married on September 29, 1921 in Montreal's Notre Dame Basilica. The newlyweds left the Basilica that day under an arch of swords held by the officers of the 22nd Battalion — all of whom had served with Vanier on the battlefields of Europe.

The Vanier marriage spanned more than four decades, produced five children and was to carry the pair to many world capitals. In 1928, they travelled to Geneva where Vanier, now promoted to Lieutenant-Colonel, served as Canada's military representative in the Disarmament Commission at the League of Nations. Three years later, he was appointed Secretary to the Canadian High Commission in London — essentially an understudy to High Commissioner Howard Ferguson. Vincent Massey — who in February 1952 would be named the first Canadian-born governor-general — took over as high commissioner two years later and Lester Pearson — a future prime minister and Nobel Peace Prize winner — became political secretary.

Georges Vanier (seated left) became secretary to the Canadian High Commission in London in 1931. Vincent Massey (seated right), a future governor-general, took over as high commissioner two years later while Lester Pearson (standing left), a future prime minister and Nobel Prize winner, became political secretary.

Epilogue

It was while Vanier was at the Canadian High Commission in London that the Canadian Government inaugurated the Canadian National Memorial at Vimy. The monument was unveiled on July 26, 1936 by King Edward VIII — it was Edward's only official visit outside the UK and came just months before his abdication. Georges not only made all the arrangements from the London side for the ceremony but he was present at the unveiling itself, joining more than 100,000 spectators including six thousand Canadians who had sailed to France for the occasion.

In 1938, Vanier was still at the High Commission working long tiring days as rumours of another war in Europe began to surface. That same year, a triple tragedy struck his family. On September 7, his mother — "my dearest Mater" — died in Montreal less than a year after she and her husband celebrated their golden anniversary. In a second and more unexpected blow, Georges' father died of a sudden heart attack two weeks later on September 21. It was Georges who wrote a brief obituary for *The Times* of London that read, in part: "They had loved and helped one another for more than fifty years and could not live apart." Then on December 8, 1938, after a year-long battle with cancer, Georges' brother Anthony died, aged only 37.

Philias and Margaret Vanier on the occasion of their golden wedding anniversary in 1937. Margaret died less than a year later and her husband soon after.

Return to France

On December 30, 1938, while Georges was still reeling from his family losses, Prime Minister Mackenzie King offered him the position of Minister and Head of Mission at the Canadian Legation in Paris. This would be his first posting as a senior diplomat and he could not have been happier that it was to his beloved France. He took up his duties on January 25, 1939. But his term of office was to be short-lived: the situation in Europe was worsening and Europe was on the brink of another war. When the German army finally invaded France on May 9, 1940, Vanier decided to evacuate his wife, her mother and the children to England. The invasion intensified with the Germans inching closer to Paris, and by June 10, Vanier reluctantly closed the Legation and he too fled to London.

After the Fall of France in the summer of 1940, Vanier returned to Canada to work as a member of the Joint North American Board of Defence. He then accepted an army post as General commanding the military district of Quebec and, at the end of 1942, returned to London as Minister to the Allied Governments in exile, including de Gaulle's French National Committee. A year later, he travelled to Algiers to assume the post of Minister to the French provisional government.

The humbling of France was to be heart-wrenching for Vanier and no one was more overjoyed than he with the news of the liberation of Paris in August 1944. Understandably, he was "moved beyond words" when the Canadian Mission in Paris was elevated to an Embassy and he was named Canada's first Ambassador to France in 1944. He returned to Paris on September 8, less than two weeks after the liberation, and served with distinction for the next ten years.

Vanier was still in Paris when he received news of the death of "my dear and old friend" "Tommy" Tremblay on March 28, 1951. He travelled to Montreal for Tremblay's funeral and spoke movingly of his old comrade-in-arms. "Tremblay embodied the true soul of the 22nd. His place in the history of our people is assured. I might even venture to say that he is the greatest French-Canadian soldier since de Salaberry[1].... (Tremblay) is living proof that the French-Canadians have not lost the admirable military qualities of their ancestors."

Epilogue

Crowning Achievement

The Vaniers returned to Canada in 1953 and moved into a small flat in Montreal where Georges, now in his late sixties, retired into relative obscurity. But that obscurity ended unexpectedly on August 1, 1959, when Prime Minister Diefenbaker asked him to accept the role of Governor-General of Canada. He was sworn into office on September 14, 1959, becoming the first French-Canadian to assume the post and the second Canadian (after Vincent Massey). During his almost eight years in office, he was to become one of the most deeply respected and beloved statesmen in the history of the country.

Georges Vanier was sworn in as Governor-General on September 14, 1959, becoming the first French-Canadian to assume the post.

As Vanier's term was drawing to a close, Prime Minister Pearson asked him to remain in office for an additional year, a period that would include extensive obligations marking Canada's Centennial year. He was, however, suffering from a weakened heart so his doctors felt it unwise to accept.

Even though Vanier's precarious health was well-known, his sudden death from heart failure on March 5, 1967, stunned the country and Canadians across the land felt a deep personal loss. More than fifteen thousand messages of sympathy reached Government House and over thirty thousand visitors passed by his flag-draped casket in Ottawa's Senate Chamber to pay their last respects.

A full state funeral took place in the capital's Notre Dame Basilica, after which Pauline Vanier and her family accompanied the coffin by train to Quebec City. Following another commemorative service in Quebec's Cathedral of Notre Dame, Georges Vanier's body was laid to rest under a simple marble slab in the Royal 22nd's memorial crypt at the Citadel.

Pauline Vanier moved to Montreal, but five years later she left Canada to join her son Jean at l'Arche, a community of men and women with handicaps that Jean Vanier had founded at Trosly, north of Paris. She remained there until her own death in 1991 when her body was returned to Quebec City and she was buried next to her husband.

The day after Georges Vanier's death, Prime Minister Lester Pearson stood before the House of Commons to pay tribute to his long-time friend: "He answered the call to arms," said Pearson "... He served for three years in France as a gallant officer of a gallant regiment whose traditions he helped to create and maintain. The Distinguished Service Order, the Military Cross and Bar and the Legion of Honour attest to his courage. His wounds attest to his sacrifices."

Soldier to the End

Georges Vanier held many high offices during his life, but it was the military that remained closest to his heart. During his years of public life, he seized every opportunity to salute his fellow soldiers. "Never have I been so proud of my compatriots than on the battlefield," he wrote several years later. "Having lived with them in the trenches for three years, I proclaim their valour." In a television interview, he paid tribute to them again:

> I saw them at Vimy, at Lens, at Méharicourt and Chérisy and at so many other places. My most poignant memory of them is at Passchendaele when they had to go forward in mud sometimes up to their knees, with dead bodies floating about in enormous shell holes.... Slowly they advanced and over and over again, slipped in the mud, fell, recovered themselves until finally they reached the firing line where duty called them.

Epilogue

Vanier delivered his last speech as Colonel of the Regiment at their fiftieth anniversary on September 26, 1964. He spoke of the qualities that constitute courageous soldiers:

> They ... are the same ones needed to guarantee the development of our country — discipline, tenacity, and moral strength. These are the qualities we need if we are to realize the vast potential of our natural and human resources.
>
> Today, half a century afterwards, we think of those who chose the road of combat, of danger and suffering, and, in too many cases, of death — the road which leads a nation to greatness. We think of those who died on the field of honour, and the words of Lacordaire spring to mind: "Oh Lord, will you not bestow a special grace upon those brave souls who arrive before You in the folds of their country's flag."

On July 1, 1998, thirty years after Georges Vanier's death, a panel of Canadians — including historians and publishers, academics and artists — was commissioned by *Maclean's* magazine to list one hundred individuals they considered to be the most significant in the history of Canada, those who made a real difference and who could be perceived as "heroes." Georges Vanier topped the list.

> A man of courage and sacrifice, in war and peace, he exemplified the best in his countrymen.... Duty, obligation and service — Vanier epitomized all these noble ideals. And as Governor-General, he represented in his person all those who went overseas to risk their lives for abstract concepts like democracy and freedom — and, yes, duty, obligation and service to a higher ideal than self. Vanier was Canada's moral compass.... an unquestioned man of probity and honour.
>
> He is the leading Hero — the most important Canadian in history.

Georges Vanier is buried beside his wife under a marble slab in the Royal 22nd's memorial crypt at the Citadel.

CHRONOLOGY

23 April 1888	Birth of Georges Philias Vanier in Montreal, Quebec.
1897-1906	Attends Loyola College, an English secondary school in Montreal.
1906-1911	Studies law at the Montreal campus of Laval University.
February 1912	Admitted to the Bar of Quebec.
1912	Joins the Montreal law firm of Dessaules and Garneau.

1914

28 June	Assassination of Austrian Archduke Franz Ferdinand.
4 August	Britain joins the war.
Early October	The first Canadian troops form the Canadian Expeditionary Force and leave for Europe.
15 October	French-Canadians gather in Montreal's Parc Sohmer to support a demand for a French-Canadian unit. By evening's end, the 22nd (French-Canadian) Battalion is born. Georges Vanier is one of its first recruits with the rank of Lieutenant.
22 October	Training begins in Montreal and in St. Jean, Quebec.

1915

12 March	Battalion leaves for Amherst, Nova Scotia to continue training.
20 May	Battalion leaves Halifax for Europe on board the *R.M.T. Saxonia*.
30 May	Battalion reaches East Sandling camp in England.
15 September	Battalion sails for France, arriving in Boulogne and Le Havre.
20 September	Battalion's first foray into the trenches near Vierstraat in Flanders (Belgium).

1916

2-3 January	Vanier leads a successful midnight raid to capture an enemy gun position. He is awarded the Military Cross (MC) for his efforts.
12 January	Vanier is promoted to the rank of Captain.
23 January	Lieutenant-Colonel T.L. Tremblay becomes commander of the battalion.
3 June	The battalion moves into the trenches at Mont Sorrel.
9 June	Vanier is knocked out by an exploding shell during the Battle of Mont Sorrel. Evacuated to rest hospital at Mont des Cats.
1 July	Beginning of the Battle of the Somme, which continues until November.
15 September	The Battle of Flers-Courcelette. The first major engagement of the Van Doos results in the successful capture of Courcelette.
5 October	Vanier returns to the front, based near brigade headquarters at Bully-Grenay.
3 November	Vanier appointed Adjutant.

1917

9 April	Capture of Vimy Ridge.
15 May	Vanier awarded Cross of the Legion of Honour.
15 August	Capture of Hill 70 at Lens.
26 October	Assault on Passchendaele.

1918

8–10 August	Battle of Amiens.
28 August	Battle of Arras. Vanier is seriously wounded at Chérisy and evacuated to the British Red Cross Hospital in Boulogne. Amputation of his left leg.
26 September	Vanier is moved to the 3rd General Hospital in Wandsworth, London.
4 November	Vanier is moved to the I.O.D.E. Hospital in London.
11 November	Armistice is declared.
5 December	The battalion crosses the Belgium/German frontier and travels to Bonn.

1919

16 May	The battalion returns to Canada on board the S.S. *Olympic*.
19 May	Demobilisation of the 22nd Battalion in Montreal.
28 June	Signing of the Treaty of Versailles.
14 July	Vanier is invested by King George V with a Bar to his Military Cross and the Distinguished Service Order (DSO).
18 July	Vanier sails for Canada aboard the S.S. *Minerva*.

Chronology

1920
1 April — Order in council passed to make the 22nd Regiment part of the permanent force of Canada.

1921
18 May — Marshal Foch becomes the first colonel of the regiment.
1 June — King George V accord the 22nd Regiment the use of the title "Royal."
29 September — Marriage to Pauline Archer.

1922
Appointed aide-de-camp to Governor-General Byng

1925
Vanier returns to Quebec to take over command of the Royal 22nd.

1928
Vanier, now Lieutenant-Colonel, becomes Canada's military representative in the Disarmament Commission at the League of Nations in Geneva.

1931
Appointed Secretary at the Canadian High Commission in London.

1944
November — Prime Minister Mackenzie King names Major-General G.P. Vanier Canadian Ambassador to Paris.

1951
Vanier succeeds Tremblay as Honorary Colonel of the Royal 22nd.

1959
August — Prime Minister Diefenbaker names Vanier Governor-General of Canada.

1967
March 6 — Death of Georges Vanier.

ENDNOTES

Prologue

1. William Makepeace Thackeray (1811–1863): A British novelist who commented on nineteenth-century social trends. He is well known for his long association with the British magazine *Punch* and for his first major novel *Vanity Fair*.

2. Father Pierre Gaume (1869–1951): A French Jesuit priest who taught at Loyola College in Montreal from 1898 to 1903. In 1914, he returned to France and from there kept in close touch with Georges Vanier during the war years. It was he who instilled in Vanier a love of Shakespeare and the English Victorian novelists that remained with him throughout his life.

3. Margaret Maloney Vanier (19 June 1865–7 September 1938) was the eldest daughter of John Maloney who came from Cork, Ireland.

4. Philias Vanier (26 July 1862–21 September 1938): Born in Montreal to an old Quebec family who were descendants of Guillaume Vanier, a citizen of Honfleur, France. Guillaume had emigrated to Canada towards the end of the seventeenth century arriving, apparently, with little more than his wife, three children and a gun. Philias brought up his family in Montreal where they lived modestly over an *épicerie taverne* at the corner of rue St. Jacques and rue de la Seigneurie. It was here that Georges, the eldest of their five children, was born on April 23, 1888. Philias later became a prominent real estate agent and moved the family to a house in downtown Montreal (810 Dorchester Boulevard),

now destroyed. He died on September 21, 1938.

One of Phileas's children died in infancy. His other children were: Georges who married Pauline Archer on September 29, 1921 and had five children: Thérèse, George (Father Benedict), Jean, Bernard and Michael. Eva who married Joseph Trudeau on January 17, 1916. They had six children. John, a Montreal businessman, who married Jeanne in September 1916 and later Cécile, with whom he had five children. Anthony, also a businessman, who married Jeanne and had three children. Frances, who married William Shepherd in June 1934. They had one son, Gyde.

5. Duke of Connaught and Strathearn (1850–1942): Governor-General of Canada from 1911–1916. As Prince Arthur he was Queen Victoria's youngest and favourite son and the uncle of King George V. His son served in the British Expeditionary Force in France from 1914–1916 and in the Canadian Corps from 1917–1918. His daughter, Princess Patricia, lent her name and considerable assistance to raising the Princess Patricia's Canadian Light Infantry — a regiment known as the Princess Pat's, or the PPCLI — which served gallantly during World War I.

Chapter 1: The Van Doos Sail for Europe — May 1915

1. David Lloyd George (1863–1945): Britain's Chancellor of the Exchequer from 1908–15 under Prime Minister Henry Asquith. He replaced Asquith as prime minister in 1916, formed a strong war cabinet and played a leading role in shaping the Treaty of Versailles. Vanier is perhaps referring to Lloyd George's speech of September 19, 1914 in which he states that "For most generations sacrifice comes in drab and [in] weariness of spirit." This same speech refers to "the great peaks we had forgotten, of honour, duty, patriotism, and clad in glittering white, the great pinnacle of sacrifice."

2. Father (Captain) Constant Doyon (1875–1927): A Dominican priest from Montreal who served for three years as chaplain of the 22nd Battalion.

3. Andrew Hamilton Gault (1882–1958): A Montreal millionaire who, in 1914, donated $100,000 to raise and equip the Princess Patricia's Canadian Light Infantry, better known as the Princess Pat's. Gault fought in the regiment overseas until he was wounded in the Battle of Sanctuary Wood in June 1916. After the war, he lived in England, serving on the staff of the Canadian forces. He returned to Canada in 1945 and served as Honorary Colonel of the Princess Pat's until his

death in 1958. There is a statue of Gault facing the War Memorial in Confederation Square, Ottawa.

4. Lady Grace Drummond: This tall, formidable woman, originally from Montreal, was the widow of Sir George Drummond, former president of the Bank of Montreal and member of the Canadian Senate. During the war years, Lady Grace was assistant commissioner and head of the Information Bureau of the Canadian Red Cross Society in London and was instrumental in turning it into a highly efficient organization. Her son, Guy Drummond, died from bullet wounds on April 22, 1915 in the second battle of Ypres.

5. Brigadier-General Sir David Watson: (b. 1869 in Quebec City) Former publisher of the Quebec *Daily Chronicle*, he commanded the 2nd Battalion of the 1st Canadian Division, which left Canada in September 1914, and the 5th Brigade until April 1916 when he was promoted to command the Fourth Canadian Division. He was knighted in January 1918.

6. Major-General Sir Richard E.W. Turner, V.C. (b. 1871 in Quebec City): A Quebec City merchant who became a popular hero in Canada after winning the Victoria Cross in South Africa. In World War I, he led the 2nd Canadian Division from August 1915 to November 1916 before becoming Chief of the General Staff.

7. Magnificat: Hymn of the Virgin Mary as it appears in the Gospel according to St. Luke. It begins "My soul doth magnify the Lord."

8. Talbot Papineau (1883–1917): A Montreal lawyer and great-grandson of Louis-Joseph Papineau, leader of the *patriote* rebels of 1837. Talbot joined the Princess Pat's as a Lieutenant, was promoted to Captain and then Major, and served on the front lines with distinction. On October 30, 1917, during the battle of Passchendaele, Papineau was struck in the stomach by a shell and died from his wounds. A gifted orator and writer and a passionate pan-Canadian nationalist, he was well known for his open letter of July 31, 1916, replying to his cousin Henri Bourassa, editor of *Le Devoir* and a vigorous Quebec nationalist who opposed Quebec's participation in WWI. The figure of Talbot Papineau is vividly portrayed in Sandra Gwyn's book *Tapestry of War*.

9. Sir Robert Borden (1854–1937): Leader of the Liberal-Conservative Party from 1901–20, he became Canadian Prime Minister in 1911 and received a knighthood from the King in June 1914. As war approached, he assured the British government that "the Canadian people will be

united in a common resolve to put forth every effort and to make every sacrifice necessary" to defend the empire. He offered notable leadership during the war years and as leader of the Canadian delegation at the Paris Peace Conference in 1919, he was primarily responsible for international recognition of the autonomous status of the dominions. Borden retired as Prime Minister in 1920

10. The Hon. Sir Sam Hughes (1858–1921): A newspaper publisher from Lindsay, Ontario, Hughes served as Minister of Militia in Sir Robert Borden's government from 1911–16. Although hailed by some as a genius of the war effort, he was an outspoken and controversial figure. Eventually, scandals and incompetence forced Borden to fire him on November 9, 1916.

11. Lord Kitchener (1850–1916): A British war hero who had been conqueror of the Sudan (1898) and South Africa (1900 and 1902), commander-in-chief in India and ruler of Egypt. When World War I broke out, he was recruited as Britain's Secretary of State for War. He startled his colleagues at his first Cabinet meeting by predicting (accurately) that the war would last for three or four years and that Great Britain would need to raise an army of several million men. It was he who successfully carried out the vast expansion of the British Army. On June 5, 1916, Kitchener drowned on the way to a high-level meeting in Russia when the *Hampshire*, the cruiser he was on, was sunk by a German mine off the Orkneys, north of Scotland. He was succeeded by Lloyd George who became Prime Minister later in the year.

12. The Dardanelles: A narrow strait separating European and Asiatic Turkey and one of the key shipping lanes in the world. When Turkey entered the war on the side of Germany, the British launched the Gallipoli campaign, which lasted from April 1915 to June 1916 and was intended to force a way through the Dardanelles to the Black Sea. The campaign ended in total failure with huge loss of life, particularly among British and Australian troops.

13. Rt. Hon. Andrew Bonar Law (1858–1923): Canadian-born leader of the Conservative opposition in the British House of Commons from 1911 to 1915 and Secretary of State for the Colonies from May 1915. Thereafter he served in coalition governments until he became Prime Minister in August 1922. His term lasted for only 209 days before he was forced to retire due to poor health and died in October 1923. He lost two sons in the 1914–18 war. A surviving son, Dick Law, became Minister of Education in Churchill's government, and was made Lord Coleraine.

Endnotes

14. Herbert Henry Asquith (1852–1928): British Prime Minster from 1908 to 1916. Dissatisfaction with his leadership during World War I led to his resignation and he was replaced by Lloyd George. He too lost a son, Raymond, who was killed in September 1916 during the Battle of the Somme.

15. Arthur James Balfour (1848–1930): A British Prime Minister from 1902 to 1905. He was foreign secretary under Lloyd George during World War I (1916–1919), and drafted the Balfour Declaration in 1917 pledging British support for a Jewish national home in Palestine.

16. Major-General Thomas Louis Tremblay (1887–1951): A graduate of Royal Military College in Kingston, "Tommy" Tremblay joined the Van Doos when it was formed in 1914. He became regimental commander in January 1916 and a few months later was assigned to lead the battalion in the Battle of Courcelette and Vimy Ridge. In 1917, he was promoted to command the Fifth Canadian Infantry Brigade. After the war, Tremblay became Colonel of the Royal 22nd in 1931. He died on March 28, 1951.

17. Father Martin Fox, s.j. (1859–1915): A French-born Jesuit priest who was one of Vanier's teachers at Loyola College. After his death in 1915, Vanier described him as a "saintly man.... I have seldom seen such a self-sacrificing man as he...."

18. Mayor Douglas: a former member of parliament and Mayor of Amherst, Nova Scotia, during the period in early 1915 when the Van Doos were training there.

19. Honorable Edgar Rhodes: Speaker in the House of Commons.

20. Judge Honoré Gervais: (1864–1915): Well-known Montreal judge and professor of International Law and Civil Procedure.

21. The *Hesperian*: A British passenger liner sunk by a German U-2 submarine on September 4, 1915. Thirty-two passengers drowned. The submarine was carrying the corpse, only recently recovered from the sea, of a traveller on one of the earlier victims of a German torpedo, the *Lusitania*.

Chapter 2: "To Be at last in France" — September 1915

1. Sir William Maxwell Aitken (1879–1964): Born and brought up in Canada, he moved to England in 1910, won a seat for the

Conservatives and was knighted in 1911 and ennobled in 1917 as Lord Beaverbrook. During the early part of World War I, he acted as official Canadian "Eyewitness," or war correspondent, and Canadian Government representative to the Canadian Expeditionary Force. He provided the chief source of published information about the activities of Canadian soldiers and published his first book, *Canada in Flanders*, which went into four printings. Shortly before gaining the title of Lord Beaverbrook, he acquired full ownership of London's *Daily Express*. Early in 1918, he was appointed Britain's Minister of Information. Some consider his greatest claim to fame to be his performance as Minister of Aircraft Production from 1940 to 1941, during the Battle of Britain.

2. "O Canadiens rallions-nous": A rough translation follows:
   Canadians let us rally together
   And by the old flag,
   Symbol of hope
   In olden days, France on our borders
   Sowed its seed of immortality.

3. Lieutenant-General Sir Edwin Alderson (1859–1927): Commander of the Canadian Army Corps from September 1914 to May 1916. He quarreled bitterly with Sam Hughes over the notorious Ross Rifle and was soon after unceremoniously fired from his position. He was replaced by General Sir Julian Byng.

4. General Joseph Joffre (1852–1931): Commander-in-chief of the French army, "Papa" Joffre deserves partial credit for the victory of the Marne in 1914. After the Germans nearly captured Verdun in 1916, Joffre was replaced by General Robert Nivelle.

5. Battle of Loos: A British offensive which took place on the Western front on September 25, 1915 with disappointing results for the Allies.

6. Champagne Drive: The British and French promise — to launch an offensive on the Western front to remove pressure from the Russians in the East — was made good on September 25, 1915. There were two separate attacks, one by the French in the region of Champagne and the other by the British at Loos.

7. The question of the Balkans: In the fall of 1915, Bulgaria joined the war and, with the Austrians and Germans, launched a major offensive against Serbia. By November 23, through the most bitter winter conditions, they had pushed the Serbians right back to a

Endnotes

corner of Kosovo from where they and thousands of refugees finally retreated southwards.

Chapter 3: "Oh, the mud of Flanders" — October 1915

1. "...is the censor looking?": Although officers letters were normally not subject to censorship, Vanier occasionally took the precaution of withholding place names by leaving a blank. Here he is referring to the Hospice of St. Antoine, a Flemish convent in Locre known for its lace-making. In fact, several of Vanier's letters had been opened and the envelopes sealed with a tab and bold black writing "Opened By Censors."

2. *The Imitation of Christ* was written by Thomas à Kempis, a German monk. (1379–1471). He lived most of his life in the Netherlands where he became an Augustinian priest. This book, which is ascribed to him, gives his thoughts on leading a more spiritual life.

3. Joseph Trudeau: The husband of Georges Vanier's sister Eva was a Montreal businessman with the firm Genin, Trudeau and Co. They married on January 17, 1916 and had six children.

Chapter 5: The Big Push — February 1916

1. Alfred Thomas Shaughnessy: Fred Shaughnessy's father, Thomas George Shaughnessy, was a champion of the Canadian Pacific Railway and its president from 1899 to 1918. He was made a baron in 1916 (giving him the title of "Lord" not, as Vanier states, a baronet, which uses the title of "Sir"). Fred Shaughnessy was company commander with the 60th Battalion when he was killed by a shrapnel bullet on March 31, 1916.

Chapter 6: Trench Warfare Intensifies — April 1916

1. Thirteen Tuesdays: A prescribed set of prayers offered each Tuesday for thirteen weeks in devotion to St. Anthony of Padua.

2. Martin's victory: Martin was elected Mayor of Montreal in 1916.

3. Rebellion in Dublin: The failure of the British government to implement home rule for Ireland, complicated by the fear in Protestant Ulster of Catholic domination, led to the Easter Rebellion (sometimes called the Easter Rising) of 1916. The militant and Catholic Sinn Fein emerged as the dominant nationalist group,

declaring themselves the Dil Eireann (Irish Assembly) and, in 1918, proclaimed an Irish republic.

4. General Sir Julian Byng (1862–1935): A British aristocrat and cavalry officer, Byng was appointed Commander of the Canadian Corps in June 1916 and led the Canadians to victory at Vimy Ridge in April 1917. He was later promoted to command the British 3rd Army. Lord Byng of Vimy became Governor-General of Canada in 1921. In the early days of his post, Byng invited Georges Vanier to join his staff as his aide-de-camp, marking the beginning of a long and close friendship. Lord and Lady Byng would later become godparents to the Vaniers first son Georges (now Father Benedict serving with the Benedictine Order in Oka, Quebec). Towards the end of his term, in 1926, Byng refused Prime Minister Mackenzie King's request for a dissolution of Parliament after the Liberals lost a vote in the House. This act precipitated a constitutional crisis and Byng left Canada under a cloud. He returned to Britain and served as Chief Commissioner of the London Metropolitan Police until his death in 1935.

Chapter 7: Convalescence in Britain — June 1916

1. Canon Frederick George Scott (1861–1944): An Anglican priest who was senior army chaplain of the Canadian 1st Division and a published war poet. His book *The Great War As I Saw It* was widely read when it was published in 1934. Scott's son, Francis (Frank) R. Scott of Montreal, also became a notable poet, as well as a civil rights lawyer, a professor of constitutional law and a founding member of the socialist movement in Canada. Another son, Henry Scott of the 87th Grenadier Guards of Montreal, was killed at Regina Trench on October 21, 1916.

2. Sir Wilfrid Laurier (1841–1919): Lawyer, journalist and politician, he served as Canada's seventh prime minister from 1896 to 1911, and was the first French-Canadian to serve in the post. Laurier vigorously supported Canadian participation in WWI and was an advocate of voluntary enrollment. When he was serving as Leader of the Opposition, he was a strong opponent of conscription and refused to form a coalition with Borden's Unionist Party, which won the election in December 1917.

3. Sir Rodolph Lemieux (1866–1937) Member of Parliament for Gaspé and later Postmaster General until his appointment to the Senate in 1930.

4. Philip Gibbs (1877–1962): British journalist whose "Eyewitness" reports from the front were legendary.

Endnotes

Chapter 8: Return to the Battlefield — October 1916

1. Joseph Chabelle, in his book *Histoire du 22e Bataillon*, published in 1952 by Les éditions Chantecler Ltée.

Chapter 9: The Campaign Heats Up — January 1918

1. General Sir Arthur William Currie (1875–1933): A former real estate agent from Victoria B.C. Was appointed Commander of the 2nd Canadian Infantry Brigade on September 29, 1914 and Commander of the 1st Canadian Division on September 13, 1915. On June 9, 1917, Currie was promoted to Commanding Officer of the Canadian Corps, becoming the first Canadian to do so. He is best known for his planning and leadership during the Last One Hundred Days (from August 8 until November 11, 1918) considered by some to be the most successful of all Allied offensives during the war. Following his wartime service, Currie returned to Canada and in August 1920 became Principal and Vice-Chancellor of McGill University, where he remained until his death in 1933.

2. The Legion of Honour: An award instituted by Napoleon I in 1802 as a way of rewarding distinguished military and civil service. The award is the most important order given by the French nation.

3. *London Gazette*: Still exists as an official newspaper. During wartime, it carried reports of war casualties and citations for bravery.

4. Georges Clemenceau (1841–1929): Twice Premier of France from 1906 to 1909 and from 1917 to 1920. As a journalist, he passionately defended Alfred Dreyfus (see below) in the Dreyfus Affair. His coalition cabinet in World War I reinvigorated French morale and facilitated the Allied victory.

5. Alfred Dreyfus (1859–1935): French army officer whose trial for treason began a twelve-year controversy, known as the Dreyfus Affair, that galvanised French political, social and intellectual life in the 1890s. After being sentenced to life-imprisonment in 1894, he was finally exonerated in 1906 by the supreme court of appeals.

6. Joseph Caillaux (1893–1944): French Finance Minister who resigned in 1914 after his wife shot and killed Gaston Calmette, editor of *Le Figaro*, who had threatened a public attack on Caillaux's private life.

7. Jean Désy: An old friend from Montreal who was attached to the

Canadian commission in Paris. He later became minister of the commission. Georges Vanier would follow in his footsteps when, in November 1944, he was appointed Canada's Ambassador to the Canadian Embassy, a post he held until 1953.

8. Canadian election result: Although this important election took place on December 17, 1917, the final results were not known until February 25, 1918. Prime Minister Borden, who was opposed to any reduction in Canada's commitment to the war effort, had announced on May 18, 1917 that the government would introduce conscription. He proposed to Liberal leader Sir Wilfrid Laurier that the Liberals and Conservatives form a Coalition Government to carry through the measure. Laurier refused, but some Liberals crossed the floor and joined the new Union Government, announced by Borden on October 19. The general election of December 1917 gave the Unionists a large majority.

Chapter 10 : "Such Frightful Carnage" — March 1918

1. Marshal Ferdinand Foch (1851–1929): Marshal of France. In 1914, Foch achieved renown when he halted the German advance at the Marne. He became chief of the French general staff in 1917 and, in April 1918, commander-in-chief of the Allied Armies. After the war, Foch was named Honorary Colonel of the 22nd Regiment and visited them in December 1921 at the Citadel in Quebec, an occasion which Vanier called "a day of glory." Foch died in Paris on March 22, 1929 and Vanier attended his elaborate state funeral, noting his impressions of the event in an article called "Memoires of Marshal Foch" carried in the *Defence Quarterly*.

2. Father J. Adolph Fortier, o.m.i. (1878–1936): Oblate priest from Ottawa who served for two years as chaplain with the 22nd battalion. He was decorated by the British with the *Croix de guerre* for his service.

3. General Douglas Haig (1861–1928): British field marshal who, in 1915, became commander-in-chief of the British Expeditionary Force. He was much criticized in Britain for the staggering losses suffered in the Battle of the Somme and the Passchendaele campaign.

Chapter 11: Casualty of War — August 1918

1. Ludendorff, Erich (1865–1937): German general and chief of staff to Field Marshall Hindenburg, he was largely responsible for German military strategy during WWI.

Endnotes

2. Chérisy: A small village four miles southeast of Arras where Georges Vanier lost his leg on August 28, 1918. He later gave the name to his eldest child and only daughter, Thérèse Marie Chérisy Vanier, born in Camberley, England on February 27, 1923.

3. Blood transfusion: Twenty-three years later in 1941, when a Red Cross Blood Clinic was set up in Quebec City, Vanier was the first person to donate blood. He said he was paying off a "debt" owing since August 1918 when a blood transfusion saved his life.

4. *Nemesis* by Paul Bourget (1852–1935). A French poet, novelist and critic, and a moulder of opinion among French conservative intellectuals in the pre-World War I period. He converted to Roman Catholicism in 1901, and is known for works of psychological analysis.

5. Victoria Cross: Instituted in 1856 by Queen Victoria, the Victoria Cross is the Commonwealth's top military decoration for gallantry and is awarded in recognition of exceptional bravery displayed in the presence of the enemy. The decoration is in the form of a bronze cross bearing the royal crest and the words "For Valour." The ribbon is dark crimson. Two members of the Van Doos received this distinguished award during WWI.

6. J'Accuse: An open letter written in 1898 by Emile Zola in response to the Dreyfus Affair. Dreyfus was a French-Jewish army officer who was falsely charged with giving military secrets to the Germans. Zola was prosecuted for libel, escaped to England and returned to France after Dreyfus had been cleared. After his death in 1902, French author Anatole France hailed him as "a moment of the human conscience." His remains were subsequently transported to the Pantheon.

7. Stephen B. Leacock (1869–1944): From the start of the First World War until the mid 1920s, Canadian-born Leacock was considered the English-speaking world's best-known humorist. *Literary Lapses* was his first book of humour, published in 1910. It was followed, in 1912, by *Sunshine Sketches of a Little Town*, which became one of the most popular of Leacock's sixty works.

Chapter 12: Continued convalescence, and Armistice — November 1918

1. Clarence Gagnon (1881–1942): Canadian painter and engraver who studied in Paris but returned to Canada in 1909, dividing his time between Montreal and Baie-St.-Paul. He was best known for his

illustration of Louis Hémon's *Maria Chapdelaine* (1933). He was a close personal friend of the Vanier family, and in 1935 painted a work specially for Georges to offer his parents. It was a snow scene about which Gagnon wrote in a letter to Vanier on June 5, 1935 that "Never before have I given so much work on a piece. I think you have lost nothing by waiting."

2. Theodore Roosevelt (1858–1919). Became 26th President of the United States on September 1901 after the assassination of William McKinley, was re-elected in 1904 and served as president until 1909. He won the Nobel Peace Prize in 1906 for helping mediate (in 1904) the end of the Russo-Japanese war. By the time of his death on January 6, 1919, he was hailed as one of the country's great presidents.

3. Sir Edward Kemp, KCMG (1858-1929). As Canadian Minister of Militia and Defence in 1916/17 and Minister of Overseas Military forces from 1917 to 1920, Kemp helped restore order to the chaos created by former Defence Minister Sam Hughes. He was made a Senator in 1921.

Epilogue

1. Charles-Michel de Salaberry: (1778–1829): Commissioned in the British Army in 1794, he raised and commanded a troop of Canadian Voltigeurs during the War of 1812. He repelled an American force in the first year of the war and, in 1813, turned back another numerically superior American advance on Montreal at the Battle of Châteauguay. Georges Vanier's wife, Pauline, was a descendant of the de Salaberry family.

ACKNOWLEDGEMENTS

Sifting through Georges Vanier's letters has been a fascinating and rewarding experience. Though the job was a daunting one, it has been lightened and guided by the help of many. Teresa de Bertodano in London was there from the start, offering professional advice and encouragement when both were sorely needed. She also introduced me to her brother, Martin, whose encyclopedic knowledge of British military history was most welcome. Journalist and author John Fraser, a long-time friend of the Vanier family, cast his careful editorial eye over the manuscript and shared it with Sandra Gwyn, who generously scanned it before her untimely death. A true professional, it was her exemplary book *Tapestry of War* that had first sparked my own interest in the period.

Dr. Jack Granatstein, former director of the Canadian War Museum, read an early draft and gave useful comments, particularly on the Canadian participation in the war. Clyde Sanger, a wise and seasoned journalist, shared his considerable expertise; our son, Christopher Cowley, offered interesting insights from his youthful vantage point while Charline Alward helped decipher and translate some of the more convoluted diary entries. A special bouquet goes to Wendy Blair, a loyal friend and gifted wordsmith.

Several Vanier family members helped unravel some of the personal history. I am particularly grateful to Gyde Shepherd, son of Frances Vanier Shepherd, and a nephew of Georges Vanier, who so generously answered my seemingly endless questions, as did Marcelle Trudeau, daughter of Georges Vanier's sister, Eva, and Lucy Vanier Vincent, another Vanier relative.

Special thanks also go to the National Archives of Canada, especially the ever-obliging Lucie Paquet, who played a large part in cataloguing the voluminous Vanier papers and cheerfully paved the way for my research. The Archives of the Royal 22nd at the Citadel in Quebec City were also fruitful and their archivist, Jacqueline Guimond, was unstinting in her time and assistance.

I owe the warmest gratitude to my husband George Cowley, above all for introducing me to Georges Vanier some thirty-five years ago when he had the privilege of working for the Governor-General for more than three years.

Finally, my thanks to the Vanier family for their support of this work, particularly Thérèse Vanier who first saw in these letters the seeds of a book and, more than anyone, helped the project become a reality.

SUGGESTED READING

The following selection of books provide background information about the period:

Berton, Pierre. *Vimy*. McClelland & Stewart, 1986.

Canadian Minister of Supplies and Services: *Valour Remembered: Canada and the First World War*. 1992.

Chaballe, Colonel Joseph. *Histoire du 22e Bataillon*. Les Editions Chantecler Ltée., 1952.

Ferguson, Niall. *The Pity of War*. Basic Books, 1999

Gagnon, Jean-Pierre: *Le 22e bataillon (Canadien-français) 1914–1919*. Les Presses de l'Université Laval, 1986.

Gilbert, Martin. *First World War*. HarperCollins, 1994.

Goodspeed, D.J. *The Road Past Vimy: The Canadian Corps 1914–1918*. Macmillan, 1969.

Gwyn, Sandra. *Tapestry of War: A Private view of Canadians in the Great War*. HarperCollins, 1992.

Keegan, John. *The First World War*. Key Porter, 1998.

Morton, Desmond and Granatstein, J.L. *Marching to Armageddon: Canadians and the Great War, 1914–1918*. Lester & Orpen Dennys, 1989.

Nicholson, Col. G.W.L. *Canadian Expeditionary Force, 1914–1919*. Dept. of National Defence, 1962.

Scott, Canon F.G. *The Great War As I Saw It*. Clarke & Stuart, 1934.

Suggested Reading

Speaight, Robert. *Vanier.* Collins, 1970.

Taylor, A.J.P. *The First World War, An Illustrated History.* Hamish Hamilton, 1963.

INDEX

Aitken, Sir Maxwell (later Lord Beaverbrook) 60, 313-314
Albert, King of Belgium 32
Alderson, Lieutenant-General Sir Edwin 62, 314
Amherst, Nova Scotia 21-24, 31, 33-34, 53, 305, 313
Amherst Daily Mirror 21
Amiens 201, 216, 220, 227, 239, 244, 245, 248-249, 306
Amiens Cathedral 249
Arc de Triumphe 99, 110
Archambault, Major J.P. 172, 251, 256, 258, 292
Archer, Pauline 297, 307, 310
Armour, Dr. Donald 269, 270-271, 278
Armistice 27, 270-271, 295, 306, 319
Arras 7, 185, 187, 216, 220-224, 226-228, 239, 249, 250-251, 306, 319
Asquith, Herbert Henry 48, 310, 313

Balfour, Arthur James 48, 313
Bank of Montreal, London 26, 159, 311
Battalion
    10th Reserve Battalion 257
    22nd Battalion ("Van Doos") 7, 16, 21-24, 31, 33-34, 41, 59-60, 62, 76, 79, 81, 88, 99, 103, 112, 122, 130, 133, 144, 151, 157, 163-168, 177, 183, 185, 187-188, 196-197, 200, 203, 206, 208-209, 218, 220, 223-224, 235, 239, 241-245, 249, 256, 262, 273, 280, 288-289, 296, 298, 306, 310, 313, 318-319
    24th from Montreal 41, 45, 110, 113, 188
    25th from Nova Scotia 34-35, 41, 72, 124, 217
    26th from New Brunswick 41, 67, 72, 75, 83, 124, 188, 251

28th Battalion 234
30th Infantry Battalion 43
69th Battalion 158, 162, 167, 187
87th Battalion 247, 316
Battle of Amiens 244, 306
Battle of Flers-Courcelette 164, 306
Battle of Hill 70 196-197, 306
Battle of the Somme (see Somme)
Bauset, Maurice 167-168, 172, 175, 199
Beaubien, Antonio 27, 69, 71, 143-144
Beaudin, Judge 42
Beaverbrook, Lord (see Sir Maxwell Aitken)
Beaudry, Lieutenant Abel 166
Blondin, Honourable L.E. 202
Borden, Sir Robert 15-16, 46-47, 311-312, 316, 318
Boulogne, France 60-62, 99, 110, 153, 184, 197-198, 253-262, 305-306
    No. 8 British Red Cross Hospital (Le Touquet) 253-255, 259-262
Boyer, Captain Guy 39-40, 50, 86, 94, 154-155, 159, 163
Bramshott Camp 154, 266
Brigade — 5th 41, 75, 111, 188, 217, 311
Brillant, Lieutenant Jean 244-245, 262
Bull, Mr. Perkins 154, 158, 163, 183, 199, 201, 206, 255, 266, 277
Byng, General Sir Julian 174, 188-189, 296, 314, 316
Belzile, Lieutenant 166
Bois de Boulogne 99, 110
Bourne, His Eminence Cardinal 54
Boyer, Captain Guy 39-40, 50, 86, 94, 154-155, 159, 163
Brady, Bernard 201, 237
Brighton Beach 51, 200
British Expeditionary Force (BEF) 16, 32, 310, 318
Brosseau, Jacques 76, 150-152
Browne, Peter S. 135, 175
Bully-Grenay 171, 173, 176-177, 196-197, 306
Burstall, Major-General 253

Caesar's Camp 41
Caillaux, Joseph 208, 317
Canadian Army Corps 62, 79, 314
Canadian Expeditionary Force 15, 314
Canadian High Commission, London 298-299, 307
Canadian National Memorial, Vimy (see Vimy)
Canadian Red Cross 39, 267, 277, 289-290, 311
Cacouna 19, 51, 274

INDEX

Carson, General 162-163, 168
Casgrain, Pierre 157
Chaballe, Joseph 166, 174, 177, 209
Champagne Drive 115, 314
Channel ports 32
Chassé, Henri 115, 130, 146, 151, 155, 159, 172, 178, 196, 199, 203, 238, 256, 271, 273-274, 296
Chérisy 27, 251, 302, 306, 319
Clemenceau, Georges 208, 317
Commander of the Order of St. Michael and St. George (C.M.G.) 236
Côté, Paul-Emile, 216
Courcelette (see Battle of Flers-Courcelette)
Crochetière, Father (Captain) Rosaire 197, 217, 222-224
Currie, General Sir Arthur William 188, 193, 202, 220, 244, 296, 317

Dardanelles 47, 59, 312
Deblois, Arthur 112
de Harding, Lieutenant-Colonel Hugues 266
de Lanaudière, Lieutenant-Colonel C. 138, 210
de Martigny, H.L. 69, 71, 152, 172, 178
de Salaberry, Charles-Michel 296, 300, 320
Department of Militia and Defence 237
DesRosiers, Lieutenant-Colonel 256-258, 274
Dessaules and Garneau 17-18, 305
Désy, Jean 212, 317
Devonport 38
Diefenbaker, John 301, 307
Division 41, 44-47, 52, 62, 68, 73, 82, 115, 137, 163, 182, 187-188, 202, 226, 238, 251, 253, 274, 311, 316-317
    4th (Canadian) Division 154, 157-160, 163, 168, 311
Dorval, C.P. 124
Douglas, Mayor 53, 313
Douaumont 176
Doyon, Father (Captain) Constant 39, 73, 96, 202, 205, 310
Dreyfous, Georges 210
Dreyfous, Jean 210
Dreyfus, Alfred 208, 263, 317, 319
Drummond, Lady Grace 39, 311
Dubrulé, Maurice 60, 69
Dubuc, Arthur-Edouard 21, 50-51, 62, 69, 71, 83, 90, 94, 101, 106-108, 111, 123, 171, 172, 174, 178, 182, 184, 186, 199, 202, 226, 230, 250-252, 255-257, 261, 273-274, 280, 285
Duke of Connaught 21, 310

East Sandling Camp 38-47, 49, 52, 54-55, 305
Elliott & Fry 115, 117

Falardeau, Jules 166
Falkenhayn, Erich von 60
Farm Street church 49
Ferdinand, Archduke Franz 15, 305
Ferguson, Howard 298
Fleet, Robbie 39
Foch, Marshal Ferdinand 220, 226, 247, 307, 318
Fontaine, Charles 174
Fortier, Father J. Adolph, o.m.i. 224, 245-246, 252, 318
Fotheringham, Lieutenant-Colonel 87
Fox, Father Martin, s.j. 53, 55, 313
French-Canadian brigade 238
Friends of the Royal 22nd 182

Gagnon, Clarence 279-280, 286, 319-320
Gallipoli 31, 59, 312
Gaudet, Frédéric 21-22, 24, 61, 73, 82, 103, 105, 112, 156, 166, 263
Gault, Major Hamilton 39, 310-311
Gaume, Father Pierre 17-18, 28, 76, 81, 90, 109, 113-117, 209-211, 309
Gauthier, Monseigneur Georges 260
George V, King 39, 294, 297, 306-307, 310
Gervais, Judge Honoré 54, 313
Gibbs, Philip 164, 190-191, 316
Gingras, L.J.Daly 112, 166, 178
Goodspeed, D.J. 191
Gorlice 60
Governor-General of Canada 21, 301, 310, 316
Grothé, Aimé 123-124, 209-210, 212
Greffard, Charles 174
Guillon Georges 200
Gwyn, Sandra 311

Haig, General Douglas 225, 228, 245, 318
Hampton, Father 55, 246
Harding, Hugues de 266
Hesperian 55, 313
Hingston, Basil 245
Hudon, Major L.E. 113, 115, 124, 142, 157, 162, 177, 289
Hughes, Right Honourable Sir Sam 46-47, 312, 314, 320

INDEX

Joffre, General Joseph 67, 314

Kaeble, Corporal Joseph 235, 260
Keegan, John 190
Kemmel 70-71, 79, 111, 115, 230
Kemp, Sir Edward 288, 320
Kennedy, Clark 93
King Edward, S.S. 71
King George V 39, 294, 297, 306-307, 310
King Edward VIII 299
Kitchener, Lord 46, 52, 312

Laflèche, L.R. 151, 159
Lake Memphramagog 19, 45, 54, 285
Lambert, P.S. 112
Lamothe, Lieutenant 199, 228, 258
Landry, Colonel 44
Languedoc, Bernard 134, 166-167
L'Arche 302
Larocque, R. 111-112
Laurier, Sir Wilfrid 16, 162, 284, 286, 291, 316, 318
Laval University 18, 212, 305
Laverdure, Armand 258
Law, Right Honourable Mr. Bonar 47-48, 312
Lawford, The 38
Leacock, Stephen B. 265, 319
Leclerc, P.E. 101-102
L'Ecole Polytechnique 211
Lefebvre, René 166-167, 172
Legion of Honour 194, 201, 302, 306, 317
Le Havre 60-62, 171
Lemieux, Sir Rodolph 162, 316
Lemieux, "Roddy" 257-258
Lemieux, Sherif 209-210
Levin, Maurice 101-102
Livesay, M. 250
Lloyd George, David 35, 48, 310, 312-313
London Gazette 107-108, 206, 317
Loos, Battle of 60, 72, 314
Loyola College 17-18, 246, 305, 309, 313
    Loyola College Review 194
Ludendorff, Erich 242, 318
Lusitania 33, 313

329

MacDougall, Stuart 205
Maclean's Magazine 14, 303
Magog (see Lake Memphramagog)
Maranda, A. 258
Marne, Battle of the 31-32, 43, 239, 314, 318
Marqueffles 195-197
Marson, Mr. and Mrs. 55, 74
Martin, Camille 17-18, 97, 105, 175, 238, 277, 286-287, 292
Martin, Mlle. Thérèse 73, 238, 286-287
Massey, Vincent 298, 301
Matt, John 101
Mayrand, M. 234
McKenna, Adrian 83, 110-111, 126
McKenna, Frank 110, 194
    Mrs. McKenna 89, 111, 116, 126, 138, 164, 194
McKenna, Ernie 126, 138-139, 144, 148, 163-164, 201
McMurtry, R. 256, 259
Mignault, Arthur 16
Mont des Cats 147-151
Mont Sorrel 122, 144, 151, 306

Napier Barracks 43
Neuville-St. Vaast 185, 202, 208
Nice, France 212-215
Nicholas II, Czar 187
North Midland Divisional Casualty Clearing Station (N.M.D.C.S.S.) 149
Notre Dame Cathedral, Paris 212
Notre Dame des Victoires 114

Painlevé, M. Paul 194
Papineau, E. Mackay 107, 124-125, 134, 159
Papineau, Talbot 44, 311
Passchendaele 14, 202-204, 208, 302, 306, 311, 318
Pearson, Lester 298, 301-302
Pelletier, George 92, 124, 136, 231, 238, 283
Penny, Trevor 250
Perkins Bull Hospital, Putney Heath, London. 154-155, 157-163, 165, 199, 275-276, 286, 288, 289, 291-293

Petit, Pierre 114, 117
Place de la Concorde 99, 110
Plante, Lucien 69, 71, 107
Pont de Briques 62

Index

Ploegsteert Wood 115
Prévost, Doctor (Captain) J.M.E. 107, 113
Princess Patricia's Canadian Light Infantry (Princess Pat's) 43-44, 310-311

Rancourt, L. 101
Reims 187, 210
Renaud, Major J. 166
Rhodes, Honourable Edgar Rhodes 53, 313
Roosevelt, President Theodore 284, 320
Ross, Gordon 139
Ross, Brigadier-General J.M. 217, 242
Routier, A.G. 155, 159, 256, 258
Roy, A.V. 71-73, 82, 117, 144
Roy, M. Maurice 211, 256, 262, 276
Roy, Honourable Philippe 276, 278, 282, 285
Royal Automobile Club, London 51-52
Royal Flying Corps (R.F.C.) 200
Royal 22nd Regiment (see "Van Doos")

Salisbury 43
Sarajevo 15
Savard, M. 234
Savoy Hotel, London 40, 51, 153, 155-156, 182-183, 198-200
Saxonia, R.M.T. 24, 34-37, 305
Scherpenberg 64, 68-70, 73, 75, 83-84, 91, 99, 230
Schlieffen Plan 31
Scott, Canon Frederick George 150, 316, 322
Second Canadian Division 41, 45, 47, 52, 115, 136, 163, 182, 188, 253, 311
Secretary of State, Ottawa 237
Shaughnessy, Fred (Alfred Thomas) 126, 202, 315
Shorncliffe 38, 43-44, 156-158, 162-163, 165, 167-168, 171
Somme, Battle of the 14, 28, 122, 154, 161, 164, 166, 171, 186, 202, 248-250, 306, 313, 318

St. Charles Orphanage 211
St. Eloi 62, 79, 122, 130, 132, 202
St. Jean, Quebec 21-22, 31, 305
St. Jean-Baptiste 43-44
St. Sebastian 109
Sullivan, Charlie 176
Summerhouse Hill 47

Tannenberg 31
Thackeray, William Makepeace 17, 309
Third London General Hospital, Wandsworth, London 261
Tremblay, Thomas Louis 50, 67, 70, 100, 105, 112-113, 116, 122, 138, 143, 164, 166-167, 174, 178, 182-184, 186, 194, 196, 199, 220, 230, 236, 242, 244, 247-249, 251, 254, 256, 261, 263, 267, 288, 293, 297, 300, 306-307, 313
Trudeau, Joseph 25, 95, 97, 106-107, 125-126, 237, 287, 293, 310, 315
Turner, Sir Richard E.W. 41, 52, 73, 82, 103, 163, 288, 291, 311
Turpen, Honourable Mr. 202

Valcartier Camp 16
"Van Doos" (see 22nd Battalion)
Vanier,
    Anthony 24, 42, 46, 73, 127, 142, 160, 184, 192, 194-195, 208, 236, 299, 310
    Margaret Maloney 11, 14, 19-20, 299, 309
    Eva (see also Joseph Trudeau) 24-25, 80, 83, 91, 95, 100, 104, 106, 108, 111, 119, 122, 125, 132, 142, 195, 201, 208, 210, 215, 237, 279, 287, 310, 315, 321
    Frances 19-20, 25-26, 28, 46, 74, 80, 99, 104, 109, 118, 121-123, 132, 140, 144, 171, 173-174, 184, 192-194, 208, 234, 239, 241, 243, 246-247, 264, 279-280, 282, 310, 321
    Guillaume 19-20, 309
    John 24, 83, 132, 141-142, 148, 159, 164, 210, 237, 279, 310
    Philias 19-20, 264, 299, 309
    Wilfrid 150
Verdun, Battle of 119, 121-125, 134, 176, 210, 314
Versailles, Treaty of 295, 306, 310
Victoria Cross 41, 73, 82, 235, 245, 260, 262, 311, 319
Vimy 14, 191, 227, 296, 302, 322, 189
    (see) Canadian National Memorial at Vimy 191, 299
Vimy Ridge 185, 187-188, 190, 192, 296, 306, 313, 316
Von Hindenburg, Paul 31, 318
Von Schlieffen, Field Marshall Alfred 31

Wallon Cappel 62-63
Walsh, J.P. 161
Watson, Brigadier-General David 41, 44, 87, 103-104, 154, 159-160, 162-163, 168, 291-293, 311
Weekes, Captain 41-42
Western front 31, 53, 60, 119, 122, 187, 190, 202, 208, 225, 230, 314
Wilson, President Woodrow 187

Index

Ypres 14, 32, 41, 62, 80, 111, 134, 163, 227, 255, 311
Ypres Salient 32, 115, 121, 129, 144

Zeppelin raid 40, 49-50, 116, 165